The Lending Library
at Connecticut College

Rent textbooks · **For the semester** · **For FREE** · SUSTAINABILITY

All books are due back to the Lending Library by the last day of finals.

Failure to do so will result in a minimum fee of $25, or the used resale price of the book on Amazon.

Questions? Email: sustainability@conncoll.edu

Book

The Lending Library runs off the generous book donations of students like YOU!

 Connecticut College Office of Sustanablity

Isaac Albéniz

COMPOSER RESOURCE MANUALS
VOLUME 45
GARLAND REFERENCE LIBRARY OF THE HUMANITIES
VOLUME 1932

Isaac Albéniz
A Guide to Research

Walter A. Clark

Garland Publishing, Inc.
A member of the Taylor & Francis Group
New York and London
1998

Library of Congress Cataloging-in-Publication Data

Clark, Walter Aaron.
    Isaac Albéniz : a guide to research / by Walter A. Clark.
        p.   cm. — (Composer resource manuals ; v. 45)   (Garland
    reference library of the humanities ; v. 1932)
        Discography: p.
        Includes indexes.
        ISBN 0-8153-2095-7 (case : alk. paper)
        1. Albéniz, Isaac, 1860–1909—Bibliography.   I. Title.
    II. Series: Garland composer resource manuals ; v. 45.   III. Series:
    Garland reference library of the humanities ; vol. 1932.
    ML134.A45C53   1998
    780'.92—dc21   98-23412
                                                                          CIP
                                                                          MN

Cover photograph of Isaac Albéniz provided by Rosina Moya Albéniz de Samsó.

Printed on acid-free, 250-year-life paper
Manufactured in the United States of America

Composer Resource Manuals

In response to the growing need for bibliographic guidance to the vast literature on significant composers, Garland is publishing an extensive series of research guides. This ongoing series encompasses more than 50 composers; they represent Western musical tradition from the Renaissance to the present century.

Each research guide offers a selective, annotated list of writings, in all European languages, about one or more composers. There are also lists of works by the composers, unless these are available elsewhere. Biographical sketches and guides to library resources, organizations, and specialists are presented. As appropriate to the individual composer, there are maps, photographs, or other illustrative matter, glossaries, and indexes.

A Señora Rosina Moya Albéniz de Samsó
No, señora, no hemos olvidado a su abuelo magnífico.

Contents

Preface

Each book in this series is necessarily different in its organization and coverage. The guiding principle in writing this resource manual on the Spanish pianist and composer Isaac Albéniz (1860-1909) has been to present the information that would have helped me in my work and to organize it as logically and accessibly as possible. When I first arrived in Spain in 1990 to begin my research on his operas, I knew absolutely nothing about the "what and where" of things and had to start from scratch. I hope that this book will obviate most of the hardships I experienced in studying the career of this fascinating composer (though other hardships certainly await the truly sedulous researcher).

The four main sections of this manual are the biography, bibliography, catalogue of works, and discography. The biography aims at a summary of moderate length and detail. So many misconceptions and fictions have clouded our understanding of Albéniz's life that my main purpose here has been to set the record straight but without detailed citation of the sources, primary and secondary, that have led to this reappraisal (one can locate that information in my book *Isaac Albéniz: Portrait of a Romantic*, B26). The biography includes a brief treatment of the evolution of his musical style and ends with an overview of the field and suggestions for further research.

The annotated bibliography consists of three parts:

1. Listing of archives and organizations devoted to Albéniz and a summary of their holdings with an emphasis on primary sources;
2. Secondary sources (books and articles);
3. Reviews of his concerts and works during Albéniz's lifetime as well as reviews of his operas after his death in 1909.

Primary sources are of the utmost importance in this kind of research, and some of the archives listed were not previously known by scholars to contain materials concerning Albéniz. This inventory can save one a great deal of time searching for documentation. Overall, the secondary literature on Albéniz is not vast, and I have included some items, such as liner notes and unpublished dissertations, that contain valuable information. Since the history of nineteenth-century music is ultimately written in the periodical literature of the time, the selective but extensive citation of articles and reviews can provide useful insights into many aspects of Albéniz's career. The catalogue of works is complete and contains pertinent information about alternate titles, dates of composition, publication, first performance (where available), and manuscript location. The discography is the first attempt at a comprehensive listing in more than forty years and includes works both in their original scoring and in transcription for other performing media.

All translations are my own. Though I have used modern Catalan spellings for persons, places, and institutions in that region, the names of Albéniz and his immediate family appear in Castilian, per the composer's own usage. Basque regions and names also receive Castilian spellings. English spellings of common Spanish place names, such as Seville, Catalonia, and Andalusia, are the rule.

It has been my great privilege to study in considerable depth the life and music of Albéniz. After more than eight years of often difficult research and writing, my admiration for his achievements and the pleasure I derive from his music have only increased. Though it is now time to move on to other pastures, I remember with utmost gratitude the enormous assistance I received from so many people and institutions, in the U.S. and throughout Europe. This book would never have been completed if they had not generously shared their time and information with me. I wish to express my appreciation to the following individuals and organizations:

London: Barbara J. Peters, head of the Latymer Archive at the bank of Coutts & Co., and the Eighth Lord Latymer, great-grandson of Francis Money-Coutts. Thanks also go to the British Library, the Westminster City Archives, and the Greater London Record Office and History Library. Dr. Clifford Bevan, the leading English authority on Albéniz, also deserves a sincere expression of thanks for sharing with me his excellent research on Albéniz's operas and English connections. *Brussels*: the library of the Conservatoire Royal, the Bibliothèque

Royale Albert Ier, and the archive of the Théâtre de la Monnaie. *Leipzig*: the library of the Hochschule für Musik Felix Mendelssohn-Bartholdy, the music library of the city of Leipzig, and the Staatsarchiv and Stadtarchiv. *Prague*: the National and Municipal Libraries, and in particular Roman Lindauer, without whose timely assistance my work would have been much more difficult. *Budapest*: Maria Eckhardt of the Liszt Ferenc Memorial Museum and Research Centre, for her thorough investigations conducted on my behalf. *Paris*: Catherine Rochon of the Conservatoire National Superieur de Musique et de Danse de Paris; the Bibliothèque Nationale and Archives Nationales for their patient assistance; and the firm of Max Eschig, for its generosity. *Barcelona*: Ayuntamiento de Barcelona; Rosa Busquets of the library of the Museu Marítim; the Arxiu Municipal; Romà Escalas and his cordial assistants at the Museu de la Música, in particular Judit Bombardó; the Biblioteca de Catalunya; and the Arxiu Històric de la Ciutat. I am also indebted to Josefina Sastre and the Biblioteca del Orfeó Català, as well as to the theater museum of the Palau Güell for their help. I benefited from the assistance of the Arxiu Diocesa of the Arquebisbat de Barcelona, the Institut Universitari de Documentació i Investigació Musicològica Josep Ricart i Matas, María Luisa Beltrán Sábat of the Institut Municipal dels Serveis Funeraris de Barcelona, and Amparo Valera of the Teatre Romea. The musicologist Dr. Monserrat Bergadà Armengol provided invaluable research support. Heartfelt thanks go to Rosina Moya Albéniz de Samsó, granddaughter of the composer, for her hospitality and largess. *Granada*: María Isabel de Falla and the Archivo Manuel de Falla for providing me access to Albéniz manuscripts in their collection. I am also grateful to Dr. Marta Falces Sierra of the Universidad de Granada for her assistance. *Madrid*: Rafael Campos and the Seretaría of the Real Conservatorio; the Biblioteca Nacional, Hemeroteca Nacional, Hemeroteca Municipal, Archivo Histórico de la Villa, Archivo del Palacio Real, Archivo General de la Administración, and the Dirección General de Costes de Personal y Pensiones Públicas, as well as the Registro Civil; Lola Higueras of the Museo Naval, and Antonio Gil of the Sociedad General de Autores de España. I also wish to thank the Sociedad Española de Musicología and the Fundación Isaac Albéniz for their assistance and encouragement. I am extremely grateful to the eminent musicologist Dr. Jacinto Torres Mulas, the foremost Spanish authority on Albéniz, whose moral support and gracious sharing of material were essential to the completion of this book. *United States*: I am very grateful to Dr. Guy Marco, General Editor of Garland's Composer Resource Manuals, for his interest in and support of this project, and for the patience of Garland's excellent staff in helping me prepare the manuscript. Thanks go to the pianist and Albéniz scholar Dr. Pola Baytelman Dobry for her generous sharing of information and invitations to lecture. I am also grateful to the libraries at the University of California, Los Angeles, and the University of Kansas for their assistance. I especially appreciate the advice of Victor Cardel and Jim Smith of the music library at KU. Dr. Daniel Politoske of the musicology division and Dr. Alan Pasco of the French department at KU also merit sincere thanks for their assistance in tracking down some materials in Paris. My overseas research was made possible by funding from the Del Amo Endowment (on two separate occasions) and the Program for Cultural Cooperation between Spain's Ministry of Culture and United States' Universities (also twice awarded). In addition, these investigations were supported by University of Kansas General Research allocation #3466. Additional research money was provided by KU in the form of a New Faculty Reseach Grant. I wish to thank my doctoral adviser, Dr. Robert Murrell Stevenson, for his encouragement and the invaluable example of his own work. Finally, thanks go to my friends Peter and Mimi Farrell and Bill Jaynes for their encouragement and assistance, and to my mother-in-law Grace Golden, my wife Nancy, and my son Robert for their patient understanding and support.

W.A.C.
Lawrence
1997

Abbreviations

Ah: Albéniz house, the current residence of Rosina Moya Albéniz
        de Samsó (the daughter of Albéniz's daughter Laura) in the
        Barcelona area.
B: Bibliography.
Bc: Biblioteca de Catalunya, Barcelona.
Bn: Biblioteca Nacional, Madrid.
C: Catalogue of Works.
D: Discography.
L: Latymer Archive, Coutts and Company, London.
Lc: Library of Congress.
LCM: *La Correspondencia Musical*.
Ls: Staatsarchiv Leipzig.
Mc: Real Conservatorio, Madrid.
Mm: Museu Municipal de la Música, Barcelona.
Oc: Biblioteca del Orfeó Català, Barcelona.
Se: Sociedad General de Autores de España, Madrid.
UMI: Ann Arbor, Michigan: University Microfilms.

Isaac Albéniz

CHAPTER ONE

Albéniz: The Man and His Music

INTRODUCTION

Numerous accounts of Albéniz's life have been written since the first one, by Antonio Guerra y Alarcón (B47), appeared in 1886. Even a cursory examination of any half dozen of them soon reveals, however, that they are all plagued by inconsistencies and contradictions. This one says he stowed away on a steamer in Cádiz and traveled to Cuba when he was but twelve; that one says that the steamer was headed for Buenos Aires, not Havana; another says that it left from La Coruña, not Cádiz. This one says that he studied for nine months in Leipzig during the years 1875-76; that one says eighteen months; another, three years. This one says that he studied with Liszt in Weimar, Rome, and Budapest; that one says that he studied with him for a year in Italy, while another says that he played for Liszt but once, in the summer of 1880. And on and on it goes.

Untying this Gordian knot has required no small expenditure of time and effort. Like Alexander, one simply has to slice through it by confronting the fact that Albéniz was in the habit of telling friends, journalists, and biographers highly elaborated versions of the truth or even outright fabrications. This was apparently a source of amusement to him, and it served the practical purpose of enhancing his credentials before the public while he struggled up the professional ladder as a pianist and composer. Those interested in an in-depth examination of Albéniz's prevarications and the documentary evidence that exists to set the record straight should consult this author's *Isaac Albéniz: Portrait of a Romantic* (B26). The summary below does not delve into these issues but rather presents a straightforward account of his career, which was remarkable enough without any embellishment. This is

intended to be more detailed than an encyclopedia entry but still easily digested in one sitting. The chronology of his life in the appendix should help bring into even clearer focus the major events of his career, according to the most recent and reliable research available.

This biographical essay continues with a brief discussion of his musical style and the rise of scholarly interest in Albéniz during the last decade. It concludes with suggestions for future research, not only on Albéniz but in the area of Spanish music since 1800.

CHILDHOOD AND EARLY CONCERT CAREER (1860-76)

Isaac Manuel Francisco Albéniz y Pascual was born on May 29, 1860, in the town of Camprodon in the Catalonian province of Girona. He was the last of four children and the only son. His siblings were Enriqueta (1850-67), Clementina (1853-1933), and Blanca (1855-74). His mother, Dolors Pascual i Bardera (1821-1900), was a native of the city of Figueres in that province.

Albéniz's father, Ángel Lucio Albéniz y Gauna, had been assigned to Camprodon in 1859 as a customs official. He hailed from Vitoria, in the Basque country, where he was born on March 2, 1817 (d. 1903). The Álava region of the Basque country was the ancestral home of the Albéniz family. Indeed, *albéniz* is a Basque word that means skinny, slender, or thread-like; it can also mean short or clever, in a devious sort of way. As a noun, it refers to a thread, strand, or a lot of hay.

Ángel remained employed in Camprodon until May of 1863. A six-month stint in Sitges, just south of Barcelona on the coast, preceded his taking up a new post at Barcelona in December of that same year, when Albéniz was three and a half years old. According to family tradition, Isaac showed a proclivity for music in his earliest years, and his sister Clementina, also a talented musician, gave him his first lessons in piano. His progress was so rapid that the two siblings made their first public appearance, at the Teatre Romea, when Isaac was but four years old (although it may have been later than this, it was definitely before 1868). He also studied piano with Narciso Olivares, a local teacher in Barcelona about whom we know next to nothing. In November 1867 tragedy struck the family when Enriqueta died of typhus. Shortly after this the family left the city.

In 1868 occurred one of the many political upheavals that plagued Spain in the nineteenth century. General Juan Prim led a conspiracy to

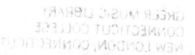

overthrow the regime of Isabel II, and his forces entered Madrid in triumph on October 3. Ángel was employed in Barcelona until January of 1868, at which time he took up a position in the customs office in Almería, on the Mediterranean coast in Andalusia. This position was terminated in August of that year, around the time of the revolution. There followed a hiatus of almost a year before he was posted to Cáceres in the western province of Extremadura. Albéniz began studying at the Real Conservatorio[1] in Madrid during the 1868-69 school year. He enrolled in first-year solfège and studied piano with José Mendizábal. But Albéniz's academic efforts were desultory, and his failure to show up for the exam in second-year solfège in June 1874 effectively terminated his formal training in Madrid.

In 1869 Albéniz composed and published his first piece, the *Marcha militar* for piano. The cover bears the printed dedication "Al Excelentísimo Señor Vizconde del Bruch," who was General Prim's twelve-year-old son. Interestingly, Ángel was appointed to his new position in Cáceres at this time, on July 29, 1869, and began his duties a month later, on August 23. This raises the likelihood that the little composition's purpose was to win the favor of Prim and that it succeeded. Or it may have been an expression of gratitude for a position already granted. We do not know.

Ángel remained in Cáceres until November 16, 1871, when his position was terminated. Shortly after Ángel's return to his family in Madrid, Albéniz began to tour the country as a child prodigy, in early 1872. He gave concerts in Andalusia and northern Castile, performing on one occasion at the Teatro Lope de Vega in Valladolid. During the spring and summer of that year he appeared in Ubeda, Jaén, Córdoba, Granada, Lucena, Loja, Salar, and finally Málaga. He reappeared in Málaga in early November, bringing his season on the road to a close.

Ángel probably assisted his son in setting up these concerts and even accompanied him during the period he himself was unemployed. Some parental guidance would have been in order because the country was in the throes of civil war during this time, and it is clear from his concert itinerary that Albéniz performed in both federal and rebel (Carlist) areas. Clearly, these concerts would have provided welcome income. Many of them were for Masonic organizations, and though Albéniz never joined a lodge, Ángel was an active Mason whose connections no doubt facilitated getting engagements. On March 15, 1873, Ángel assumed a new post in the federal office of General

Accounts and Auditing. Once Ángel was settled in Madrid and working regularly, he expected his son to resume serious studies. But this Albéniz clearly did not want to do, and a spate of performances in the provinces ensued during the following academic year (1873-74), taking the young artist to El Escorial, Ávila, Toro, Salamanca, Peñaranda de Bracamonte, Valladolid, Palencia, León, Oviedo, Avilés, Gijón, Orense, Logroño, and Barcelona, where he played at the salon of the Bernareggi piano firm on October 18, 1874.[2]

Ángel must not have approved of this behavior, but he could not have been trying very hard to curtail it, either. In any case, we cannot yet confirm or refute the traditional stories of Albéniz's having run away from home to go on this tour. We can be reasonably certain that it came to an end as the result of his sister Blanca's suicide. An aspiring singer, she had failed in her audition for the Teatro de la Zarzuela in Madrid and killed herself in a fit of despair on October 16. Albéniz's concertizing ceased for six months after this tragedy.

However, several of Ángel's friends had been so impressed with young Albéniz's triumphs in Spain that they arranged a concert tour for him in the New World, which they hoped would provide money for his future education. Albéniz performed extensively in the Greater Antilles in the summer and fall of 1875. He traveled there on April 30 with his father, who had been appointed to the post of Inspector General in Havana. He gave successful concerts in San Juan, Mayagüez, and Cáguas, Puerto Rico, during the spring and summer. He then made his way to Cuba and created a sensation in Santiago and Havana, where he resided with his father at least until November. Arrangements were then made for him to enroll in the Leipzig Hochschule für Musik Felix Mendelssohn-Bartholdy so that he could fully realize his potential.

FORMAL STUDIES AND CONCERT CAREER (1876-89)

Albéniz began his studies at Leipzig on May 2, 1876, and terminated them a short time later, on June 24 of the same year. He studied theory and composition with Carl Piutti, piano with Louis Maas as well as Salomon Jadassohn, and voice with Henry Schradieck. He attended theory lectures by Oscar Paul and participated in a chamber ensemble (under the supervision of Schradieck). His professors were almost unanimous in stating that he attended regularly at the beginning and was diligent. Why he withdrew so soon, then, is a matter of speculation.

One possibility is that he was discouraged by difficulties with the language. Another has to do with family resources. Ángel entered another hiatus in his work beginning July 9, 1876, and he did not resume his duties in Havana until February of 1877. His pay was suspended during this time, and he returned to Spain. This loss of income probably created financial hardship and necessitated calling Albéniz home from Leipzig.

In the summer of 1876 it was obvious that if young Albéniz were to continue his formal education abroad, he would require financial assistance. Albéniz met Guillermo Morphy, secretary to King Alfonso XII, during the summer of 1876. Morphy was himself a composer and musicologist who had studied with François Fétis at Brussels. He was in a good position to judge musical talent and was impressed by Albéniz's accomplishments and potential. He secured a grant for the aspiring pianist so that he could study at the Conservatoire Royal in Brussels. Albéniz was admitted to the Conservatoire on October 17, 1876, and eventually became a student of Louis Brassin. In addition to piano, Albéniz studied harmony with Joseph Dupont and solfège with Jan Lamperen. Albéniz tied with Louvain native Arthur de Greef for first place ("with distinction") in the July 1879 piano competition in Brassin's class. He terminated his studies at the Conservatoire shortly thereafter, in September. He returned to Barcelona a local hero and gave a concert at the Teatre Espanyol on September 12, 1879, that had the critics singing his praises.[3] He gave several more successful concerts in that city before rejoining his family in Madrid.

In the summer of 1880, Albéniz set out to realize his dream of studying with Franz Liszt. He made his way to Budapest via Prague and Vienna, but Liszt was not in Budapest at that time. Albéniz wrote in his diary that he played for him on August 18, 1880, but this was pure fabrication, and he probably never met, much less studied with, Liszt. Why Albéniz fabricated the encounter is uncertain, but he probably wanted to justify to his family—and perhaps to posterity, of which he was keenly aware even early in life—what turned out to be little more than a sight-seeing excursion. Albéniz threaded his way back to Madrid through Vienna and Paris. Overall, his lack of artistic success on this trip was a disappointment to him, and he even contemplated taking his own life as a result. (Despite his normal ebullience, there was a depressive streak in his personality, and one readily perceives this in much of his music.) During this year Albéniz entered the reserves of the

Spanish army.[4] His fascination with military trappings may have gotten the best of him, or perhaps the service was obligatory, but it in no way slowed down his concert career. Fortunately, in the early 1880's there was a lull in Spain's almost incessant civil war, and he was never called up.

By December 1880 Albéniz was back in Havana and Santiago giving concerts. He then made his way to Granada in July of the following year. He had performed there nine years earlier, as a boy of twelve; now, he was a grown man and an artist of impressive stature. Albéniz had a great love of Granada, which he expressed in some of his most popular piano pieces. He gave private performances in the homes of Granada's leading citizens, music lovers already familiar with his talents.

More appearances followed in Santander and Zaragoza that fall, followed by a December concert in Pamplona. One searches in vain in the press for a single negative assessment of his performances during this period. The audiences were ecstatic about his technique and musicianship, and the critics lavished their encomiums on him. January of 1882 found Albéniz still in the north country. He performed in Bilbao between the two acts of Joaquín Gaztambide's zarzuela *El juramento*. Shortly after this performance, Albéniz entered into a new musical arena by composing his own zarzuelas (Spanish operettas). Today nothing remains of these early works except their titles. *Cuanto más viejo*, composed to a one-act libretto by a Señor Zapino, premiered in Bilbao at the Coliseo in February 1882. Though it was a hit, it did not remain in the repertoire, and we know practically nothing about the story or the music.

We know little more about a second zarzuela, *Catalanes de gracia*, also in one act, with a libretto by Rafael Leopoldo Palomino de Guzmán. It premiered at the Teatro Salón Eslava in Madrid in late March 1882 and continued to draw large audiences well into April. But despite this success, by May Albéniz was back on the concert trail, where he remained at least until November. No evidence of a putative third zarzuela, *El canto de salvación*, has yet surfaced.

After a rousing triumph in Córdoba in May, Albéniz moved on to San Fernando, Cádiz, and Seville. On August 7 he performed on the opposite side of the country, in Valencia. Other appearances took him to Málaga, Pontevedra, and Vigo, where he performed with a sextet including his friends Enrique Fernández Arbós (violin) and Augustín

Rubio (cello). Not one to rest on his laurels for very long, Albéniz continued on to Cartagena to give several concerts. His last known performance in 1882 took place in Madrid at the elegant salon of the Círculo Vasco-Navarro, where he played his well-rehearsed repertoire of Chopin, Scarlatti, Boccherini, Beethoven, Raff, and Mendelssohn. The following year Albéniz moved to Barcelona and continued his concertizing from there. Around this time the young pianist met, briefly courted, and married Rosina Jordana Lagarriga (1863-1945)—one of his students and the daughter of a prominent family in the Catalonian capital—and adopted a more settled lifestyle. The nuptials took place on June 23, 1883, at the church of Mare de Déu de la Mercè, in the Gothic quarter of Barcelona near the harbor.[5] (With the intercession of Ángel, Albéniz was able to free himself of his military obligations, receiving his discharge from the reserves on June 7.) Albéniz did not, however, allow matrimony to keep him off the concert circuit. In September he journeyed to Santander to join Arbós's sextet, which was busy giving concerts on the north coast. After a successful appearance in La Coruña, the group moved on to Vigo, Santiago de Compostela, and Orense. However, after La Coruña the tour was a failure and drew small audiences. Albéniz parted company with the group and passed through Madrid on his way back to Barcelona.

It was most likely during this Barcelona period that Albéniz made the acquaintance of Felip Pedrell and studied composition with him. He knew that he had yet to acquire any real technique as a composer and that he would have to grapple with the complexities of form, counterpoint, and orchestration before he could aspire to anything higher than the charming little entertainments he was already capable of writing. By 1883, the Catalan Pedrell (1841-1922) had already established a solid reputation as an opera composer and musical nationalist. Albéniz himself certainly was unstinting in his praise of Pedrell as a teacher as well as a composer. In his letters to Pedrell, Albéniz addressed him as "Dear Master" and signed himself "your eternally affectionate disciple."[6]

Aside from the adulation his apprenticeship aroused, the most important point usually made about Albéniz's contact with Pedrell is that it reinforced his determination to use the musical folklore of his own country as the basis for composition. Pedrell was an advocate of musical nationalism who believed that folk song formed the ideal foundation for Spanish art music. To be sure, Pedrell was not a Catalan nationalist but pan-Spanish in his outlook, and it was this philosophy to which Albéniz also adhered.[7] Thus, the 1880's witnessed Albéniz's increasing output of charming and distinctive Spanish-style pieces for the piano, which received an enthusiastic reception by the concert-going public in Spain and elsewhere. Many of these works have found a permanent place in the piano repertoire, though they are most frequently heard in transcription for the guitar. They are so convincing that it is indeed easy to take their originality completely for granted. These works represent Albéniz's characteristic blend of indigenous and non-Spanish elements: lively rhythms, modality, elementary formal structure, and haunting melodic arabesques couched in poignant, chromatic harmonies reminiscent of Chopin. Though he continued to write light pieces in the salon style so popular at that time, Albéniz's "Spanish" pieces represent the first flowering of his unique creative genius.

Albéniz signed a lucrative contract to entertain at the Café Colón in Barcelona. Here he was persuaded by acquaintances to speculate on the stock market, and he lost a considerable amount of money. But he simply gave more concerts to make good his losses. He toured southern France and northern Spain, appearing in Marseilles, Toulon, Biarritz, Cauterets, and Arcachón. Concerts in the Catalonian capital during 1883 included appearances at the Teatre Espanyol in January, at the Tívoli in February, and at the Liceu in May.[8] It was probably during one of these appearances that Rosina first heard him perform. Unfortunately, we know little about his activities in 1884 in Barcelona. Albéniz's final appearance there took place on March 22, 1885, for a benefit at the Liceu. On August 8, 1885, he gave a recital at the Casino Luchón, and part of the proceeds went to aid the poor.[9]

Albéniz's first child, named after his deceased sister Blanca, was born in 1884 in Barcelona. A second child was born during the summer of 1885 in Tiana, a hamlet outside Barcelona. The boy was named Alfonso, after the king who had made possible Albéniz's studies in Brussels. Soon thereafter, Albéniz moved his growing family to Madrid, where he gave concerts for the royal family and established his reputation as a popular composer as well as a virtuoso.

One of the most important concerts Albéniz ever gave took place at the elegant and fashionable Salón Romero in Madrid on Sunday, January 24, 1886, when he was twenty-five years old. It was in conjunction with this appearance that Guerra y Alarcón's biography of

Albéniz appeared in print. Most of the information for this account was provided to the author by Albéniz himself, and critics reviewing the concert borrowed from it extensively. Word of his smashing success at the Salón Romero spread throughout the country, and Albéniz received numerous invitations from various cities in Spain to perform. But triumph soon blended with tragedy when Albéniz's twenty-month-old daughter Blanca died of a fever on April 4, 1886.

In spite of this heartbreak, on July 17 and 19 he was back on stage in San Sebastián appearing with a sextet (not Arbós's group) and in a recital for two pianos, with a local pianist accompanying him. In 1886 Albéniz also performed in Zaragoza. On March 21, 1887, he again appeared at the Salón Romero performing many of his own works; several of his students also appeared performing his latest compositions. On September 20, 1887, he ventured across the waters of the Mediterranean to perform in Palma de Mallorca, where the local press saluted his artistry.

For the rest of Albéniz's tenure in Madrid until 1889 we have as yet little information. We can safely assume that life settled into a routine of concerts, teaching, and dealing with family matters. He spent many evenings at Morphy's home, in the company of Tomás Bretón, Arbós, and other musical notables. The piano pieces of this period represent most of the genres of salon music: mazurkas, waltzes, barcarolles, pavanes, minuets, romances, polkas, polonaises, serenades, etudes, and caprices. We know these figured prominently in his concerts during the 1880's and 90's, and nearly all of them bear dedications to students, friends, and family. The majority of these pieces were suitable for amateur use and served the dual purpose of bringing in income and spreading his name. Benito Zozaya and Antonio Romero in Madrid and Juan Ayné in Barcelona published most of them. In addition, Albéniz wrote all of his seven sonatas during this time, though only nos. 3-5 are complete. Nothing remains of 2 and 6, while only single movements of 1 and 7 (a scherzo and minuetto, respectively) are extant. Number three bears a dedication to the pianist Manuel Guervós, who premiered it at the concert in the Salón Romero on March 21, 1887. Number four is dedicated to his "beloved Maestro" Count Morphy (Alfonso XII gave him this title in 1885) and was premiered by Luisa Chevalier at this same concert.

The most enduring and popular of his compositions from this period are, however, his Spanish-style pieces. Albéniz freely adapted from Spanish folk music certain generic rhythmic and melodic elements that give the works their flavor. He felt a special attraction to flamenco, the exotic folk music of Andalusia (where he toured extensively during his youth and returned later as a tourist). This was certainly a source of inspiration for several numbers in *Recuerdos de viaje* and the *Suite española No. 1,*[10] which contain some his finest pieces from this period.

However, Albéniz did not confine himself to works for piano in the 1880's, and he wrote some excellent vocal music, including *Rimas de Bécquer*, on poems of the celebrated Sevillan poet Gustavo Adolfo Bécquer, and the *Seis baladas*, to Italian texts of the Marquesa de Bolaños. Two choral works also flowed from his pen during the Madrid years: the oratorio *El Cristo* (lost),[11] and *Salmo VI: Oficio de difuntos* (1885), for SATB chorus, composed upon the death of his patron Alfonso XII.[12] A number of orchestral works were published in piano reduction as well, including the *Rapsodia española* for piano and orchestra and the Concerto No. 1 for Piano and Orchestra in A Minor ("Concierto fantástico"). Not only was Albéniz reviving the sonata in Spain, but he was establishing a tradition of concerto writing that would blossom in the next century. He was also helping foster Spanish symphonic music, though the *Escenas sinfónicas catalanas* of 1889 remained unpublished, and his most important contribution, *Catalonia*, would not appear for another decade.

As a result of his many accomplishments, on March 30, 1886, the Queen Regent appointed Albéniz to the position of assistant professor of piano at the Real Conservatorio. Several months later, on November 11, 1886, the Dirección General de Bellas Artes made Albéniz a member of the Royal Order of Isabel the Catholic, and the actual ceremony took place on the 22nd at the Royal Palace. On this occasion he received the designation of Ordinary Knight Commander. He was made a Full Knight Commander two years later.[13]

In the summer and fall of 1888 Albéniz made several highly successful appearances at the Exposición Universal in Barcelona, and these served as a springboard for the next phase of his career. The piano manufacturer Erard and Co. invited Albéniz to give a series of concerts in the French section of the exposition, and he performed no less than twenty recitals between August 20 and October 11. He appeared in Madrid on March 7, 1889, at the Teatro de la Comedia with the orchestra of the Sociedad de Conciertos conducted by Tomás Bretón.

He then performed again in Vitoria. Oddly, though Albéniz seems to have played up his Basque heritage for all it was worth when he concertized in that region, he rarely did so elsewhere. His only pieces inspired by Basque folklore are two *zorticos* for piano, based on the popular dance in 5/8 meter.

THE LONDON YEARS (1889-93)

Albéniz as a composer and soloist was bound to outgrow the peninsula and seek a larger arena for his talents. Erard invited him to perform in their hall in Paris on April 25, 1889. The concert was devoted exclusively to his own works, and he was accompanied by the orchestra of Édouard Colonne in his Piano Concerto No. 1. Those in attendance at the performance included Debussy, Ravel, Fauré, and Dukas. Albéniz's pianism and style of writing were a revelation to them in the way he was able to evoke from the piano the characteristic sounds of the Spanish guitar.

In Madrid on July 23, 1889, Rosina gave birth to a second daughter, this one named after another of Albéniz's deceased sisters, Enriqueta. But Albéniz was concertizing in Britain at the time. He made his first known appearance in London at Prince's Hall in Piccadilly on June 13, 1889. In July, Albéniz performed at 19, Harley St., including in his program works by himself and his friends Arbós, Ruperto Chapí, and Bretón. With characteristic generosity, Albéniz had already determined to serve as a pathfinder for Spanish composers and performers in the concerts he gave and organized during his tenure in London. Other performances during this year took place at the Derby Drill Hall, at one of Edgar Haddock's Musical Evenings in Leeds, at a Royal Amateur Orchestral Society concert (with Arbós and Pablo Sarasate), at the Lyric Club, and at the Crystal Palace. He played at St. James's Hall in October, where he presented his own compositions in addition to works by Bach, Scarlatti, and Chopin. Perhaps the highlight of his concerts in London in 1889 was a December performance at a *conversazione* of the Wagner Society, held in the Institute over Prince's Hall. His renditions of Brassin's transcriptions earned him the praise of George Bernard Shaw, who reviewed the concert (B168).

His reputation now well established, in early 1890 Albéniz set out on a tour of the provinces with a group of performers, serving as both soloist and accompanist. Their travels took them to many cities, including Brighton, Lancaster, Leeds, Bradford, Halifax, Huddersfield, Sheffield, Chatham, Rochester, Stourbridge, Manchester, Birmingham, Bristol, and Glasgow. Despite these peregrinations, Albéniz was probably present when his third daughter and last child, Laura, was born April 20, 1890, in Barcelona. But June found him once again in London, now resolved to settle in the city that had received him so favorably.

Later that month, Albéniz signed a contract with a London businessman, Henry Lowenfeld, who would now serve as his manager and hold exclusive rights to the publication of his music. This arrangement also provided Albéniz with a spacious house at 16 Michael's Grove, Brompton, a district traditionally populated by accomplished musicians and actors. It would provide ample room for Albéniz's wife and three children, who now moved to London to join him.

Lowenfeld likely provided financial support for our pianist/composer's ensuing ambitious concert ventures. Albéniz organized two orchestral concerts at St. James's Hall in November 1890. The first program, on the 7th, attracted only a small audience due to the large venue, competition from Hans Richter's concert series there, and inclement weather. The second of Albéniz's orchestral extravaganzas took place on November 21 and was greeted by the press and public with more enthusiasm. Buoyed by this success and enjoying the financial backing of Lowenfeld, Albéniz set about to organize a series of ten concerts in St. James's Hall the following year, from January through June. These programs featured not only Albéniz but many of his friends, including Arbós and the Hungarian violinist Tividar Nachez.

But Albéniz did not confine his appearances to England during these years. In early February 1892, he and the Belgian violinist Eugène Ysaÿe appeared in one of the Valleria concerts at the Philharmonie in Berlin. Nearly a month later, on March 1, Albéniz presented a solo program at the Singakademie in Berlin, one to which the critics had ambivalent reactions (see B211-20). In this same year he performed with Arbós in Brussels and made another tour in England with Arbós and the Czech cellist David Popper.

The year 1892 represented the apex of his career as a concert pianist, and after this time he gave himself over more and more to serious composition. He did continue to concertize over the next few years but far less actively than had been his custom. The chief impetus for this development lay in his growing occupation with musical theater in London. His initial foray into this arena came in the form of incidental music to poems by Paul-Armand Sylvestre, read by the celebrated actress Sarah Bernhardt. Sylvestre's *Poèmes d'amour* were arranged as a series of twelve *tableaux vivants* by Cyprien Godebski and premiered on Monday afternoon, June 20, 1892, at the Lyric Club, Barnes. Albéniz had begun composing the work only a week earlier, on June 14, and finished the manuscript but a day before the concert.

He next became involved in a production of the operetta *Incognita*, an English adaptation of Charles Lecocq's *Le Coeur et la main*, which opened October 6, 1892, and ran for 101 performances.[14] For this production the work was expanded from two acts to three, and Albéniz composed a finale for Act II, entitled "Oh! Horror! Horror!"

In the summer of 1892 Albéniz began work on an operetta entirely his own entitled *The Magic Opal*, on a text by Arthur Law, a popular English librettist of the day. The work premiered on January 19, 1893, at the Lyric Theatre. It initially proved so successful that a touring company was formed only three weeks after the premiere to perform *The Magic Opal* in other cities, opening at the Royalty Theatre in Glasgow and continuing on to Edinburgh, Manchester, Brighton, Hull, Liverpool, Newcastle, Sheffield, and Leeds, finally closing at the Bolton Theatre Royal on May 20. In spite of all this, the London run ended ignominiously on February 27. This was due in part to the mediocre libretto, but financial difficulties lay at the heart of the matter, as production expenses consistently outstripped ticket receipts.

Albéniz and company undertook a revision of the work, renamed *The Magic Ring*, which reduced the number of characters, simplified the plot, and cut some numbers and added others. It premiered at the Prince of Wales's Theatre on April 11, 1893, conducted by the composer. Unfortunately, this also failed to hold the public's attention. However, Albéniz's activities on the London stage did not end with *The Magic Ring*. He soon took an active part in the production of the two-act musical comedy *Poor Jonathan*, an English-language adaptation of Karl Millöcker's *Der arme Jonathan*.[15] *Poor Jonathan* premiered at the Prince of Wales's Theatre June 15, 1893. Albéniz not only conducted the work but contributed several musical numbers in addition to those by Millöcker. Yet again, however, his efforts were not enough to make a success of the production.

Albéniz did not cease to compose piano music during his London tenure, and several of his best-loved works were written for his concerts in Britain, including the lovely *Zambra granadina* and *España: Six Feuilles d'album*, which contains the ever-popular "Tango." *Chants d'Espagne* (or *Cantos de España*) includes some of the most celebrated and widely performed of his works, especially the "Prélude," a war-horse in the guitar repertoire. Although this piece was later inserted by publishers into the *Suite española No. 1* under the title "Asturias (Leyenda)," it is important to understand that this work was inspired by Andalusian flamenco and has absolutely nothing to do with folk music of the Asturias region in the north.

Sometime during the year 1893, Albéniz entered into a revised agreement with Lowenfeld that now included a third party. This man was Francis Burdett Thomas Nevill Money-Coutts (1852-1923), a London lawyer, poet, librettist, and wealthy heir to the fortune of the Coutts banking family.[16] This was a collaboration in which Money-Coutts supplied Albéniz with a large income in exchange for Albéniz's setting his poetry and librettos to music. Over time they became very close friends, and Money-Coutts supported Albéniz without any consideration of his operatic output.

According to the extant contract of 1893, Albéniz was obliged to confine his professional collaboration to Lowenfeld and Money-Coutts. When Lowenfeld dropped out of the deal the following year, Albéniz was committed to working only for Money-Coutts. This has prompted many biographers to characterize the arrangement as a "Faustian pact" in which Albéniz was forced to set mediocre texts that were out of sympathy with his temperament. But that is a gross exaggeration. We will see that Albéniz never felt himself constrained to work only for Money-Coutts and that he set librettos by other writers, or at least left several such projects in various stages of completion. One such project that he finished was a zarzuela for Madrid in 1894 on which he began serious work in late 1893. This coincided with his decision to leave London on a trip to Spain before moving permanently to Paris.

Exactly when he left London and how long he remained in Spain before taking up residence in Paris remain unanswered questions. But Albéniz clearly did not intend to build on the substantial foundation of success he enjoyed in London. Without the monetary assistance of Money-Coutts, Albéniz would have had great difficulty making this move, especially as he now intended to devote himself to composition and to perform much less often, thus greatly reducing what had been his principal source of income.

PARIS (1894-97)

Albéniz's first assignment from Money-Coutts was to set the libretto for an opera, eventually entitled *Henry Clifford* (it had many preliminary working titles), whose action takes place during the Wars of the Roses in fifteenth-century England. Albéniz began work on this new opera about the time he decided to leave London, for reasons of health, in the fall of 1893. Another motivation for the change of locale was that Rosina did not care for the climate and ambiance of London. She much preferred Paris, which she found more congenial to her temperament and where she could speak French, in which she was more fluent than English. He was no doubt also attracted to Paris as the artistic and intellectual capital of Europe.

Exactly when Albéniz settled in Paris is uncertain, but it was sometime before August 1894. We know he performed a great deal of chamber music in Barcelona during the fall and winter, and it bears pointing out that Albéniz was not only a brilliant soloist but a sensitive and knowledgeable interpreter of chamber music. Yet he did not remain in Barcelona more than a few months, at most. He had indicated already in London that he had no desire to resettle in Spain, and he never made a secret of his disenchantment with the state of culture and politics in his homeland (given his socialist and atheistic leanings, this is not hard to comprehend).

Albéniz's successful performances in Paris in 1889 were a living memory, and now, five years later, many influential people welcomed him back with open arms. Among these were Ernest Chausson and his wife Jeanne, who helped introduce him to Parisian musical society through their *soirées*, which attracted the city's brightest musical luminaries. At these functions Albéniz often improvised at the piano, charming the guests with his distinctively Spanish style. His own home became a mecca for Spanish writers, artists, and musicians. He participated in concerts given by the Société Nationale de Musique and eventually enrolled in the Schola Cantorum, where he studied counterpoint with Vincent d'Indy starting in October 1896. He also taught piano there from 1897 to 1900. It was at the Schola that he made the acquaintance of Erik Satie, Albert Roussel, and Déodat de Séverac.

He attended the 1894 premiere of Debussy's *Prélude à l'après-midi d'un faune*, as well as the opera *Pelléas et Mélisande* (1902), and cultivated an admiration for that composer's music. Albéniz's rapport with Paris and French culture became second in importance only to that with his homeland. In Paris he entered a new stage in his career as a composer, one marked by increased sophistication and technical ability.

By January of 1894 Albéniz had completed work in Barcelona on the piano-vocal score for the second act of *Henry Clifford*. Albéniz and Money-Coutts remained in frequent contact, and sometimes the Englishman would visit his Spanish friend in Paris to discuss details of the work. While progress continued on the new opera, Albéniz was busy with other projects. On September 13 he performed for the family of the Grand Duke of Wladimiro and other notables at the Miramar Palace in San Sebastián. But his chief occupation during the summer of 1894, in Paris, was finishing work on a one-act zarzuela entitled *San Antonio de la Florida*, with a text by his friend Eusebio Sierra, for performance in Madrid that fall.

At that time, there were two basic kinds of zarzuela, the *género chico* ("small genre") and *género grande* ("large genre"). The work by Albéniz and Sierra belongs to the former category in that it consists of a single act, divided into two scenes, and lasts an hour and forty-five minutes. The drama is characteristically comic and frivolous and presents a love story set during a period of political instability under the reign of Ferdinand VII, in 1823.[17]

The zarzuela premiered October 26, 1894, at the Teatro de Apolo. It ran until November 11 of the same year, receiving a total of fifteen performances. It was revived briefly before Christmas, receiving five more performances (December 17-21) before closing for good. All in all it was an average run; respectable, but not a big hit. The critics were unanimous in condemning the libretto, and they found Albéniz's music too sophisticated for the genre. The work would not be revived in Madrid until 1954 and then only for a short run.

However, Albéniz and Sierra also hoped to score a success with a Spanish adaptation of *The Magic Opal*, now to be called *La sortija* ("The Ring"). It is difficult to tell exactly how much the work was modified for performance in Madrid, but most of the operetta seems to have remained in its original version. Of course, the text was translated into Spanish, by Sierra. The operetta premiered on November 23, 1894, at the Teatro de la Zarzuela, but it received a cool reception from the public and elicited outright hostility from the critics, who castigated the authors for being "too foreignized." *La sortija* was a fiasco and folded after only three nights. Albéniz left for Paris, disillusioned and disheartened, before the end of its run.

Though he was embittered by the failure of the Madrid productions, Albéniz hoped his next stage work would fare better in Barcelona. He focused his efforts on finishing the score for *Henry Clifford* in time for its premiere at the Gran Teatre del Liceu in 1895, where it ran for five performances from May 8 through May 12. The production was sung in Italian under the title *Enrico Clifford*. The critics raved about the score but found the libretto inappropriate for Albéniz's musical personality. The opera promptly slid into obscurity and has never again been produced. *San Antonio de la Florida* was performed at the Tívoli in Barcelona on November 6 of that same year at a benefit concert for the soprano Angeles Montilla.[18] But the critical reaction was at best mixed.

Albéniz was not easily daunted. He determined to heed the counsel offered by friends and critics and set a libretto more in harmony with his nationalist inclinations. He prevailed on Money-Coutts to craft a libretto based on a Spanish work, the celebrated novel *Pepita Jiménez* (pub. 1874) by Juan Valera. At last he had a vehicle he believed would bring him the "glory and profit" the critics had predicted for him.

"PEPITA JIMÉNEZ" (1896-97)

After gaining Money-Coutts's approval of the project, Albéniz got in touch with Valera (1824-1905). However, Valera's initial response was highly negative, for he believed that the novel was unsuitable for the stage and would inevitably be misrepresented and distorted. But he did not stand in the way of the opera's progress, and Money-Coutts completed the libretto well before September of 1895, when the surviving manuscript of the score is dated.

The premiere took place in Barcelona on Sunday, January 5, 1896, at the Gran Teatre del Liceu. The work was performed in Italian, the custom at the Liceu, just as *Henry Clifford* had been. The opera received two performances on the 5th, one on the 6th, two on the 8th, and one each on the 11th, 12th, and 19th of January, on which day it closed. Despite the praise many well-meaning critics heaped on the work, it found no place in the repertoire and would not be produced again in Spain during Albéniz's lifetime.

So, in the spring of 1897, Albéniz travelled to the German-speaking world to promote *Pepita Jiménez*. He had established useful connections over the years with important people there, including the editors at Breitkopf und Härtel in Leipzig, who published the opera. It premiered at the Königliches Deutsches Landestheater Neues Deutsches Theater in Prague on June 22, 1897. In Albéniz's own mind the performance was less than satisfactory, but the notices were generally positive, and he was greatly encouraged by this. Appearing as it did at the end of the regular season, *Pepita Jiménez* ran only two nights (it was performed once more on the ensuing Friday, the 25th of June). It did not find the permanent place in the theater's repertoire Albéniz had hoped for and was never produced there again. He seems, however, to have been resigned to this, as he had his sights set on new possibilities. Albéniz signed a contract with Angelo Neumann (director of the Neues Deutsches Theater) for the composition of a stage work to be based on a libretto entitled *La voglia* by José Echagaray. He signed another contract with Neumann to write a ballet on the novel *Aphrodite* of Pierre Louÿs.[19] Neither of these commitments bore the slightest fruit.

During this period of intense involvement with the theater, he also took increasing interest in music for solo voice. While in London in 1892, he composed "Il en est de l'amour" to a text by M. Costa de Beauregard, which was followed three years later by the *Deux Morceaux de prose de Pierre Loti* ("Crépuscule" and "Tristesse"). In 1896 Albéniz began collaborating with Money-Coutts on songs as well as operas. Among these are *To Nellie: Six Songs* (Nellie was Money-Coutts's nickname for his wife). Other Money-Coutts songs from this time include "Will You Be mine?" and "Separated" (the only extant numbers from a collection of six songs that was not published during his life). "The Gifts of the Gods" later appeared with "The Caterpillar" as a set of two songs.[20] One other song (also unpublished during his life) was "Art Thou Gone for Ever, Elaine" (composed in 1906). But Albéniz was not confined to Money-Coutts's poetry, and around this same time he composed the lovely "Chanson de Barberine" to a text by Alfred de Musset. But, in fact, his future was more than ever bound up with that of his benefactor, and the following four years would absorb him in a project beyond the dimensions of anything he had previously attempted.

"MERLIN" (1898-1904)

The next product of Albéniz's professional association with Money-Coutts was an operatic project on a truly grand scale. This was a trilogy based on *Le Morte d'Arthur* by the fifteenth-century English author Sir Thomas Malory. The constituent parts of the *King Arthur* trilogy were to be *Merlin*, *Launcelot*, and *Guenevere*. Though it is tempting to see this as a misguided effort, one could also view the project as consistent with Albéniz's ever-waxing devotion to Wagnerism, a love affair that went back perhaps as far as his days as a student of Louis Brassin in Brussels. Albéniz attended performances of Wagner's operas whenever possible, and detailed annotations made by him in his personal copies of the full scores to the *Ring* cycle reveal a profound knowledge of the music.[21] Albéniz's commitment to Wagnerian principles in the trilogy is apparent in his use of leading motives and their presentation and development almost exclusively in the orchestra. It is also apparent in his avoidance of simultaneous singing and his treatment of the voices, i.e., in the emphasis on clarity of declamation and renunciation of *fioritura*.

When precisely the Arthurian project commenced is not known. The librettos were published in 1897 by John Lane in London. *Merlin* was finally published, in piano-vocal format, by Édition Mutuelle in 1906. Unfortunately, Albéniz completed only the piano-vocal score of the first of *Launcelot*'s three acts and some of the orchestral score for Act II. Marginalia in the libretto represent his furthest progress with the four acts of *Guenevere*. *Merlin* was never staged during Albéniz's lifetime. The Prelude to Act I, however, was well received at its premiere in Barcelona on November 14, 1898, during the third in a series of four concerts Vincent d'Indy conducted with the Asociació Filarmònica. *Merlin* finally premiered on December 18, 1950, at the Tívoli in Barcelona, performed by the Club de Fútbol Junior.

The year 1898 was one of severe health problems for Albéniz, which were even reported in the Barcelona press. He devoted that summer to seeking relief at a health spa in Plombières. His intestines had always been a source of discomfort, and his penchant for overeating only made matters worse. This was also a period of personal loss. In 1899 his friends Ernest Chausson and Count Morphy both died. The following year his beloved mother passed away (his father, with whom he had a complex and trying relationship, died in 1903). Charles

Bordes had appointed Albéniz to teach piano at the Schola Cantorum in 1897; however, on account of his intense involvement with composition, Albéniz was now less interested in teaching than he had been before, and ill health forced him to resign the position around 1900.

Albéniz's association with the Schola Cantorum inspired his most humorously charming work for piano, *Yvonne en visite!*, whose two movements bear the titles "La Révérence" ("The curtsy") and "Joyeuse Rencontre, et quelques pénibles événements!!" ("Joyous encounter, and some painful events!!"). It appeared in a collection of pieces for children "small and large" by musicians at the Schola Cantorum. Albéniz became involved with another important musical institution in Paris at this time, the Société Nationale de Musique, and his services as a performer and composer were in demand at their concerts. Albéniz's single most important work for orchestra, *Catalonia*, premiered at a concert of the Société Nationale de Musique on May 28, 1899, in the Nouveau-Théâtre. It was initially conceived as a "Suite Populaire" of compositions inspired by his native province. But he abandoned work on the other pieces and contented himself with the first number.

Albéniz occupied three different residences during his Paris years. The first was at 49, rue d'Erlanger (building no longer standing) until about 1905, when he moved for a short time to 21, rue Franklin. The years 1906-09 were spent at 55, rue de Boulainvilliers in a fashionable, upscale district. The building, completed in 1905, was virtually brand new in the year Albéniz moved there and still stands today. Thus, though he also had addresses elsewhere in France and Spain, Paris was his "home base," and he became a fixture in the French capital's cultural life. Although he had reservations about French modernism, Albéniz held Debussy in high regard (contrary to what some biographers have asserted) and was very close to Séverac, d'Indy, and Dukas. He became an especially intimate friend of Fauré.

In 1899 Albéniz began an extensive reorchestration of *Pepita Jiménez*, no doubt inspired by the lessons he had learned from the other orchestral works of this period and from Dukas, who mentored him on this subject. Albéniz's interest in orchestral writing during this time received further impetus from another collaboration with Money-Coutts. The Englishmen wrote several letters to him about a series of poems entitled *The Alhambra* that Albéniz had evidently requested for setting to music and that were based on the composer's suggestions.

Albéniz decided not to use these poems for songs and commenced a suite of pieces for orchestra inspired by them. At some point, Albéniz again changed his mind and chose to write the suite for piano rather than orchestra, but he completed only the first number, "La vega." José Vianna da Motta, the work's dedicatee, premiered it at a Société Nationale de Musique concert on January 21, 1899. This work signals a dramatic change in his nationalist style and is a clear harbinger of *Iberia* in its impressionist harmony and sophisticated formal design. However, Albéniz was by no means ready to give up on opera yet. He was convinced of the merit of his efforts in that arena, including *Merlin*, a production of which he did everything in his power to secure. His aspirations began to take material form in June 1901 when he, Enric Morera, and Enric Granados entered into an agreement to establish a Teatre Líric Català in Barcelona. [22] The plan was to produce a series of twelve presentations of their works the following spring at the Teatre de Novetats, including *Merlin* as well as Morera's *Emporium* and Granados's *Follet*. Morera, however, soon betrayed the confidence of his friends and applied to Chapí in Madrid to have his opera produced at the Teatro Lírico in that city. At some point Albéniz approached the Liceu about producing *Merlin*. But he merely encountered the suspicion and hostility of the theater's management, which insisted on his submitting the score to a panel of "experts" for evaluation. Albéniz and Granados gave up in disgust, and the entire Catalan lyric theater project came to naught. The whole episode merely reinforced Albéniz's hostility towards Spain.

Albéniz rarely remained long in one place. In the spring of 1902 he left Barcelona and followed Morera to Madrid in hopes of gaining an audience for *Merlin* or *Pepita Jiménez*. His desire now was to settle in Madrid, not only for the sake of a possible *Merlin* premiere but because he was determined finally to make his mark as a *zarzuelero*. In 1902 he committed to composing a three-act zarzuela entitled *La real hembra* ("The Royal Woman") with a libretto by Cristóbal de Castro, a Madrid journalist who had signed a contract with the Circo de Parish for the work. Albéniz planned to spend the summer near Santander to make the translation of *Merlin* with the help of Sierra, as well as to work on *Launcelot* and a new operatic project, *Rinconete y Cortadillo*, based on an episode from *Don Quijote* (libretto by Henri Cain). In addition to the prospect of *Merlin* in the fall and the new zarzuela, he was attempting to bring *Pepita Jiménez* to the capital city. But Madrid's theaters had no real interest in this work. *Rinconete y Cortadillo* never made the journey from mind to manuscript, and Castro finished only the first act of the libretto for *La real hembra* before leaving town and losing interest in the project. Albéniz got no further than the prelude and first two scenes. Finally, Chapí did not live up to whatever assurances he had given Albéniz, and *Merlin* was never produced in Madrid. Albéniz gave up and retreated once again to the north.

The fall of 1902 was spent recuperating from his habitual malaise, this time in the beauty of the Swiss Alps with Money-Coutts and Nellie. November found Albéniz and his traveling companions in Milan searching for a publisher for *Merlin*. In the following year Albéniz used the extremely generous allowance Money-Coutts was giving him to establish yet another residence, at the Château St. Laurent in Nice. So, Albéniz would now divide his remaining time on earth between Paris, Nice, and Tiana, just as his hero Liszt had spent his twilight years in Weimar, Rome, and Budapest.

Albéniz liked to discuss philosophical issues, and his correspondence with Money-Coutts reveals a lively dialogue on politics and religion. Despite his lack of formal education, Albéniz was fluent in Spanish, French, English, Italian, and Catalan, knew some German, and was well read. His library included novels of Daudet and Flaubert, the writings of Berlioz, plus the works of Voltaire, Byron, Hugo, Racine, Corneille, de Musset, Molière, Balzac, Plato, Louÿs, Maeterlinck, France, Plutarch, Shakespeare, Goethe, and Schiller (these last two in French translation). He also read works of contemporary Catalan authors, such as Santiago Rusiñol and Àngel Guimerà. He loved to collect books, and the generous income from Money-Coutts facilitated his buying. In addition, he collected fans and paintings. Though he could have built a valuable collection of impressionist paintings, he preferred to patronize Spanish artists. His daughter Laura become a noted artist in her own right, and her designs appeared on the first edition of *Iberia*.

With his interest in literature, Albéniz was not oblivious to the fact that his talents would be better devoted to librettos more consonant with his love of Spain. In 1899 he began composing a one-act lyric drama entitled *La Sérénade* (author unknown), but he soon abandoned the project. In this same year he commenced work on another lyric drama, *La morena* ("The Dark Woman"), with a text by Alfred Mortier. This, too, was left incomplete.

A reversal in Albéniz's operatic fortunes was on the way, but once more it would take place outside Spain. Ironically, it would prove the beautiful sunset and not the glimmering sunrise of his theatrical ambitions. Albéniz, dispirited by his inability to succeed as an opera composer, would thereafter pour his declining energies into writing once again for the piano, a decision greatly supported by friends and family alike. The result of this was, of course, his immortal masterpiece *Iberia*.

"IBERIA" (1905-09)

In 1905 Albéniz finally succeeded in securing a production of *Pepita Jiménez* and his zarzuela *San Antonio de la Florida*[23] at the Théâtre Royal de la Monnaie in Brussels, with which he had kept up a long correspondence on this very matter. They premiered together on January 3, 1905, with additional performances on January 6, 10, 13 and February 1. The production was apparently a huge success, though its total of five performances might not suggest this. There were attempts on the part of Fauré and others to secure a production of *Pepita Jiménez* in Paris, but this would not happen until 1923, long after Albéniz's death. *Merlin* was performed privately in a concert version on February 13, 1905, in Brussels (with the composer at the piano), but Albéniz was not successful in getting it produced anywhere. Though *Merlin* would remain unfamiliar to the Belgian public, the possibility of a new stage work materialized as a result of the Brussels triumph. Ramon Cattier was a journalist with *La Gazette* in the Belgian capital, and he and Albéniz laid enthusiastic plans for an opera entitled *La loba* ("The She-Wolf"). But the project never advanced beyond the planning stage.

This episode in Belgium marked both the high point and the end of Albéniz's musico-theatrical career. A combination of discouragement with the continued lack of interest in Spain in his operas and inability to get a production of *Merlin* anywhere persuaded him that his waning strength should be focused on what he did best, writing for the piano. However, his theatrical ventures had by no means been a waste of time and effort. First, they had brought forth from his pen some of his finest numbers, especially in *Pepita Jiménez*. Second, they had given him the best composition lessons he could have gotten, and he was now far beyond where he had been fifteen years earlier in terms of his handling of texture, sonority, and large-scale form.

So, Albéniz now set about to compose a monumental set of works for the piano entitled *Iberia*, whose creation would occupy him during the years 1905-08. It belonged to what the composer referred to as his "second manner," of which "La vega" was a clear premonition. But whether *Iberia* should actually be called a "suite" is open to question. Albéniz's title simply refers to them as twelve *nouvelles impressions* ("new impressions") for piano. Performers usually program at most a few of them on a concert; all together they make for a long evening (total playing time is about eighty-five minutes). It could more justifiably be called a collection, as the pieces are quite distinct and are not laid out in a sequence of any significance. The harmonic and rhythmic richness and complexity of these pieces are quite extraordinary, especially in comparison to his piano pieces of the 1880's and 90's. They abound in hand crossings, counter-rhythms, difficult leaps, and nearly impossible chords, while the innumerable double accidentals make them difficult to read. As a result, *Iberia* requires almost superhuman technique, and Albéniz himself was hardly capable of playing it.

The twelve pieces of *Iberia* are arranged into four books of three pieces each. Every number evokes a peninsular locale, city, festival, or song and dance, largely concentrating on the south of Spain. The first book, consisting of "Evocación," "El puerto," and "Fête-Dieu à Séville" (the original title, but usually referred to as "El Corpus en Sevilla"), bears a dedication to Madame Jeanne Chausson and was composed in December 1905. In the autograph score, "Triana," which he composed less than a month after the first book was complete, appears as the first selection in Book Two (dedicated to Blanche Selva), followed by "Almería" and "Rondeña," which were composed later that year. This chronological order was reversed in the first published edition, however, so that "Rondeña" leads off Book Two followed by "Almería" and "Triana." Albéniz wasted little time in commencing work on Book Three (dedicated to Marguerite Hasselmans), completing the three numbers "El Albaicín," "El polo," and "Lavapiés" during November and December of 1906 while spending the winter in the temperate climate of Nice. The final book (dedicated to Madame Pierre Lalo) took longer to finish. "Málaga" and "Eritaña" were composed in the summer of 1907 in Paris, but the final number, "Jerez," which occupies the middle position in the book, was not completed until January 1908. The explanation for this is quite simple. Albéniz had originally planned to conclude the collection with *Navarra*, a work he left incomplete at his death (it was finished by Séverac). He felt the style of *Navarra* did not fit in with the other numbers, so he composed "Jerez" as a substitute.

The four books of *Iberia* were premiered at various locales in France by the French pianist Blanche Selva, dedicatee of the second book. But in fact the Catalan pianist Joaquim Malats was Albéniz's favorite interpreter of these pieces, and they were composed for him. Though Selva was the first to present entire books in concert, Malats premiered several of the individual numbers in Spain. Albéniz laid great plans for a tour that would take Malats and *Iberia* throughout Europe. He was especially keen to have a Spaniard introduce the works. But Malats fell ill and could not realize these plans. Albéniz's letters to Malats certainly reveal the composer's uncommonly great admiration and affection for his countryman (see B94).

The papers in France took scant notice of Selva's premieres, but in Spain the critics gave unqualified praise to the works. This surprises, given the previous hostility of the Spanish press towards Albéniz's "foreignized" music and anything "Frenchified." In truth, the work's sympathetic reception in Spain was probably aided by the composer's ill health and premature death. Then again, purely instrumental music did not raise the critics' hackles the way stage works did, especially when it was played by an artist of Malats's stature. In the case of musical theater, Albéniz was running up against a long tradition and a deeply entrenched establishment. But in the sphere of piano music, he himself had defined the tradition and could do as he pleased.

It is important for us to remember that Albéniz's declining health made concertizing or holding any kind of regular job nearly impossible. The continued generous support from Money-Coutts permitted Albéniz to compose *Iberia*, and the Englishman never exerted pressure on him to finish the Arthurian trilogy. By the period of *Iberia*, then, Albéniz's association with Money-Coutts had ripened into a deep friendship and was not merely a business association. Their collaboration did produce one more work, the *Quatre Mélodies* for solo voice and piano of 1908, dedicated to Gabriel Fauré.

With the completion of *Iberia* and *Quatre Mélodies*, Albéniz began a precipitous decline into terminal illness. He spent the summer of 1908 in Bagnoles de l'Orne taking the waters and relaxing. Albéniz and his family then spent a trying winter on the Riviera, where they had gone in the futile hope that its mild climate would stimulate a recovery. A brief return to Paris in the spring and the ministrations of various specialists there did little to retard the deterioration of his health. A regular stream of visitors came to see him, and Dukas appeared religiously every day. Albéniz's heart was sorely taxed by excessive urea in his blood, due to the inefficiency of his kidneys. Now the family retreated once again to the south, this time to the French Basque country on the Atlantic side of the Pyrenees, in the small resort town of Cambo-les-Bains. Here he and his wife and daughters settled into a suite in the Château St. Martin. Though Money-Coutts could not come to see him, there were several other visitors during this final struggle. Pau Casals paid a visit, in the company of Alfred Cortot and Jacques Thibaud. The most heartening development was a surprise visit by Albéniz's dear friend Granados, who read a letter from Debussy informing Albéniz that, upon the recommendation of himself, Fauré, Dukas, and d'Indy, the French government had awarded him the Croix de la Légion d'Honneur.

However, the intense emotion of Granados's visit may have caused Albéniz's condition to worsen, and death moved much closer to his doorstep. On May 18, 1909, he was given an injection of morphine to ease his pain, but this had the unintended consequence of causing arrhythmia and initiated the end. He closed his eyes forever at exactly eight o'clock that evening. In eleven more days he would have reached his forty-ninth birthday.

Albéniz's body was embalmed and interred temporarily in Cambo-les-Bains before being sent by train to Barcelona, where elaborate funeral preparations had been made by Granados and others. His cortege wended its way through the city on June 6, accompanied by the police, dignitaries, and a band, while thousands of ordinary citizens thronged the streets and showered the hearse with flowers, as a gesture of affection and respect for one of Catalonia's greatest musicians. He was then buried in the Cementiri del Sud-Oest, on the seaward side of historic Montjüic.

THE MUSICAL LEGACY OF ALBÉNIZ

Albéniz continues to be a vital presence in the canon of western music. Thousands of recordings of his music have been made, and no less than forty publishing houses have printed his works. And he exerted a discernible influence on succeeding composers, especially in Spain.

Yet, his output was undeniably uneven in quality, and the only part of it to hold a place in the repertoire is a portion of the piano music. The rest of the piano pieces, stage works, and songs have slid into obscurity. Despite the enormous creative energy he poured into his operas in particular, his reputation has reaped relatively little benefit from them.

Though Albéniz himself broke his output down into two "manners," it makes more sense to divide it in the traditional fashion of early, middle, and late. The early works include his zarzuelas of 1881-2 (now lost), the many salon pieces of the 1880's, and the suites of Spanish pieces composed up to 1894, including such well-known collections as *Recuerdos de viaje*, *España: Six Feuilles d'album*, and *Chants d'Espagne*. The works of the middle period include all the stage works, the piano piece "La vega," and the orchestral work *Catalonia*. These last two works are clear premonitions of Albéniz's late period, represented chiefly by *Iberia* and *Quatre Mélodies*.

Albéniz's three-phase career as a composer can be seen, then, to correspond roughly to the final three decades of his life, from 1880 through 1909. Each decade brought with it a new level of development, culminating in an undisputed masterpiece, *Iberia*. The other conspicuous feature of his career is that, aside from his beginnings as a zarzuela composer, the first decade was devoted largely to the composition of works for piano, while the second decade was given over to musical theater. The final creative period presents a return to piano composition. This seeming ABA form poses, however, an important variation in the *da capo*. For Albéniz the composer of *Iberia* was light years beyond Albéniz the composer of *Recuerdos de viaje* in terms of musical sophistication and technical control, something he himself acknowledged. To be sure, some aspects of *Iberia* are observable in the early nationalist works, e.g., the use of Spanish dance rhythms, modality (especially the Phrygian mode), characteristic melodic and rhythmic flourishes, the descending minor tetrachord, and evocations of flamenco *cante jondo* and guitar. But many of the chief characteristics of *Iberia* are completely absent in the early period.

In terms of formal structure, the early nationalist works are almost without exception in simple sectional forms, usually ABA. The characteristic *modus operandi* regarding thematic material is repetition, not development. Albéniz's melodies, no matter how charming, were suited to little more than transposition, a characteristic Romantic device. By contrast, eight of the twelve pieces of *Iberia* are in freely adapted sonata form. Albéniz's juxtaposition of contrasting material and development of ideas create a richness and variety unprecedented in his early piano works. This is aided in part by melodies built from motivic cells that render them more capable of development. The early works offered harmonies that were suited to the melodic material in their charm and poignancy but that rarely ventured beyond the conventional. *Iberia*, on the other hand, reveals the influence of contemporary French music in its chromaticism, use of whole-tone scales, and its myriad modes and modal mixtures. Dissonance is far more prominent, and the use of augmented-sixth chords for modulating to distant tonal areas is conspicuous. There is also a high concentration of added-note sonorities and the use of secundal and quartal harmonies, which do not occur in the early suites.

Although Albéniz's style was always characterized by lively rhythms, *Iberia*'s use of superimposed meters, rapidly shifting meters, and complex patterns of accentuation represents a quantum leap over his earlier practice. The textures of *Iberia* and the early works are essentially homophonic, but those of *Iberia* are much more animated and often exhibit a contrapuntal use of countermelodies, especially during development sections. Finally, the virtuosic exploitation of the resources of the piano, the sheer range of timbres and effects Albéniz elicits from that instrument in *Iberia*, finds no parallel in the compositions from the early period.

This dramatic evolution in his style sets him apart from most of his contemporaries in Spain, who composed for a domestic market that was not noted for its sophistication. His tremendous growth was largely the product of his lengthy residence in Paris and exposure to a very high level of musical culture. It also emanated from his experience as an opera composer, through which he achieved greater mastery of large-scale forms and an appreciation of the expressive possibilities of orchestral sonority. He exhibited remarkable versatility and wrote operas in several of the major styles of his day: English operetta in *The Magic Opal*; French and German operetta in the additional numbers for *Incognita* and *Poor Jonathan*; Spanish operetta (zarzuela) in *San Antonio de la Florida*; Italian grand opera in *Henry Clifford*; Spanish national opera in *Pepita Jiménez*; and Wagnerian opera in *Merlin*. This wealth of experience was crucial in propelling Albéniz to a new level of composition. Unfortunately, these works have not held a place on the stage because of the weakness of their librettos and because of

Albéniz's penchant for investing musical interest in the orchestra and relegating the singers to delivering the text in a recitative that lacks the expressive range of Wagner or Verdi. The same could be said of the majority of his songs, which make so many demands on the pianist that the declamatory vocal line appears almost incidental. (There are a few happy exceptions to this, however, such as "The Caterpillar" and "To Nellie." In these cases, the voice has a charming melody supported by an unobtrusive piano accompaniment.)

If we consider Manuel de Falla as the central point towards and from which we measure the progress of Spanish nationalism in music, Albéniz is Falla's most important predecessor. Falla owes an obvious debt to Albéniz in such masterpieces as *La vida breve*, *Noches en los jardines de España*, and *Fantasía bética* in their blending of southern Spanish folklore and elements of French modernism. Joaquín Turina's style shift was the direct result of Albéniz's influence, and in such guitar works as *Ráfaga*, *Fandanguillo*, and the Sonata reverberations of Albéniz's Franco-Hispanic style are clear. In the music of Joaquín Rodrigo and Federico Moreno Torroba, we clearly hear the echoes of Albéniz's works. It was indeed he who defined what Spanish art music of our time would sound like.

Moreover, Albéniz occupies an important position in the overall cultural history of his homeland. As he spent more time outside of Spain and consequently came under the influence of Wagner and French music, he aligned himself with the forward-looking internationalists in Spain who sought a closer incorporation of their country into European culture (as opposed to the xenophobic *españolismo* of the conservative faction). Rodrigo has said of Albéniz that what he represents is "the incorporation of Spain, or better said, the reincorporation of Spain into the European musical world."[24] This was best summed up by Albéniz himself when he declared that Spanish composers ought "to make Spanish music with a universal accent."[25] *Iberia*, then, exhibits a political and philosophical dimension we might otherwise overlook. It is more than beautiful music; in its novelty and scope it is a summing up of Albéniz's view of Spanish culture and its proper place in European civilization.

CURRENT STATE OF RESEARCH

Given his importance, then, one is fairly amazed to discover that the scholarship on Albéniz has traditionally been neither wide nor deep. However, in recent years musicologists have begun to show increasing interest in him, and with the contributions of Baytelman, Bevan, Falces Sierra, Mast, and Torres, the study of his life and music has reached a new level. However, much work remains to be done. In particular, there are wide swaths of the piano music that have scarcely been considered. Indeed, nearly twenty years have passed since the last major study of *Iberia* (by Kalfa, B59), and even this is not available outside of the library of the Sorbonne in Paris. An up-to-date study of this work, utilizing the latest theoretical approaches, is greatly needed. However, the earlier works also present many opportunities for scholars and performers alike. "La vega," his greatest single work for piano (and this author's favorite), has never been the subject of even the briefest publication, and recordings of it are few. Yet, it is a pivotal work in his output, and in its formal and harmonic complexity more than worthy of substantial analysis. The same holds true for his sonatas and concertos, as well as *Catalonia*. Moreover, critical editions of Albéniz's music are almost wholly lacking, though this situation is beginning to change. [26]

Adherents of the "new musicology" might easily fault Hispanists for their tendency to produce work of a conservative nature, seemingly oblivious to the most recent trends. There is no doubt that much can and must be done in the area of gay and feminist criticism as well as with issues of race and culture. Critical reception has been shown by Carol Hess [27] and others to form a particularly significant intersection of politics and culture. However, those unfamiliar with this field need to understand that much of the rudimentary musicological work we take for granted in other areas of study (published correspondence, collected works, reliable catalogs and biographies, critical editions) is largely absent in the field of Spanish music history 1800-present. Thus, along with an up-to-date analytical and critical examination of this repertoire, there will always be a need for more traditional kinds of research.

The study of Albéniz, at any level of detail, quickly reveals that there are numerous possibilities for research in related areas. Albéniz's early career demonstrates that there was a rich concert life in the provinces as well as in Madrid and Barcelona during the nineteenth century, and this would merit deeper study. The enormous impact of

French and Italian musical theater in nineteenth-century Spain throws into sharp relief the revival of the zarzuela beginning around 1850 and continuing well into the twentieth century. This golden age is rich in outstanding composers and works (Albéniz certainly made a contribution to it, albeit minor), but the literature in English is very sparse and not as abundant in Spanish as one would expect. Though the movement towards national opera in Spain never reached a critical mass, there are several works by Bretón, Granados, Pedrell, and Falla that would reward thoughtful study. Twentieth-century composers other than Falla have been grossly neglected. Joaquín Rodrigo, for instance, wrote one of the most popular concertos of the twentieth century (the *Concierto de Aranjuez* for guitar and orchestra), while Moreno Torroba, Turina, and the Halffter brothers (Rodolfo and Cristóbal) all produced substantial bodies of work. Despite the fact that some excellent research has been done on several of these composers, they all remain wide open for further study.[28]

Above and beyond these considerations, the enormous impact of Spanish music outside the Iberian peninsula (especially in France and Russia) has been routinely underestimated by musicologists treating European art music of the nineteenth and twentieth centuries.[29] This is partly due to the fact that Spanish musical folklore is *terra incognita* to most scholars outside Spain, and without an intimate knowledge of the many genres (e.g., *bulerías*, *sevillanas*, *fandango*) it can prove rather difficult to get to the heart of classical works based on them. Thus, though Spanish-style music often seems facile, it is a mistake to conclude that any serious analysis would be pointless, especially in the case of a composer as intelligent and resourceful as Albéniz. This situation reflects the ongoing separation between historical musicology and ethnomusicology and the difficulties involved in bridging the two disciplines. With the ascendancy of rock 'n' roll as the dominant form of musical expression during the last forty years and the advent of the "classic rock" phenomenon, we have reached a point where this separation is a luxury we can no longer afford. If musicologists now feel compelled to take seriously such icons of popular musical culture as Madonna and Elvis, then composers of accessible classical music inspired by folklore, like Albéniz, certainly merit close scrutiny as well.

In short, anyone researching not only Albéniz but Hispanic music in all its dazzling variety will find ample opportunities for rewarding work. As they say in Spanish, "¡Vale la pena!"–it is worth the effort!

NOTES

1. This was its original name (founded in 1830) and the one it bears today. During Albéniz's studies there, however, it was known as the Escuela Nacional de Música y Declamación.

2. Independent confirmation of this concert is to be found in the manuscript *Concerts Celebrats á Barcelona 1797-1901 de Música Simfónica i de Camera*, located in the Institut Universitari de Documentació i Investigació Musicològica Josep Ricart i Matas in Barcelona. This is an important source of information concerning concert life in nineteenth-century Barcelona.

3. Reference to this is made in *Concerts Celebrats á Barcelona*. . . .

4. His military papers are in the Mm, carpeta 1, but they do not provide the exact date of his enlistment.

5. The Arxiu Diocesa of the Arquebisbat de Barcelona states that the marriage certificate was destroyed during the Spanish Civil War (1936-39).

6. See four letters in the Bc, M964, dated April 20, 1891, November 23, 1901, January 24, 1902, and June 29 (no year, but during the London period). It is this last one that bears the affectionate signature.

7. Pedrell's *Por nuestra música* (Barcelona: Juan Bta. Pujol, 1891) was a virtual manifesto of Spanish musical nationalism in opera and exerted considerable influence on Albéniz and his compatriots. Pedrell based his philosophy in part on Wagner, and in part on the writings of the eighteenth-century Spanish theorist Padre Antonio Eximeno.

8. According to *Concerts Celebrats á Barcelona*. . . .

9. A program of this concert is in the Bc, M987, v. 2.

10. This influence is especially apparent in "Rumores de la caleta (Malagueña)" from *Recuerdos de viaje* and in "Sevilla (Sevillanas)" from the *Suite española No. 1*. To be sure, Albéniz also evoked songs and dances from regions other than Andalusia, such as the Aragonese *jota* and Cuban *habanera*.

11. This oratorio was probably never completed.

12. The king died on November 5, 1885, of consumption.

13. The two letters informing him of these honors are in the Bc, M986 ("D"). The actual notices of appointment are in the same collection, under "V" (Varia). Most other sources assert that he was also made a Knight of the Order of Carlos III, but the author has as yet found no documentation to support this.

14. The original premiered in Paris at the Nouveautés on October 19, 1882.

15. The original work, with a text by H. Wittmann and J. Bauer, premiered January 4, 1890, in Vienna.

16. He became the Fifth Lord Latymer in 1912. His surnames are usually, but not always, hyphenated. His publications often appear under the name Coutts (pronounced "coots"). He also adopted the pen name "Mountjoy."

17. The exact year is not given in either the score or libretto from the original production. The year 1823 is stated in the French libretto published for the 1905 staging in Brussels.

18. Angeles Montilla had sung the role of Lolika in the Madrid production of *La sortija* and was credited by some critics with saving the performance from being a complete disaster.

19. *La voglia* ("The Wish") was actually an idea for a libretto that Neumann hoped Echegaray would consent to write. *Aphrodite* was a popular novel (pub. 1896) depicting courtesan life in ancient Alexandria.

20. Though most catalogs list these as a group of two songs, based on the Édition Mutuelle publication of 1913, "The Caterpillar" was composed in 1903, six years after the first publication of "The Gifts of the Gods." Moreover, Albéniz always took his poems for groups of songs from the same collection. "The Gifts of the Gods" comes from Money-Coutts's *Poems* (1895), whereas "The Caterpillar" appeared in *Musa Verticordia* (1895). Both songs were translated into French by Henry Varley for the 1913 edition (entitled "Les Dons des dieux" and "La Chenille").

21. Published Mainz: Schott, n.d. These have surfaced in the library of La Escuela Superior de Canto in Madrid. They bear Albéniz's stamp, dated April 16, 1896. The scores were eventually bequeathed to Enrique Arbós, who then gave them to the school. I thank Prof. Jacinto Torres for bringing them to my attention.

22. The actual contract is located in the Mm, carpeta 4, and is dated June 18, 1901.

23. Now entitled *L'Hermitage flueri*, in a French translation by Lucien Solvay and Robert Sand. In marked contrast to the reception accorded it in Spain, the Brussels critics had nothing but praise for the zarzuela's elegance, humor, and popular melody.

24. From the program notes of a concert at the Liceu commemorating the centenary (Barcelona: Juan A. Pamias, 1960).

25. In Víctor Ruiz Albéniz, *Isaac Albéniz* (Madrid: Comisaria General de Música, 1948), 102.

26. In 1996 the Instituto Complutense de Ciencias Musicales (ICCMU) in Madrid published a modern edition of the two-act version of *Pepita Jiménez*, edited by José Soler. This appeared felicitously on the centenary of the opera's premiere in Barcelona. At this writing, an *urtext* and facsimile edition of *Iberia*

is being prepared by Jacinto Torres Mulas and Guillermo González and will soon be published by Schott in Spain (EMEC-EDEMS). It has already been recorded by González on a Naxos CD (8.554311/12). See also the performance edition of Antonio Iglesias, *Iberia: doce nuevas impresiones* (Madrid: Alpuerto, 1993). Pola Baytelman has recorded her critical edition (unpublished at this writing) of *Iberia* on a CD for Élan (82288). A performance edition of *Merlin*, edited by Jose María de Eusebio, will soon be available from Editorial Piles in Valencia. Our understanding of archival sources for modern editions has recently been enhanced by Jacinto Torres Mulas, "Concentración vs. dispersión de fondos documentales. El desdichado caso de Isaac Albéniz," *El patrimonio musical: Los archivos familiares (1898-1936)* (Trujillo, Cáceres: Ediciones de la Coria, 1997). This same author has shed light on the sources and publication history of the *Suite española No. 1* and *Chants d'Espagne* in his liner notes for a recording of two-guitar arrangements of these masterpieces by Carmen María Ros and Miguel García Ferrer (Opera Tres CD-1026-ope, 1997).

27. "Manuel de Falla's *The Three-Cornered Hat* and the Advent of Modernism in Spain" (Ph.D. dissertation, University of California, Davis, 1994).

28. In particular, see William Craig Krause, "The Life and Works of Federico Moreno Torroba" (Ph.D. diss., Washington University, 1993). Notable work on Spanish opera composers has been done by Francesc Cortès i Mir, "El nacionalismo musical de Felip Pedrell a través de sus óperas: Els Pirineus, La Celestina y El Comte Arnau" (Ph.D. diss., Universitat Autònoma de Barcelona, 1996), and Elizabeth Seitz, "Manuel de Falla's Years in Paris, 1907-14" (Ph.D. diss., Boston University, 1995).

29. Indeed, Carl Dahlhaus's *Nineteenth Century Music*, trans. by J. Bradford Robinson (Berkeley and Los Angeles: University of California Press, 1989) includes no discussion at all of Spain or Spanish composers. An insightful recent study into the relationship between Spanish nationalist composers (including Albéniz) and French impressionism is by Celsa Alonso, "Nazionalismo spagnolo e avanguardia: la presunta praticabilità dell'Impressionismo," *Musica/Realtà* 15/44 (1994), 81-106. The important role played by Spanish musicians in Paris around 1900 is the subject of Montserrat Bergadà Armengol, *Les pianistes catalans à Paris entre 1875 et 1925: Contribution à l'étude des relations musicales entre la France et l'Espagne* (Ph.D. diss., Université François Rabelais, Tours, 1997).

CHAPTER TWO

Bibliography

PART A: PRIMARY SOURCES (HOLDINGS AND LOCATION OF ARCHIVES AND ALBÉNIZ ORGANIZATIONS)

This is not intended as a detailed catalogue of the holdings listed below, as the author does not have permission to publish such an inventory and a thorough list would overwhelm the necessary limits of this book (there are over 600 letters in the Biblioteca de Catalunya alone). However, these entries will give any researcher a general understanding of the primary source materials that are currently accessible, their location, and the name of a person to contact (where available).

1. Biblioteca de Catalunya
    Sección de Música
    Carrer de L'Hospital, 56
    08001 Barcelona
    Spain
    Contact Person: Joana Crespi

    Correspondence: Letters to Albéniz are ordered alphabetically under sig. M986 and include items from such figures as Louis Bertrand, Tomás Bretón, Ernest Chausson, Édouard Colonne, Mathieu Crickboom, Vincent d'Indy, Paul Dukas, Manuel de Falla, Gabriel Fauré, Enric Granados, Pierre Louÿs, Joaquim Malats, Camille Mauclair, Francis Money-Coutts (under 'C'), Enric Morera, Guillermo Morphy, Joaquín Nin, Felip Pedrell, Francis Planté, Joseph Ropartz, Darío Regoyos, Déodat de Séverac, Eusebio Sierra, Joaquín Turina, José Vianna da Motta, and Ignacio Zuloaga. Under "Varia" one finds the certificate of his winning first prize in the 1879 piano competition at the Brussels conservatory, documents pertaining to his appointment to the Royal Order of Isabel the Catholic, and his comments on auditioning hopefuls at the Paris Conservatoire in 1907. Four letters from Albéniz to Pedrell are in M964. *Newspaper Clippings:* Two volumes under sig. M987 contain many reviews of his concerts and operas from the period 1889 to 1894, during his tenure in London. They also include some concert programs. *Printed materials:* Scores from his library, many with dedicatory inscriptions by the composer. Represented are works by Tomás Bretón, Emanuel Chabrier, Ernest Chausson, Paul Dukas, Manuel de Falla, Vincent d'Indy, Jules Massenet, Enric Morera, Déodat de Séverac, and Joaquín Turina. *Manuscripts:* All the operas (M974-83) and symphonic works (M984). "La vega" from *The Alhambra: Suite pour le piano*; "Evocación," "El Albaicín," "Málaga," "Jerez," and "Eritaña" from *Iberia*; and *Navarra* (M980). Various opera numbers and the incomplete second piano concerto (M985).

2.   Biblioteca del Orfeó Català
     San Francesc de Paula, 2
     08003 Barcelona
     Spain
     Contact Person: Josefina Sastre, Director

     Printed material: Programs from Albéniz's 1888 concerts at the Exposición Universal in Barcelona, and from the premiere of *Merlin* in 1950.
     Manuscripts: "Rondeña," "Fête-Dieu à Séville," "Almería," "El polo," and "Triana" from *Iberia; San Antonio de la Florida* (piano-vocal score in copyist's hand); Act I of *Henry Clifford* (piano-vocal score in copyist's hand); "Will You Be Mine" and "Separated," the only extant numbers from *Six Songs*.

3.   Museu Municipal de la Música, Barcelona
     Avgda. Diagonal, 373
     08008 Barcelona
     Spain
     Contact Person: Romà Escalas, Director

This archive includes some of the most important documentation pertaining to his life and work. Most of the materials are kept in large file boxes called *carpetas*. Correspondence not located in these files is organized numerically and kept in folders called *lligalls* (a register is available). Items of interest include:

Correspondence to him and/or his family from: Breitkopf und Härtel, Max Eschig, Enric Granados, Joaquim Malats, Francis and Helen Money-Coutts (up to 1923), Michel Raux Deledicque (one of his biographers), Juan Valera, and Ignacio Zuloaga. Also includes Albéniz's letters to his wife, Rosina, and letters from Granados to Malats.

Newspaper Clippings: The "Arxiu carpeta premsa" and "Arxiu premsa biogràfic" include newspaper clippings of reviews (many without newspaper title or specific date) of his performances, operas, his reviews of others' works, and articles about him (before and after his death) and his funeral ceremonies.

Personal Items: Numerous photographs of him and important figures in his life (Tomás Bretón, Felip Pedrell, Guillermo Morphy, Enric Granados), the album he took with him on his early concert tours (containing inscriptions and reviews), journals and diaries, military papers (and those of his maternal grandfather), baptism and death certificates, and other documents pertaining to his death.

Printed materials: Programs of concerts and operas (during and after his life), and of events connected with the centenary of his birth in 1960. Poems by his father, Ángel. His scores and books on music. Journal articles on Albéniz.

Manuscripts: *San Antonio de la Florida* (piano-vocal score, in copyist's hand but autographed by Albéniz), *Henry Clifford* and its working version "The Shepherd Lord" (full and piano-vocal scores), *Fantasie espagnole pour le piano* (same as "La vega" from *The Alhambra: Suite pour le piano*), *La Sérénade* (incomplete piano-vocal score), Prelude to *Merlin* (full score), *Launcelot* (incomplete full score of Act II), *Poèmes d'amour* (parts only), and "Lavapiés" from *Iberia*. Reproductions of this last manuscript are for sale at the musuem.

4. Rosina Moya Albéniz de Samsó
   San Antonio, 1
   08394 San Vincenç de Montalt
   Barcelona
   Spain

   The granddaughter of the composer retains his extensive
   library (except for music scores and books on music) and his
   sizeable collection of paintings and fans.

5. Archivo de la Dirección de Costes de Personal y Pensiones
   Públicas
   Argumosa, 41
   28012 Madrid
   Spain

   Detailed records of Ángel Albéniz's employment in the
   revenue department of the Spanish government from 1847 to
   1881. His personal file also includes documents pertaining to his
   retirement in 1881 and the dispensation of his pension after his
   death in 1903. These documents provide valuable information
   about the family's residences during Albéniz's early life.

6. Fundación Isaac Albéniz
   Juan Bravo, 20-6° Dcha.
   28006 Madrid
   Spain
   Contact person: Cristina Pons, Director

   This organization was founded by the pianist Paloma
   O'Shea to promote performance and scholarship devoted to
   Albéniz. It organized a traveling exhibition on Albéniz in 1990
   and has issued several important publications. It remains an
   important source of information for Albéniz researchers.

7. Instituto de Bibliografía Musical
   c/ Santa Isabel 15, 5°
   28012 Madrid
   Spain
   Contact Person: Dr. Jacinto Torres Mulas

Dr. Torres publishes through his Instituto the only editions available of various works by Albéniz, including his *Salmo VI*, *Rapsodia española* (original orchestration), and the songs "Will you be mine," "Separated," and "Art Thou Gone for Ever, Elaine?," all to texts of Money-Coutts. He is also a leading authority in this field and has amassed a large amount of research material. He is willing to assist other researchers.

8. Real Conservatorio Superior de la Música
Doctor Mata, 2
28012 Madrid
Spain
Contact Person: José Soto, Director of the Archive

Manuscripts: *Salmo VI*, "Cataluña" and "Cuba" from the *Suite española No. 1*, and examination records containing references to Albéniz's studies there (*Actas de los Exámenes de 1865-66 á 1871-72 y 72-73 á 77-78*). Several first editions.

9. Hochschule für Musik Felix Mendelssohn-Bartholdy
Grassistrasse 8
Postfach 100809
04008 Leipzig
Germany
Contact Person: Frau Piech, Head Librarian

Record of admission (no. 2513) and Lehrer Zeugniß (also no. 2513), which lists courses taken and provides comments of the professors.

10. Staatsarchiv Leipzig
Schongauerstraße 1
04329 Leipzig
Germany

The archive of the publisher Breitkopf und Härtel is located here and includes the correspondence to and from Albéniz (the originals of some of the letters from Breitkopf und Härtel are located in the Mm). There are over fifty letters and cards from 1896 through 1906.

11. Latymer Archive
    Coutts & Co.
    440 Strand
    London WC2R 0QS
    Great Britain
    Contact Person: Barbara J. Peters, Archivist

    Retains the 1893 contract between Money-Coutts, Lowenfeld, and Albéniz that became the basis for a much-fictionalized "pact of Faust" between the Spaniard and his wealthy English benefactor. Also contains useful documents pertaining to Money-Coutts's own theatrical investments and speculations, his estate, and his payments to Albéniz.

12. Conservatoire Royal de Bruxelles (Administration Archives)
    30 rue de la Régence
    1000 Brussels
    Belgium

    Demande d'Admission (no. 886) listing period of study, addresses, and courses taken.

13. L'Association Internationale Isaac Albéniz
    52 rue La Fayette
    F-75009 Paris
    France
    Contact Person: Dr. Jacqueline Kalfa, President

    This organization has done considerable research on Albéniz and retains some materials donated by Diane Albéniz Ciganer, one of the composer's descendants.

PART B: SECONDARY SOURCES (BOOKS AND ARTICLES)

This bibliography includes only published materials. Exceptions to this rule are doctoral documents available through UMI and unpublished Ph.D. dissertations. It does not include recording or performance reviews, master's theses, term papers, or D.M.A. documents not registered with UMI. It also does not include short articles (of one to two pages) of no substance. However, longer items of little originality or value are cited so that one can know not to pursue them. Encyclopedia or dictionary entries do not appear unless they are of unusual substance and length. Liner notes and concert programs of importance are included. Only publications in Catalan, English, French, German, Italian, and Spanish appear.

14. Albéniz, Isaac. *Impresiones y diarios de viaje.* Ed. by Enrique Franco. Madrid: Fundación Isaac Albéniz, 1990. 70 p. ISBN 847506311X. ML410.A3 A3 1990. In Spanish.

    The first publication of Albéniz's travel journals and diaries. The initial entries are from 1880 and record his journey to Budapest in search of Franz Liszt, with whom he hoped to study. The second set of journal entries deals with his journey to Prague in 1897 and the production of *Pepita Jiménez* there in that year. In 1898 Albéniz began a diary in which, until the final entry in 1903, he expatiated on a wide variety of subjects. Unfortunately, this edition was rendered from a typewritten copy made by the composer's daughter Laura. There are some deletions and a number of other discrepancies between this version and the original manuscripts (in the Mm). Unfortunately, these errors persist in the printed edition.

15. Andrade de Silva, Tomás. "El Piano de Albéniz." *Música (Revista de los Conservatorios),* 2 (October-December 1952), 71-82. In Spanish.

    A treatment of the daunting technical problems posed by *Iberia,* describing it as "anti-pianistic" in its nearly impossible chords, leaps, and rhythms. Proceeds to a brief discussion of the particular challenges of each number in the collection, along with some reflections on their musical style.

16. Aparicia, María Pilar. "'Pepita Jiménez,' correspondencia Valera-Albéniz." *Boletín de la Real Academia Española* (1975). Reprinted in Enrique Franco, ed. *Albéniz y su tiempo*, pp. 80-100. Madrid: Fundación Isaac Albéniz, 1990. ISBN 8475063136. ML141.A53 1990. In Spanish.

    During the period 1895-98 Albéniz corresponded with the noted Spanish author Juan Valera concerning his plans to convert Valera's novel *Pepita Jiménez* (1874) into an opera. Only Valera's letters have survived, but they reveal his misgivings about the novel's dramatic merits. He declared that even if Mozart were to set it to music, "it would be a disaster." He further insisted that mixing his novel with Albéniz's music would be like "mixing a partridge with custard," a recipe in which both ingredients would be ruined. Though he did give grudging consent to the project and rejoiced in its success, to the end he believed there were others of his works more suitable for the stage.

17. Arbós, Enrique Fernández. *Arbós*. Madrid: Ediciones Cid, 1963. 538 p. ML410.A73 A3 1963. In Spanish. [Excerpt entitled "Santander, 1883" appears in Enrique Franco, ed. *Albéniz y su tiempo*, pp. 63-67. Madrid: Fundación Isaac Albéniz, 1990. ISBN 8475063136. ML141.A53 1990. In Spanish.]

    The autobiography provides useful insights into the period when Arbós and Albéniz were students together at the Conservatoire Royal in Brussels (1877-79) and their later collaborations in England during the early 1890's. In this excerpt from his autobiography, Arbós (the renowned violinist and conductor who was also a close friend of Albéniz's) discusses their joint concert tour in northern Spain in 1883 and makes some amusing observations about Albéniz's mannerisms, especially his eating habits.

18. Aviñoa, Xosé. *Albéniz*. Series: Conocer y reconocer la música de. Mexico City: Daimon, 1986. 84 p. ISBN 9686024867. In Spanish.

This pocket-size work contains a cursory biography and discussion of his music as well as a catalogue of his works, discography, chronology, and glossary. Includes only a few footnotes and no musical examples, index, or bibliography.

19. Baytelman, Pola. *Isaac Albéniz: Chronological List and Thematic Catalog of His Piano Works.* Detroit Studies in Music Bibliography, 72. Warren, Mich.: Harmonie Park Press, 1993. 124 p. ISBN 0899900674. ML134.A45 A12 1993. In English. Reviewed by Frances Barulich, *Notes of the Music Library Association* 51/3 (1995): 939-42; Gertraut Haberkamp, *Die Musikforschung* 43/1 (1995): 93; Walter Aaron Clark, "Recent Researches in Spanish Music 1800 to the Present," *Inter-American Music Review* 16/1 (Summer-Fall, 1997), 87-88.

   A reworking of her doctoral document (Pola Baytelman Dobry, *Albéniz: Chronological Listing and Thematic Catalogue of His Piano Works.* D.M.A. thesis, University of Texas, Austin, 1990. 106 p. UMI Order No. AAC 9116798), this is the first thematic catalog of Albéniz's music ever published and the first monograph on him in English. Presents a summary of biographical issues, including recent research casting doubt on some aspects of the existing record. Discusses style periods, publishers, and detailed examination of the piano music in chronological order listing performance, publication information, and special details. The chronology of Albéniz's compositions is often difficult to determine, and some problems persist in her ordering. Concludes with a discography and several other appendices, including a chronology of his life and lists of piano works by collection and by grade of difficulty. Contains many reproductions of cover designs from first editions.

20. Bevan, Clifford. "Albéniz, Money-Coutts and 'La Parenthèse londonienne.'" Ph.D. dissertation, University of London, 1994. 296 p. In English. Reviewed by Walter Aaron Clark, "Recent Researches in Spanish Music 1800 to the Present," *Inter-American Music Review* 16/1 (Summer-Fall, 1997), 86-87.

   Bevan explores in detail Albéniz's operatic collaboration with the wealthy Englishman Francis Burdett Money-Coutts.

The dissertation provides short biographies of both men up to 1893, with an emphasis on Albéniz's years in London 1890-93 and the formation of their relationship. The three operas Albéniz composed to librettos by Money-Coutts—*Henry Clifford*, *Pepita Jimenez*, and *King Arthur* (a trilogy)—are examined in a comparative way in terms of their production, reception, textual and musical structure, and influences. Also provides a brief examination of Albéniz's songs on texts of Money-Coutts. The appendices include plot summaries and a thorough catalogue of manuscript and published sources. The text is provided with numerous musical examples.

21. Bretón, Tomás. "En la muerte de Albéniz." *ABC* (May 21, 1909): 4-5. Reprinted in Enrique Franco, ed. *Albéniz y su tiempo*, pp. 121-24. Madrid: Fundación Isaac Albéniz, 1990. ISBN 8475063136. ML141.A53 1990. In Spanish.

    A homage to the recently deceased composer with personal recollections of the author's acquaintance with the young Albéniz. Praises his eventual accomplishments as both a pianist and composer.

22. Camín, Alfonso. "De Nueva York a Budapest." *Norte* (Revista Mexicana) (1951). Reprinted in Enrique Franco, ed. *Albéniz y su tiempo*, pp. 41-49. Madrid: Fundación Isaac Albéniz, 1990. ISBN 8475063136. ML141.A53 1990. In Spanish.

    A brief biography of Albéniz that is completely dependent on earlier, often unreliable, secondary sources. The author invents dialogue to make the article a better read. It is useful for some of the historical and cultural background information it contains, including a poem by the Nicaraguan poet Rubén Darío.

23. Clark, Walter Aaron. "Albéniz en Leipzig y Bruselas: Nuevas luces sobre una vieja historia." *Revista de Musicología* 14/1-2 (1991): 213-18. In Spanish.

    An examination of records of Albéniz's study at the Hochschule für Musik Felix Mendelssohn-Bartholdy in Leipzig and at the Conservatoire Royal in Brussels. Contrary to his various claims to have studied nine, eighteen, or thirty-six months in Leipzig, he was there for less than two months. He began his studies at Brussels in September of 1876, shortly after his departure from Leipzig.

24.   — — —. "Albéniz in Leipzig and Brussels: New Data from Conservatory Records." *Inter-American Music Review* 11/1 (Fall-Winter, 1990): 113-17. In English.

English version of the above article (slightly condensed). Casts doubt on Albéniz's having met and played for Liszt, who was not in Budapest at the time Albéniz claimed to have met him there.

25.   — — —. "'Cavalleria Iberica' Reassessed: Critical Reception of Isaac Albéniz's Opera *Pepita Jiménez.*" *Actas del XV Congreso de la Sociedad Internacional de Musicología,* in *Revista de Musicología* 16/6 (1993): 3255-62. In English.

A reception history of Albéniz's best-known and most successful opera, which was produced in Barcelona, Prague, Brussels, Paris, again in Barcelona, and finally in Madrid. Although reviewers praised its local color and rhythmic vitality, they faulted Albéniz's preference for the orchestra over the voices and the libretto's lack of dramatic interest.

26.   — — —. *Isaac Albéniz: Portrait of a Romantic.* Oxford: Clarendon Press, 1998. 325 p. ISBN 019816369X. In English.

The first book-length examination in English of the life and works of the composer (in press at this writing). Begins with a history of Albéniz biography and confronts the issue of Albéniz's prevarications about his early career and the inconsistencies and discrepancies that, as a result, plague all biographical accounts. The biography traces his family history and then attempts, on the basis of much new and previously overlooked documentation, to provide an accurate account of Albéniz's remarkable early career as a touring prodigy and his metamorphosis into a full-time composer of considerable importance. Includes a critical examination of his major compositions for piano, voice, orchestra, and the stage, with an emphasis on his handling of folkloric material. Study of his music's critical reception is supported by ample citation of press notices. Also amply cited are letters to and from the composer and his own diary entries, which tell a great deal about his relationships and inner life. The biography concludes with a critique of his legacy, his role in Spanish music history, and his status in Spain today. Contains a genealogical chart and list of works as well as numerous musical examples.

27.   — — —. "Isaac Albéniz's Faustian Pact: A Study in Patronage." *Musical Quarterly* 76/4 (December 1992): 465-87. In English.

Examines in detail Albéniz's relationship with the wealthy Englishman Francis Burdett Money-Coutts, the inheritor of a banking fortune who became a writer of poetry and librettos and hired Albéniz to set them to music. All biographers have railed at Money-Coutts for seducing Albéniz into a "pact of Faust," which supposedly forced him to expend his energy on projects that were alien to his nature. This article debunks that view and shows, through their correspondence and other documentation, that there was no compulsion in the arrangement and that it emanated from a deep bond of friendship between the two men. Albéniz benefited to the extent that he did not have to worry about money and was therefore able, during his final, illness-ridden years, to devote himself to composing his *chef d'oeuvre*, *Iberia*.

28.   — — —. "'Spanish Music with a Universal Accent': Isaac Albéniz's Opera *Pepita Jiménez*." Ph.D. dissertation, University of California, Los Angeles, 1992. 380 p. UMI Order No. AAC 9317432. In English.

An in-depth study of Albéniz's most successful opera. Begins with an examination of problems in the biography of Albéniz's early life, then a study of his career as an opera composer and his relationship with Francis Burdett Money-Coutts, the librettist. Chapters on the transformation of the novel into a libretto and on manuscript and published sources are followed by an analysis of the music and the opera's critical reception. The final chapters treat the work's significance in the context of Albéniz's evolution as a composer and in the development of Spanish national opera. Appendices include the English libretto of the 1896 version and a catalog of his stage works. Concludes with an index.

29. Collet, Henri. *Albéniz et Granados.* Paris: Librairie Félix Alcan, 1926 (slightly revised edition, 1929). Rev. ed., Paris: Éditions Le Bon Plaisir, 1948. 233 p. ML390.C69 1948. Spanish trans. by P. E. F. Labrousse, Buenos Aires: Tor-S. R. L., 1948. Reprint of 1929 ed., Paris: Éditions d'Aujourd'hui, 1982. 244 p. ISBN 2730701958. ML390.C69 1929. In French.

This was a groundbreaking work that set the standard for all biographies to follow. Collet was the first to examine Albéniz's life and works in their entirety. The biographical section includes many anecdotes by acquaintances of the composer who were still alive when Collet wrote the book. Collet also borrows heavily from Guerra y Alarcón (B47), Albéniz's first biographer. The section on his music was the first to form a comprehensive overview of his *oeuvre* and includes a cursory analytical appraisal of the major works and an estimate of their critical reception. Collet, however, had limited access to primary sources and did not consult closely with the Albéniz family in the final stages of preparation. Thus, it contains many errors, which most succeeding biographers were unsuccessful in correcting.

30. ———. "Isaac Albéniz y Joaquín Malats." *Revista musical catalana* 6/72 (December 1909): 377-79. In Spanish.

Examines the relationship between Albéniz and the illustrious Catalan pianist Joaquim Malats, who premiered several numbers from Albéniz's *Iberia*. The correspondence between the two men reveals the uncommon respect and affection Albéniz, himself a pianist of the highest caliber, had for Malats. It also makes it clear that Albéniz wrote *Iberia* for him and with his special abilities in mind.

31. Condesa de Castellá. *La Suite Iberia.* Barcelona, n.d. 8 p. In Spanish.

This booklet presents brief summations of the twelve numbers of Albéniz's masterpiece for piano. They are aimed at the general reader but present a few genuine insights into the music. Mostly of limited value.

32. Debussy, Claude. "Concerts Colonne—Société des Nouveaux Concerts." *Bulletin Français de la Société Internationale de Musique* 9/12 (December 1, 1913): 42-44. In French.

In 1913 Debussy attended a concert of Spanish works performed by Spanish musicians. Albéniz's *Iberia*, a work with which he had long been familiar, was on the program, and he singles it out for special honors. Of particular merit is "Eritaña": "Never has music attained to such diverse, such colorful impressions." He goes on to state that "in this *Iberia* collection . . . Albéniz has given his best."

33. Domenech Español, M. "Isaac Albéniz." *Revista de Música* (Buenos Aires), 2 (1928): 150-55. In Spanish.

Begins with a discussion of Spain's curious lack of preeminence in music, given its illustrious history in literature and the visual arts. Focuses on Albéniz as one of the "geniuses" of Spanish music who helped create a distinctive national style. Briefly surveys his life and works, with special attention to the nationalist piano music, especially *Iberia*.

34. Falces Sierra, Marta. "Albéniz en Inglaterra, una etapa oscura." *Revista de Musicología* 14/1-2 (1991): 214-19. In Spanish.

Examines Albéniz's years in London 1890-93 to shed light on a period of his career that biographers have either given short shrift or misunderstood altogether. Focuses on his relationship to Money-Coutts, the wealthy financier who aspired to write poetry and librettos.

35. ———. *El pacto de Fausto: Estudio lingüístico-musical de los lieder ingleses de Albéniz sobre poemas de Francis Money-Coutts.* Granada: Universidad de Granada, 1993. 247 p. ISBN 8433816438. ML410.A3 F35 1993. In Spanish. Reviewed by

Walter Aaron Clark, "Recent Researches in Spanish Music 1800 to the Present," *Inter-American Music Review* 16/1 (Summer-Fall, 1997), 85-86.

The first thorough study of an overlooked portion of Albéniz's output. She begins with an examination of the sources and biographical problems, then continues with a look at Albéniz's London period during the early 1890's. This establishes the foundation for a critical examination of the so-called "pact of Faust" and Albéniz's relationship to Francis Burdett Money-Coutts. For it was to poems of Money-Coutts that Albéniz composed most of his songs, and an analysis of these forms the principal substance of the rest of the book. After presenting the manuscript and published sources, she focuses on the relationship between musical phrasing and poetic structure. (Falces is a philologist at the University of Granada, where she received her doctorate.) The book concludes with several appendices, including a copy of Albéniz's contract with Money-Coutts and reproductions of the songs treated in the book.

36. Fernández-Cid, Antonio. "Matices diferenciales y nexos afectivo-musicales de Enrique Granados e Isaac Albéniz." *Notas de Música (Boletín de la Fundación Isaac Albéniz)* 1 (December 1988): 16-19. In Spanish.

Examines the relationship between the two dominant figures in Spanish music ca. 1900, based on personal recollections of friends and family. Points out the affectionate respect and admiration the two Catalan musicians had for one another.

37. Fornet, Emilio. *Isaac Albéniz.* Series: Figuras de la raza 2/24. Madrid: A. Marzo, 1927. 55 p. In Spanish. ML410.A328 F72. In Spanish.

An insubstantial biography intended for a general readership with limited knowledge of music.

38. Franco, Enrique, ed. *Albéniz y su tiempo.* Madrid: Fundación Isaac Albéniz, 1990. 152 p. ISBN 8475063136. ML141.A53 1990. In Spanish and Catalan.

A catalog of the 1990 traveling exhibition organized by the Fundación. It contains articles and essays about Albéniz and his times. This was clearly an outgrowth of the earlier *Imágenes de Isaac Albéniz* (B39) but includes much new material as well as some items previously published. Richly illustrated with photographs and drawings of Albéniz and imporant figures and locales in his life story. (The articles and essays about Albéniz appear singly in this bibliography.)

39. — — —. *Imágenes de Isaac Albéniz*. Madrid: Fundación Isaac Albéniz, 1988. 50 p. ISBN 8475062504. ML410.A3 I4 1988. In Spanish.

A collection of essays, articles, and poems dealing with Albéniz. Includes many photographs as well as passages from his travel diaries. This was the first major publication of the Fundación and includes some items not found in their subsequent publications (these appear singly in this bibliography).

40. — — —. "La Suite Iberia di Isaac Albéniz." *Nuova Rivista Musicale Italiana* 7 (1973): 51-74. In Italian.

Offers useful insights into each of the numbers of the famous collection. Traces the folkloric origin of some of the thematic material and touches on salient aspects of Albéniz's handling of the piano.

41. Gallego, Antonio. "Isaac Albéniz y el editor Zozaya." *Notas de Música* (*Boletín de la Fundación Isaac Albéniz*) 2-3 (April-June 1989): 6-14. In Spanish.

Explores Albéniz's relations with the Madrid editor Benito Zozaya, who published much of Albéniz's piano music during the 1880's when Albéniz was residing in the capital. Zozaya was also the publisher of *La Correspondencia Musical*, in which notices of Albéniz's concerts regularly appeared and which is one of the most important sources of information about his activities during this period.

42. Gallego, Julián. "Albéniz: La España que (acaso) fue." *Notas de Música* (*Boletín de la Fundación Isaac Albéniz*) 1 (December 1988): 27-28. In Spanish.

    Deals with Albéniz's romantic longing for a Spain that existed mostly in the realm of idealized reminiscence. This longing finds poignant expression in *Iberia*, whose musical depictions of various locales in Spain such as "Málaga" and "Almería" do not correspond to present or historical reality.

43. Gauthier, André. *Albéniz*. Trans. from French to Spanish by Felipe Ximénez de Sandoval. Madrid: Espasa-Calpe, 1978. 123 p. ISBN 8423953300. ML410.A3 G38 1978. In Spanish.

    Gauthier succeeded Laplane as the foremost French biographer of Albéniz. The biographical material is completely dependent on earlier secondary sources. Offers helpful synopses of Albéniz's stage works as well as a balanced discussion of *Iberia*. The discography and bibliography, however, are so cursory as to appear mere afterthoughts.

44. Gilson, Paul. "Albéniz à Bruxelles." *Notes de musique et souvenirs*, pp. 11-19. Brussels: Collection Voilá, 1924. Reprinted Brussels: Éditions Ignis, 1942. In French. Reprinted in Enrique Franco, ed. *Albéniz y su tiempo*, pp. 29-32. Madrid: Fundación Isaac Albéniz, 1990. ISBN 8475063136. ML141.A53 1990. In Spanish.

    Gilson was a friend of Albéniz and recorded his impressions of their first meeting in this article. Must be taken with a grain of salt, as the author declares that Albéniz did not introduce himself until after they had had supper together. But his recollections of Albéniz's loquacity and vivactiy agree with other accounts.

45. Gómez Amat, Carlos. *Historia de la música española*. Vol. 5: Siglo XIX, pp. 305-17. Madrid: Alianza Música, 1984. ISBN 8420685054. ML315.A48. In Spanish.

    Amat devotes an entire chapter to Albéniz, but from a biographical standpoint it suffers from reliance on accounts that

are not altogether accurate. The discussion of the music is very
limited and not furnished with any musical examples.

46. Grew, Sydney. "The Music for Pianoforte of Albéniz." *The
     Chesterian* 6/42 (1924): 43-48. In English.

     Surveys the piano works of the composer and treats the
     "startling difference" between his earliest works and *Iberia*.
     Lauds the genuineness of his Spanish style, declaring that the
     works of non-Spaniards in that vein have "either perverted our
     taste for Spanish music or obscured our vision, the incomplete or
     false making us unable to apprehend the character of the true and
     absolute." Recommends that musicians familiarize themselves
     with Spanish folklore to gain a fuller appreciation of Albéniz's
     music, claiming that "he will always most please men and
     women of high intellectual ardour."

47. Guerra y Alarcón, Antonio. *Isaac Albéniz, notas crítico-
     biográficas de tan eminente pianista*. Madrid: Escuela
     Tipográfica del Hospicio, 1886. Extract in G. Arteaga y Pereira,
     ed. *Celebriades musicales*, pp. 650-52. Barcelona: Centro
     Editorial Artístico, 1886. Original reprinted Madrid: Fundación
     Isaac Albéniz, 1990. 47 p. ISBN 8475063136. ML410.A3 G84
     1990. In Spanish.

     The first biographical account of Albéniz, issued in
     conjunction with his sensational concerts in Madrid in 1886.
     Information for the booklet came straight from Albéniz but does
     not agree in many particulars with accounts he later dispensed to
     other journalists, friends, family members, and biographers or
     with the actual historical record as revealed in primary sources.
     Includes useful lists of his repertoire, compositions, and his
     extraordinarily ambitious program at the Salón Romero on
     January 24 of that year.

48. Guzmán, Juan Pérez. "Los Albéniz." *La Época* (May 21, 1909).
     Reprinted in Enrique Franco, ed. *Albéniz y su tiempo*, 23-28.
     Madrid: Fundación Isaac Albéniz, 1990. ISBN 8475063136.
     ML141.A53 1990. In Spanish.

Guzmán was a friend of the family first in Barcelona and then in Madrid during Albéniz's young years. Deals with Albéniz's early education, flight from home, concert tours, and the suicide of his sister Blanca.

49. Heras, Antonio de las. *Vida de Albéniz*. Barcelona: Ediciones Patria, 1940. 182 p. ML410.A3 H3. In Spanish.

Superficial biography consisting of short chapters and providing no footnotes or bibliography. Distillation of secondary sources with little discussion of the music and no musical examples.

50. Iglesias, Antonio. *De la dificultad del gran piano de Isaac Albéniz*. Madrid: Editorial Alpuerto, 1988. 25 p. (Offprint of an article that appeared in the III. Boletín de la Reial Acadèmia Catalana de Belles Arts de Sant Jordi in Barcelona.) In Spanish.

Intriguing study of the technical difficulties that abound in Albéniz's piano work *Iberia*. Among these problems are frequent hand crossings, intertwining of the fingers of both hands, superabundant accidentals (especially double flats), and the exaggerated use of tempo and dynamic markings. Yet, for all his specificity in these respects, Albéniz neglected to include metronome markings and was stingy with fingerings, leaving that job for performers and editors. Thus, every performer must arrange certain passages of the work to make it playable.

51. ———. *En torno a Isaac Albéniz y su "Iberia."* Madrid: Real Academia de Bellas Artes de San Fernando, 1992. 46 p.

The text of a lecture given at the Real Academia de Bellas Artes de San Fernando on April 5, 1992. Presents an overview of Albéniz's career and accomplishments and treats the particular significance of his greatest work, *Iberia*. Deplores the ongoing neglect, both official and scholarly, of Albéniz in his homeland and calls for greater recognition of his importance. Includes the text of a response by Antonio Fernández-Cid, who concurs with and elaborates upon themes presented by Iglesias. The fifteen pages of footnotes contain some useful information.

52.   ———. "Isaac Albéniz." *Enciclopedia Salvat de los grandes compositores*. Volume 4: La música nacionalista, pp. 230-50. Pamplona: Salvat S.A. de Ediciones, 1982. ISBN 8471374617 (v. 4). In Spanish.

The lengthiest entry on Albéniz in any encyclopedia. Though the biography is based on the canon, it is very detailed and contains valuable data. Includes many photographs and illustrations as well as a list of works.

53.   ———. *Isaac Albéniz (su obra para piano)*. Madrid: Editorial Alpuerto, 1987. 2 vols. 425 p. (v. 1) and 488 p. (v. 2). ISBN 8438101119 (v. 1) and 8438101208 (v. 2). ML410.A3 I3 1987. In Spanish.

Another in this author's series of studies of Spanish piano music. Presents detailed examination of Albéniz's large piano output. The works are placed in alphabetical rather than chronological order. The book is enhanced by musical examples, poems, and photographs, and concludes with a list of works, discography, and bibliography.

54.   Istel, Edgar. "Isaac Albéniz." Trans. by Frederick H. Martens. *Musical Quarterly* 15 (1929): 117-48. In English.

A summary of Albéniz's life and works, based in part on Collet (B29) and in part on the author's acquaintance with the composer's widow, Rosina. Istel deprecates Albéniz's attempts to compose opera, especially *Merlin*, and finds *Iberia* to be unconvincing in its complexity and hence mere "studio music." Albéniz was best at "singing his little song beneath the eternally smiling sun of Spain, freely and happily, with no concern for academic demands." Istel reserves his venom, however, for Money-Coutts and the "Faustian pact," which he holds "responsible for Albéniz's untimely end." The article contains musical examples and some useful insights into the music. Istel is correct in claiming that Albéniz's stage music has little to offer that "his best piano compositions do not adequately reveal."

55. Jankélévitch, Vladimir. "Albéniz et l'État de verve." *Mélanges d'histoire et d'esthétique musicales. Offerts à Paul-Marie Masson*, vol. 1, pp. 197-209. Paris: Bibliothèque d'Études Musicales, 1955. In French.

Essay on Albéniz's musical style. Ideas are often couched in lyrical prose that seems specific but offers few substantial insights. Though there is a minimum of modern theoretical terminology, the text is illustrated with musical examples.

56. ———. *La Présence lointaine. Albéniz, Séverac, Mompou.* Paris: Éditions du Seuil, 1983. 158 p. ISBN 2020064510. ML390.J24 1983. In French.

An expansion of the above article. He states that "the distance is great between the charming 'tiles' of the second act of *Pepita Jiménez*, which relies on enumerative and amplified juxtaposition, and the third and fourth books of *Iberia*, which develop through a kind of organic growth, like tropical plants." Albéniz is the "poet of mystery" and the "magician of flat keys." Resorts to the standard observation that in his compositions for the stage Albéniz, a "phenomenal pianist, . . . never ceased to feel and think through his rapport with the keys."

57. Jean-Aubry, Georges. "Isaac Albéniz (1860-1909)." *Musical Times* 58 (1917): 535-38. In English.

Presents a biographical summary interlaced with personal recollections of the composer. Extensive treatment of *Iberia* and its merits in relation to piano warhorses of the nineteenth century by Chopin, Liszt, Schumann, Franck, etc. Explores Spain's indifference to much of his work. "The life-work of Albéniz is perhaps the only image around which all Spain, whether from North or South, assembles. One and all of the young composers of Spain owe to him a debt."

58. Kalfa, Jacqueline. "Isaac Albéniz à Paris." *Revue Internationale de Musique Française* 9/26 (June 1988): 19-37. In French.

Treats in detail Albéniz's Paris years (1894-1909) and his relationship with notable musicians and institutions, including

Chausson and d'Indy, the Société Nationale de Musique, and the Schola Cantorum. Discusses his relationship with Debussy and the influence they exerted on one another. Albéniz was no mere hanger-on but an active participant in the Parisian musical scene around 1900 and was greatly admired for his virtuosity and the vibrant originality of his music.

59. ———. "Inspiration hispanique et écriture pianistique dans *Iberia* d'Isaac Albéniz." Thèse de 3e cycle de musicologie, Université de Paris-Sorbonne, 1980. 624 p. In French.

An exhausitve study of the pianistic style of Albéniz's most important composition. It begins with a general introduction to the work, followed by five chapters devoted to Spanish music from the era of Domenico Scarlatti through the revival of the zarzuela, with an emphasis on folk music and nationalism. Chapters six through twenty deal with Albéniz's handling of local color, articulation, notation, modality, evocation of the guitar, and his harmonic language, particularly the use of non-harmonic tones. Chapters twenty-one through twenty-three treat the form of the pieces, particularly in relation to the use of variation and improvisation in Spanish folk music. The final three chapters discuss the performance and reception of the work as well as its influence on other composers (Granados, Turina, Falla, and Ohana). The dissertation concludes with appendices pertaining to documentation (programs, correspondence, transcriptions, and press reviews) and terminology. The bibliography is followed by a discography, tables of musical examples and illustrations, and an index of names.

60. Laplane, Gabriel. *Albéniz, sa vie, son oeuvre*. Preface by Francis Poulenc. Geneva: Éditions du Milieu du Monde, 1956. 222 p. ML410.A3 L3. In French. *Albéniz: vida y obra de un músico genial*. Trans. into Spanish by Bernabé Herrero and Alberto de Michelena. Paris: Editorial Noguer, 1958. 240 p. ML410.A3 L318 1958.

Laplane's biography was the most thorough effort ever undertaken. Its three sections and nineteen chapters include not only a biographical discussion but an excellent treatment of his musical style and a survey of his works. It concludes with a useful bibliography (a rarity in this field) as well as the customary discography and chronology of Albéniz's life. Still, it is far from a reliable source of information and is rife with errors and the usual misconceptions, the result of too great a reliance on secondary sources and a reluctance to treat the composer's autobiographical dispensations with the necessary circumspection.

61. Lebrun, Vera. "A Great Spanish Composer." *Radio Times* (April 17, 1936): 11. In English.

Discusses Albéniz's London connections and presents the most accurate estimate of the amount of compensation Money-Coutts paid him to set his librettos and poems to music, about £1,200 a year. Lebrun was married to Albéniz's only son, Alfonso.

62. Llongueres, Joan. "Cómo conocí a Isaac Albéniz." *Evocaciones y recuerdos*. Barcelona: Dalmau, 1944. Reprinted in Enrique Franco, ed. *Albéniz y su tiempo*, pp. 111-13. Madrid: Fundación Isaac Albéniz, 1990. ISBN 8475063136. ML141.A53 1990. In Spanish.

Relates interesting anecdotes about his acquaintance with Albéniz and confirms, among other things, Albéniz's close relationship with Barcelona modernists and his fluency in Catalan, which some sources deny.

63. Llopis, Arturo. "En el centenario de Isaac Albéniz." *Destino* (February 13, 1960): 13-17. In Spanish.

An article based on conversations with Mariano Perelló, the Catalan violinist who was a friend of Albéniz. Perelló became acquainted with Albéniz during the final years of the composer's life, and this article's value lies in the credible anecdotes it provides of Albéniz's personality and relationships with others. Albéniz was by this account especially eager to help young, aspiring Spanish musicians like Perelló, but he was generous with everyone. Once, while the two were walking down the

street together in Barcelona, Albéniz gave a few pesetas to a
poor old woman, then exhorted Perelló to "learn to be generous."

64.   Llorens Cisteró, José María. "El 'Lied' en la obra musical de
      Isaac Albéniz." *Anuario Musical* 15 (1960): 123-40. In Spanish.

The first and only detailed study of all of Albéniz's art
songs. Though the majority of these were written to texts by the
English poet Francis Burdett Money-Coutts (see Falces Sierra,
B35), Albéniz composed several other songs to Italian and
French texts. This article examines the songs in chronological
order treating their genesis and style, with numerous musical
examples. Albéniz's songs have not gained the same popularity
as his piano music because he invests most of the musical
interest in the piano accompaniment (which is often virtuosic),
while the voice declaims the text in a recitative that is
unmemorable. There are exceptions in which the piano is
subordinate to a lyrical vocal line, e.g., "To Nellie" from *To
Nellie: Six Songs* (to poems by Money-Coutts) and the earlier
Seis baladas (to Italian texts by the Marquesa de Bolaños).
These are his most effective works in this genre.

65.   ———. "Isaac Albéniz a través de unas cartas inéditas." *San
      Jorge*, 38 (April 1960): 26-31. In Spanish.

The extant correspondence of Albéniz numbers in the
hundreds of letters. Among these are missives from many
distinguished contemporaries in France and Spain, and this
article presents brief excerpts from several of them. Included are
passages by Alfred Bruneau, Enric Granados, Gabriel Fauré,
Joaquim Malats, Enric Morera, and Tomas Bretón concerning
both his performances and compositions. Unfortunately, these
quotes do not bear the date and provenance of the letter;
however, they bear out the wide range of personal and
professional contacts of the composer and the high esteem and
affectionate regard in which he was held. Pedrell, his erstwhile
teacher, asked him to "remember those who love you for your
genius, your constant work, and your goodness of heart."

66. ———. "Notas inéditas sobre el virtuosismo de Isaac Albéniz y su producción pianística." *Anuario Musical* 14 (1959): 91-113. In Spanish.

    Excerpts from letters, poems, and articles concerning Albéniz's remarkable gifts as a performer and improviser at the piano. Includes commentary from the album he took on his early concert tours in which admirers incribed their encomiums. Also provides substantial quotes from letters by Francisco Barbieri, Vincent d'Indy, Henri Gillet, and Charles-Marie Widor congratulating him on his performances and his own compositions. Albéniz was a notable interpreter of eighteenth-century music, especially Scarlatti and Bach, and he was also a sensitive chamber musician whose rendering of Brahms won particular praise from his fellow musicians. Also includes passages from the correspondence between Albéniz and Joaquim Malats in regard to *Iberia*, as well as from his earlier letters to Enrique Moragas concerning "Granada" from the *Suite española No. 1*. Also represented are Tomás Bretón, Manuel de Falla, Enric Granados, and the author Camille Mauclair. The article concludes with some dedications to Albéniz found in scores by d'Indy, Lluís Millet, and Ignacy Paderewski.

67. Lucena, Luis Seco. "En la Alhambra." *Cuadernos de la Alhambra*. Granada, 1982. Reprinted in Enrique Franco, ed. *Albéniz y su tiempo*, pp. 105-09. Madrid: Fundación Isaac Albéniz, 1990. ISBN 8475063136. ML141.A53 1990. In Spanish.

    Fascinating account of Albéniz's concerts in Granada in 1882 and his enthusiasm for the Alhambra. Albéniz created a sensation in the city and later expressed his love of Granada in several of his most popular compositions for the piano.

68. Marliave, Joseph de. *Études musicales*. Paris: Librairie Félix Alcan, 1917, pp. 119-38. ML60.M16. In French. Reprinted in Enrique Franco, ed. *Albéniz y su tiempo*, pp. 33-40. Madrid: Fundación Isaac Albéniz, 1990. ISBN 8475063136. ML141.A53 1990. In Spanish.

Compares Albéniz to Schumann in his Romantic technique but classical restraint, particularly in using folklore. Like Schumann, his inspiration is "noble and elevated." Regards *Merlin* as an error and a waste of time that should have been spent on piano composition.

69. Martínez, Julia. *Falla. Granados. Albéniz.* Series: Temas españoles, 6. 2nd ed., pp. 21-30. Madrid: Publicaciones Españolas, 1959. ML390.M3. In Spanish.

Intended for a general readership, it contains no footnotes or other references and is a summary of common secondary sources. Describes his music as "the fruit of an improvisation unaware of the rules and ignorant of technical names," a gross exaggeration of statements by Felip Pedrell and irrelevant to Albéniz's mature works.

70. Mast, Paul Buck. "Style and Structure in 'Iberia' by Isaac Albéniz." Ph.D. dissertation, University of Rochester, Eastman School of Music, 1974. UMI Order No. AAC 7421529. In English.

The most exhaustive and detailed analysis ever of Albéniz's greatest work, Mast begins with a distillation of secondary sources in presenting a portrait of Albéniz as a man and artist. A chapter on Spanish folk music, mainly flamenco, serves as a necessary introduction to an extensive summary of the work's principal stylistic features. He then proceeds systematically through the four books of *Iberia* in discussing the formal structure of each number, with emphasis on his adaptation of sonata form to his folkloric style. The conclusion is a useful recapitulation of the major points. This is followed by a works lists, bibliography, discography, and an index to musical examples and Spanish terms.

71. Menéndez Aleyxandre, Arturo. *Albéniz, primer universalizador de la música española.* Barcelona: Gráf Valero, 1960. 10 p. In Spanish.

Text of a lecture given in commemoration of the centennial of Albéniz's birth. Credits Albéniz with elevating Spanish music from the trivial and the commonplace to the level of high art. "The music of Albéniz is folkloric in a lofty and exceptional sense . . . his music is Iberian in its etymology and universal in its potency and destiny."

72. Mitjana, Rafael. "Merlín." *Revista Musical de Bilbao* (October 1902). Reprinted in Rafael Mitjana. ¡*Para música vamos!*, pp. 202-07. Valencia: Casa Editorial F. Sempere, 1909. ML315.5.M5. In Spanish. Also reprinted in Enrique Franco, ed. *Albéniz y su tiempo*, pp. 77-80. Madrid: Fundación Isaac Albéniz, 1990. ISBN 8475063136. ML141.A53 1990. In Spanish.

Favorable assessment of Albéniz's Wagnerian opera *Merlin*, the only finished part of a projected trilogy entitled *King Arthur* with librettos by Money-Coutts. Praises the dance numbers in Act III as well as Albéniz's overall mastery of technique, structure, and setting of the text. Compares the "profundity" of its conception with Wagner's *Ring*.

73. Montero Alonso, José. *Albéniz. España en "suite."* Barcelona: Silex, 1988. 189 p. ISBN 8477370095. ML410.A3 M6 1988. In Spanish.

Basically a summary of secondary sources, especially Collet (B29), Laplane (B60), and Ruiz Albéniz (B87). Contains little in the way of original research, and the bibliography is largely confined to items in Spanish. Strictly biographical with no discussion of the music. The concluding works list and chronology are useful; however, there is no index.

74. Moragas, Rafael. "Epistolario inédito de Isaac Albéniz." *Música* 1/5 (May-June 1938): 38-45. In Spanish.

Letters from Albéniz to his friend Enrique Moragas throw valuable light on the genesis of several of his works, including "Granada" from the *Suite española No. 1*, "La vega" from the incomplete *The Alhambra. Suite pour le piano*, and the reorchestration of *Pepita Jiménez*. Also reveals his plan (unrealized) to set Joaquín Dicenta's play *Juan José* as an opera.

75. Morales, Pedro G. "Notes for an Essay on Albéniz." *Essays on Music.* Ed. by Felix Aprahamian, pp. 5-9. London: Cassell & Co., 1967. ML55.A65. In English.

The author knew Albéniz, who told him that he used to perform the overture to Rossini's *Semiramide* with his back to the piano, and "that trick saved me more than once from starvation." There is some truth to this, but otherwise the account is anecdotal and loose with facts.

76. "Necrologie." *Bulletin Français de la Société Internationale de Musique* 5/7 (July 15, 1909): 717. In French.

This obituary-tribute to the late pianist and composer reveals the tremendous attraction Albéniz had for Parisians, both as a man and a composer. Refers to the possibility of a production of Albéniz's opera *Pepita Jiménez* at the Opéra-Comique, something that would not happen until 1923. Deplores "indolent Spain's" continuing neglect of the "genius of one of its most glorious sons." This was probably a reference to the lack of interest there in his stage works, an indifference that persists to this day.

77. Nectoux, Jean-Michel. "Albéniz et Fauré. Correspondence inédite." *Tilas (Travaux de l'Institut d'Études Ibériques et Latino-Américaines)*, pp. 159-86. Strasbourg, 1977. In French.

The only complete publication of the extensive correspondence (twenty-two cards and letters) from Fauré to Albéniz and his family (in the Bc, sig. M986, "F"). These make it clear that they were the most intimate of friends and greatly admired one another. In addition, there are three poems by Fauré to Albéniz that reveal his wit and humor as well as affection for the Spaniard.

78. Newman, Ernest. "Albéniz and his 'Merlin.'" *The New Witness* 10/254 (September 20, 1917): 495-96.

Though not premiered until 1950 (in Barcelona), Albéniz's opera *Merlin* found an early advocate in Ernest Newman, who extolled the "magical beauty" of the music. He recommended the score "to anyone who is on the look-out for something at once original, strong and beautiful" and who could appreciate with him the fact that "the best opera on our sacrosanct British legend has been written by a Spaniard."

79. Pedrell, Felipe. "Albéniz. El hombre, el artista, la obra." *Músicos contemporáneos y de otros tiempos*, pp. 375-81. Paris: P. Ollendorf, 1910. ML60.P373. Also in *Revista Musical Catalana* 6 (May 1909): 180-84 (in Catalan), and *La Vanguardia* (June 15, 1909) (in Spanish). Reprinted in Enrique Franco, ed. *Imágenes de Isaac Albéniz*, pp. 20-22. Madrid: Fundación Isaac Albéniz, 1988. ISBN 8475062504. ML410.A3 I4 1988. In Spanish.

Albéniz briefly studied composition with Pedrell in Barcelona during the early 1880's. In this article Pedrell provides fascinating insights into this apprenticeship and Albéniz's distinctive musical personality. Pedrell claims that Albéniz was uncomfortable with the rules and regulations of composition, which only stymied his creativity. Pedrell overstates the case for Albéniz's lack of formal training and unfamiliarity with music theory, but Albéniz was a diffident orchestrator, and Pedrell gently chides him for using the orchestra as an extension of the piano. Pedrell has unqualified praise for Albéniz's pianistic gifts and applauds the "Spanish fragrance, flavor, and color" in *Iberia*, a nationalist impulse that Pedrell had helped inspire in Albéniz. Laments the ingratitude shown to Albéniz by his homeland, a refrain repeated many times by other commentators as well.

80. Pena, Joaquim. "Musichs que fugen." *Joventut* 3 (1902): 383-85. In Catalan.

Pena recounts a dinner given in Albéniz's honor before his departure from Barcelona for Madrid in 1902. The event was held at the Hotel Sant Jordi de Vallvidrera, and many friends and luminaries were in attendance, including the conductor Crickboom and the critic Suárez Bravo. In spite of the festive mood, Albéniz expressed with some bitterness his reasons for moving to Madrid. He found in Barcelona an environment hostile not only to him but to artists like Pedrell, Vives, and Morera, all of whom had likewise fled to the capital city. The final straw, however, was the Liceu's rejection of *Merlin*. This, perhaps more than any other single reason, impelled him to abandon Barcelona.

81.   Plá, Josep. "El poeta Moréas y Albéniz." *Vida de Manolo contada por él mismo*. Barcelona: Ediciones Destino, 1947. In Spanish. 151 p. [Excerpt entitled "La generosidad" appears in Enrique Franco, ed. *Imágenes de Isaac Albéniz*, pp. 17-19. Madrid: Fundación Isaac Albéniz, 1988. ISBN 8475062504. ML410.A3 I4 1988. In Spanish.]

This is Chapter 17 of Plá's book and deals with Albéniz and the renowned Symbolist poet Jean Moréas (né Yánnis Papadiamantópoulos, 1856-1910). In this excerpt from that chapter, Plá recounts the kindness and generosity Albéniz showed to the young Spanish sculptor Manolo Hugué, the subject of the biography. Albéniz's home was a haven of warmth and hospitality for many Spanish writers, artists, and musicians trying to establish their careers in Paris around 1900.

82.   Preckler, Mercedes Tricás, ed. *Cartas de Paul Dukas a Laura Albéniz*. Bellaterra: Universidad Autónoma de Barcelona, 1983. 77 p. ISBN 8474880548. In Spanish. Reviewed by Frances Barulich, *Notes of the Music Library Association* 41/3 (1985): 515-16.

Paul Dukas was an intimate friend of the Albéniz family and maintained a close relationship with it for many years after the composer's death. His letters (sixty-nine in all, covering the period 1906-35) to Albéniz's daughter Laura (who served as her father's secretary before his death) make clear the affectionate regard in which he held the Spanish composer and shed some light on the production of *Pepita Jiménez* in Paris.

83.   Raux Deledicque, Michel. *Albéniz, su vida inquieta y ardorosa*. Buenos Aires: Ediciones Peuser, 1950. 437 p. In Spanish.

Raux Deledicque was a Frenchman who had briefly met Albéniz in 1908 before moving to Buenos Aires in 1914. His is the first and last attempt to write a novelistic biography of Albéniz, in which he invents large amounts of dialogue and fills in the "cracks" with unsubstantiated claims and sheer fiction. The lengthy book includes no serious discussion of the music, and scholarly rigor is lacking (no footnotes, index, bibliography). The author did correspond with Albéniz's descendants, who in turn sent him much of the archive to examine. Therefore, the book cannot be entirely disregarded.

84. Redford, John Robert. "The Application of Spanish Folk Music in the Piano Suite 'Iberia' by Isaac Albéniz." D.M.A. document, University of Arizona, 1994. 75 p. UMI Order No. AAC 9426340. In English.

Heavily indebted to Mast's dissertation (B70) and otherwise rather superficial, this work's chief value lies in its examination of folkloric references in *Iberia* through citation of examples from collections of Spanish folksong. Although Albéniz rarely quoted folksongs verbatim, these examples serve as useful points of reference in identifying to which types of song and dance themes from *Iberia* belong.

85. Reig, Ramón. "Isaac Albéniz." *Revista de Gerona* 5/6 (Primer Trimestre de 1959): 55-56. In Spanish.

Reig relates interesting anecdotes about his meeting with Arthur de Greef, the Belgian pianist who tied for first place with Albéniz in the 1879 piano competition at the Conservatoire Royal in Brussels, where they were both students of Louis Brassin. De Greef declared that the jury could not decide between them, so evenly matched were they, and eventually declared them both winners "with distinction." (There was a total of four contestants on this occasion.) This is an aspect of that competition not revealed in any other account.

86. Reverter, Arturo. "Albéniz-Arbós: Amistad, relación musical, escenarios." *Notas de Música (Boletín de la Fundación Isaac Albéniz)* 2-3 (April-June 1989): 23-27. In Spanish.

Enrique Fernández Arbós was a celebrated conductor and violinist whose orchestrations of several numbers from *Iberia* have found their way into the standard orchestral literature. Reverter explores the close personal relationship between these two giants of Spanish music, which began when they were students at the Brussels conservatory in the 1870's and ripened during their numerous concerts together in Spain and England during the following two decades.

87. Roda, Cecilio de. "La 'Suite' Iberia." *Programas de Conciertos, Sociedad Madrileña* (1911-13). Reprinted in Enrique Franco, ed. *Albéniz y su tiempo*, pp. 73-76. Madrid: Fundación Isaac Albéniz, 1990. ISBN 8475063136. ML141.A53 1990. In Spanish.

Program notes for *Iberia* (the excerpt in Franco presents only "Evocación," "El Puerto" and "Triana"). The author's insights into the folkloric references are useful and are supported by brief musical examples. Conveys the fact that Albéniz was no ethnographer and mixed these references in a "capricious" manner without regard to consistency or authenticity.

88. Ruiz Albéniz, Víctor. *Isaac Albéniz*. Madrid: Comisaría General de Música, 1948. 143 p. In Spanish.

This brief biography is by Albéniz's nephew (the son of his sister Clementina), a doctor who attended Albéniz on his deathbed and who eventually gave up medicine to work as a music critic in Madrid. It is neither comprehensive nor entirely accurate, but it does present some interesting glimpses into Albéniz's private life based on family records as well as on the author's own relationship with the composer. Of special interest are passages from Albéniz's letters to Clementina, letters that are not otherwise available to the researcher. His account of Albéniz's final days is the most detailed and reliable in any biography.

89. Ruiz Tarazona, Andrés. *Isaac Albéniz: España soñada*. Madrid: Real Musical, 1975. 75 p. ISBN 8438700098. ML410.A3 R8. In Spanish.

Another brief biography aimed at a general musical readership, it has no bibliography or index. Still, it is one of the few to stress Albéniz's Basque ancestry on his father's side. Otherwise, the book is very dependent on earlier and often undependable sources.

90. Sagardía, Ángel. *Albéniz*. Series: Gent Nostra, 46. Barcelona: Editions de Nou Art Thor, 1986. 51 p. ISBN 8423953300. ML410.A3 G38 1978. In Catalan.

A small book intended for the general public, it nonetheless contains some insights into the latter period of Albéniz's life, especially regarding the premieres and reception of his stage works. Of greatest interest, perhaps, are several reproductions of drawings by Albéniz's daughter Laura, a noted artist.

91. — — —. *Isaac Albéniz*. Series: Hijos ilustres de España. Plasencia, Cáceres: Editorial Sánchez Rodrigo, 1951. 120 p. In Spanish.

A major biographical effort. Though it is reasonably detailed, it lacks the footnotes and bibliography that would enhance its reliability and utility. Nonetheless, the author's placement of Albéniz's life and music in a larger cultural and historical context is informative, though the music itself does not receive a close examination. As with all other biographies, reliance on secondary sources and not on rigorous scrutiny of documentation is a major liability.

92. Saint-Jean, J. "Isaac Albéniz (1860-1909)." *Revue Française de Musique* 10/1 (1912): 3-16; 79-83. In French.

One of the most extensive pre-Collet accounts. Provides a biographical overview that relies heavily on earlier sources, especially Guerra y Alarcón (B47). Stresses the importance of his association with Felip Pedrell and his leading role in Spanish musical nationalism. Gives an overview of his output and includes a reproduction of the "Zortzico" from *España: Six Feuilles d'album* for piano, dedicated to Albéniz's friend Ignacio Zuloaga, the Basque artist. Concludes with an assessment of his

late works, especially *Iberia*, and compares him favorably to
Schumann and Debussy, among other notable figures in the arts.

93.   Salazar, Adolfo. "Isaac Albéniz y los albores del renacimiento
       musical en España." *Revista de Occidente* 12/34 (April-June
       1926): 99-107. In Spanish.

       Basically a review of Collet's recently issued biography of
       Albéniz and Granados (B29). Questions Albéniz's supposed
       assimilation of Debussian impressionism, because Albéniz was
       too wedded to the "Lisztian rhapsody" style. In addition, he did
       not possess the technical command of Debussy, and his penchant
       was for "direct, immediate effect," rather than the subtleties and
       complexities of impressionism.

94.   Salvat, Joan. "Epistolari dels nostres músics: Isaac Albéniz a
       Joaquim Malats." *Revista Musical Catalana* 30/357 (September
       1933): 364-72. Reprinted in Enrique Franco, ed. *Albéniz y su
       tiempo*, pp. 129-36. Madrid: Fundación Isaac Albéniz, 1990.
       ISBN 8475063136. ML141.A53 1990. In Catalan.

       The correspondence between these two titans of Catalan
       pianism reveals Albéniz's uncommon affection and respect for
       his compatriot. The correspondence deals mostly with the
       creation and interpretation of *Iberia*, several numbers of which
       Malats premiered in Spain (though Blanche Selva was the first to
       perform each book in its entirety). *Iberia* was clearly written
       with Malats in mind, and his performance of it gave Albéniz
       complete satisfaction.

95.   Saperas, Miquel. *Cinc compositors catalans: Nicolau, Vives,
       Mossèn Romeu, Lamote, Albéniz*, pp. 163-200. Barcelona: Josep
       Porter, 1975. ML390.S2. In Catalan.

       Though he relied heavily on secondary sources, Saperas
       examined material in the archives as well. His biography offers
       some information of value, especially in regard to the critical
       reception of Albéniz's music and his relationship to other major
       figures in Catalan culture in the nineteenth century.

96. Seifert, W. "In Memoriam." *Musica* 13 (June 1959): 402-03. In German.

Assays Albéniz's importance, crediting him with bringing international recognition to Spanish national music and being the most significant predecessor of Manuel de Falla.

97. Selleck-Harrison, Maria B. "A Pedagogical and Analytical Study of 'Granada' ('Serenata'), 'Sevilla' ('Sevillanas'), 'Asturias' ('Leyenda') and 'Castilla' ('Seguidillas') from the 'Suite Española', Opus 47 by Isaac Albéniz." D.M.A. essay, University of Miami, 1992. 172 p. UMI Order No. AAC 9314534. In English. Reviewed by Walter Aaron Clark, "Recent Researches in Spanish Music 1800 to the Present," *Inter-American Music Review* 16/1 (Summer-Fall, 1997), 88-90.

The first in-depth study of this portion of Albéniz's output, including not only detailed analyses of the music but useful guidance for the practice and execution of each of the numbers. The biography is a distillation of secondary sources and contains the usual errors. Though the author commendably questions the contradictions she finds, a thorough investigation of purely biographical issues was beyond the scope and focus of her work. Concludes with an extensive discography of this suite.

98. Serra Crespo, José. *Senderos espirituales de Albéniz y Debussy*. México City: Costa Amic, 1944. 196 p. ML410.A3 S4. In Spanish.

A slender volume consisting of short chapters in which the author stresses the importance of Wagner and folklore in the nationalist music of Albéniz. In particular, Pedrell's *Por nuestra música* (1891) is viewed as an influential manifesto, uniting these two elements into a coherent philosophy that had a strong impact on Albéniz.

99. Solà-Morales, J. M. de. "La sang gironina-gaditana d'Isaac Albèniz." *Annals de l'Institut d'Estudis Gironins* 25/2 (1981): 233-53. In Catalan.

Detailed study of Albéniz's genealogy, tracing his family on both mother's and father's sides back to the seventeenth century. Demonstrates beyond doubt that Albéniz's father was Basque and that there was no connection between his family and that of Mateo and Pedro Albéniz. Contains records of the military service of his maternal grandfather, a war hero who served four decades in the Spanish army.

100. Sopeña, Federico. "Gracia y drama en la vida de Isaac Albéniz." *Historia y Vida* 2/12 (March 1969): 122-33. In Spanish.

Biographical summary making extensive use of correspondence already available in Víctor Ruiz Albéniz's monograph (B88).

101. Torres Mulas, Jacinto. "The Long Sleep of Pepita Jiménez." Trans. by Derek Yeld. Liner notes for *Pepita Jiménez*. Harmonia Mundi (HMC-901537), 1995. In English.

An informative treatment of the genesis and checkered performance history of Albéniz's most successful opera for this concert suite of numbers from *Pepita Jiménez*.

102. — — —. "Isaac Albéniz en los infiernos." *Scherzo*, 80 (December 1993): 150-53. In Spanish.

This first appeared as the prologue to the dissertation by Marta Falces Sierra (B35). It deals with the issue of Albéniz's supposed Faustian pact, in which biographers have portrayed Money-Coutts as Mephistopheles, Albéniz as Faust, and Rosina as Marguerite. Also touches on the subject of Albéniz's connection to Freemasonry.

103. — — —. "The 'Classical' Inspiration of Isaac Albéniz." Trans. by Christine Losty. Liner notes for *Isaac Albéniz: Sonatas para piano nos. 3, 4, 5/L'Automne*. Harmonia Mundi, France (987007), 1994. In English.

These notes present the interesting story behind the genesis and publication history of Albéniz's piano sonatas from the

1880's. Though of high quality, they lie outside his nationalist style and have received scant attention from performers.

104. —␣—␣—. "La metamorfosis de Isaac Albéniz: de intérprete a creador." Liner notes for *Albéniz: Klavierwerke/Piano Pieces*. Koch-Schwann (3-1513-2), 1996. In Spanish. (The translation by J & M Berridge is a summary.)

From 1886 to 1892, Albéniz made the transition from a brilliant interpreter of music to a noted composer. The recording includes several rarely heard gems from this period (such as the *Siete estudios en los tonos naturales mayores* and *Les Saisons*), and the liner notes provide important and detailed information about the genesis, publication history, and musical style of these pieces.

105. —␣—␣—. "La producción escénica de Isaac Albéniz." *Revista de Musicología* 14/1-2 (1991): 167-212. In Spanish.

This was the first systematic study of the stage works of Albéniz, including their genesis, production history, alternate titles, and sources. It was first presented as a paper at the 1990 national meeting of the Spanish Musicological Society in Granada.

106. —␣—␣—. "Un desconocido 'Salmo de difuntos' de Isaac Albéniz." *Revista de Musicología* 13/1 (January-June 1990): 279-93. In Spanish.

Torres discovered this work in manuscript at the Real Conservatorio in Madrid. It was composed on the death of Alfonso XII, the Spanish king who had sponsored Albéniz's studies abroad. The article presents its history, salient musical charcteristics, and includes a reproduction of the original manuscript. Torres has since published the work in a modern edition through the Instituto de Bibliografía Musical.

107. Turina, Joaquín. "Encuentro en Paris." *Arriba* (January 14, 1949). Reprinted in Enrique Franco, ed. *Albéniz y su tiempo*, pp.

115-16. Madrid: Fundación Isaac Albéniz, 1990. ISBN 8475063136. ML141.A53 1990. In Spanish.

Provides interesting anecdotes about Albéniz based on their friendship, which began in 1907. Includes insights into the genesis of *Iberia* and Albéniz's awareness of contemporary trends in harmony and increased use of dissonance. Also makes clear Albéniz's generosity to Turina in helping him get his Quintette published and in encouraging him to found his composition on the basis on Spanish folk music.

108. Verastegui, Alejandro de. "Isaac Albéniz, oriundo Vitoriano." *Boletín de la Real Sociedad Vascongada de los Amigos del País* 17/1 (San Sebastián: Museo de San Telmo, 1961): 43-49. In Spanish.

Brief biographical sketch commemorating the centenary of his birth (written in 1960). Notable for the emphasis it places on Albéniz's Basque ancestry, insofar as his father was a native of Vitoria. Contains intriguing details about his early life, especially in Barcelona, but without substantiation.

109. Villalba Muñoz, P. Luis. "Imagen distanciada de un compositor-pianista." *Gaceta de Mallorca* (1909). Reprinted in Enrique Franco, ed. *Albéniz y su tiempo*, 51-61. Madrid: Fundación Isaac Albéniz, 1990. ISBN 8475063136. ML141.A53 1990. In Spanish.

Rehash of the usual anecdotes about Albéniz's early career, gleaned from secondary sources. Offers an unflattering (and inaccurate) assessment of the composer, declaring that Albéniz did not possess the "technique of the art of composition" and that counterpoint in particular remained "inaccessible to his character as a free artist."

PART C: CONTEMPORARY PERIODICAL LITERATURE

(Reviews and articles of interest in newspapers and journals during Albéniz's lifetime and reviews of his operas after his death)

The following is an extensive but necessarily selective compilation based on research conducted for purposes other than tracking down every article and review ever published (an impossible task). The first section deals with reviews of his concerts. These give us valuable insights into his pianistic technique and style. They also provide generally reliable information about his activities (though the biographical information is usually suspect). The second section is devoted to reviews of his stage works, including productions that took place after his death, and of *Iberia*. (The press in general took far less interest in premieres of his instrumental music.) In a few instances, several citations are grouped under one number. Though they are without annotation, there is some value in knowing they are available (in all cases they appear under the heading of the opera to which they pertain). Aside from clippings found in the archives mentioned in Part A, the papers and journals cited below were consulted in the periodicals section of the following libraries: Barcelona: Arxiu Històric de la Ciutat and Biblioteca de Catalunya; Brussels: Bibliothèque Royale Albert Ier; London: British Library; Madrid: Biblioteca Nacional, Hemeroteca Municipal, and Hemeroteca Nacional; Paris: Bibliothèque National; Prague: National Library. (NB: All reviews by George Bernard Shaw are reprinted in Dan H. Laurence, ed. *Shaw's Music: The complete musical criticism in three volumes*. New York: Dodd, Mead & Co., 1981.)

I. Reviews and articles dealing with his concert career from 1872 to 1894, in chronological order (page number and author given where available).

110. *Correo de Teatro* (Barcelona) (July 23, 1869). In Spanish.

Account of his meeting with the Vizconde del Bruch to present him with the *Marcha militar*, Albéniz's first published composition, which bears a dedication to the twelve-year-old Viscount.

111. *Correspondencia Teatral* (Valladolid) (February 15, 1872). In Spanish.

> Review of his concert at the Teatro Lope de Vega, where he was a sensation. Reports that he has been giving concerts in northern Castile as well as Catalonia and Andalusia. "Words fail us in praising such mastery, such feeling, such perfection . . . he will be one of the glories of Spanish art."

112. *Artísta de La Habana* (September 23, 1875). In Spanish.

> Favorable report on his concerts in Havana, one given on the ship *Manzanillo* for various luminaries, including editors of the paper *La Bandera*.

113. *Artísta de La Habana* (October 10, 1875). In Spanish.

> Report on a recital given in his home at Amargura 14 in Havana. It was well received by the "distinguished" invitees. Gives notice of an upcoming concert at the Teatro de Tacón.

114. *El Espectador de La Habana* (November 6, 1875). In Spanish.

> Review of his concert at the restaurant El Louvre, in which he played several virtuosic numbers, including a fantasy on themes from *The Barber of Seville*, executed with his back to the piano (several accounts report his ability to do this).

115. *Diario de Cádiz* (August 23, 1878). In Spanish.

> Reports on his concert activities in Brussels, where he was a student at the Conservatoire Royal. Rhapsodizes that "under his able and agile fingers, the piano sighs, cries, and sings."

116. *Diario de Barcelona* (August 24, 1879). In Spanish.

> Favorable review of his performance at the Navas piano factory.

117. *Gaceta de Catalunya* (August 24, 1879). In Spanish.

> Also praises his recital at the Navas piano factory.

118. *Publicidad de Barcelona* (September 16, 1879). In Spanish.

Review of his recent concert at the Teatre de Novetats, in which the reviewer praises his "excellent hand position, clarity and cleanness of execution, admirable contrasts in tone color, and equality in repeated notes, tremolo, and arpeggios."

119. *Publicidad de Barcelona* (September 28, 1879). In Spanish.

Favorable assessment of his program at the salon of the piano makers Raynard y Maseras, where he gave his standard recital of Bach, Scarlatti, Mendelssohn, Chopin, and Weber.

120. *Crónica de Barcelona* (September 30, 1879). In Spanish.

States that he is now moving to Madrid. Places Albéniz in the "classical school" of pianists.

121. *Anunciador de Vitoria* (May 4, 1880). In Spanish.

Rejoices in his concert and hails him as a true "Vitoriano" (his father was from Vitoria). The casino presented him with a set of gold buttons.

122. *Diario de La Habana* (December 1880). In Spanish.

Review of his concert at El Louvre, a benefit for a local charity. He performed the Liszt *Spanish Rhapsody* as well as a Beethoven trio, which had to be repeated at the audience's insistence.

123. *El Bien Público* (February 10, 1881). In Spanish.

Review of his concert at the Círculo Español in Havana, at which he conducted an orchestra in selections from *Le Pré aux clercs* by Hérold. Also played Mendelssohn G-minor concerto.

124. *Santiago de Cuba* (February 15, 1881). In Spanish.

Review of his concert at the Teatro de la Reina, in which the reviewer prases the perfection, taste, and feeling of a "delicate soul."

125. *LCM* 1/14 (April 6, 1881), 6. In Spanish.

Reports on his concerts in Santiago and states that he had toured Germany and the U.S. before his arrival in Cuba. (There is no other evidence to support this claim.)

126. *LCM* 1/31 (August 3, 1881), 6. In Spanish.

Account of his concert in Santander, declaring that under his hands "the instrument reveals all of the divine mysteries of music."

127. *LCM* 1/46 (November 16, 1881), 7. In Spanish.

Report of his concert in Zaragoza on November 11, 1881, which was "applauded frenetically." Liszt's *Rigoletto Paraphrase* was the highpoint of the concert.

128. *LCM* 1/49 (December 7, 1881), 7. In Spanish.

Account (taken from *El Navarro*) of his December 3 concert in Pamplona in which his program of Scarlatti, Liszt, Mendelssohn, and his own works was "listened to until the final note amidst the most religious silence."

129. *LCM* 2/57 (February 1, 1882), 6. In Spanish.

Quotes from *El Porvenir Vascongado* (January 25, 1882) that Albéniz performed in between acts of Joaquín Gaztambide's zarzuela *El juramento* ("The Judgement") in Bilbao, which was a benefit for a local charity. His music was well received, though the numbers are not specified.

130. *LCM* 2/61 (March 21, 1882), 6. In Spanish.

States that Albéniz has just returned from a successful tour of various provincial capitals.

131. *LCM* 2/73 (May 24, 1882), 6. In Spanish.

Reports on Albéniz's concerts in the Gran Teatro in Córdoba, which were well received.

132. *LCM* 2/76 (June 14, 1882), 7. In Spanish.

Account (from the Cádiz *La Palma* of June 10) of his concert at the casino in San Fernando, where he played twelve works and three improvisations on melodies submitted by the audience.

133. *LCM* 2/77 (June 21, 1882), 6. In Spanish.

Review of his concert at the Academia de Santa Cecilia in Cádiz, for a gathering of "famous artists and well-known aficionados." He organized the successful concert himself.

134. *LCM* 2/80 (July 12, 1882), 8. In Spanish.

Glowing report of his concerts in Seville at the Jardines de Eslava.

135. *LCM* 2/81 (July 19, 1882), 6. In Spanish.

Encomiastic account of further concert triumphs in Cádiz.

136. *LCM* 2/85 (August 16, 1882), 6. In Spanish.

Albéniz in Valencia for a concert on August 7 (reported in the local paper *La Nueva Alianza*), where his program of Boccherini, Liszt, and his own pieces was "frenetically applauded."

137. *LCM* 2/90 (September 20, 1882), 6. In Spanish.

Albéniz's concert in Alcoy (as reported in *El Serpis*) prompted "a very noisy tribute" to his artistry. After the recital, he was serenaded at his hotel by a local orchestra.

138. *LCM* 2/97 (November 8, 1882), 6. In Spanish.

Report on Albéniz in Cartagena, where he is giving a series of successful concerts.

139. *LCM* 2/98 (November 15, 1882), 6-7. In Spanish.

Review of a November 10 recital in Cartagena, featuring "very difficult pieces" rendered with "delicate taste."

140. *LCM* 2/101 (December 6, 1882), 6. In Spanish.

Account of Albéniz's welcome participation in a program at the home of Señora Duquesa de Medinaceli in Madrid.

141. *LCM* 2/103 (Decmber 20, 1882), 5. In Spanish.

Review of his concert at the Círculo Vasco-Navarro in Madrid, which featured works by Scarlatti, Boccherini, Beethoven, Raff, and Mendelssohn and was warmly applauded.

142. *La Ilustración Musical* 1/2 (April 14, 1883), 4. In Spanish.

Review of Albéniz's concert at the salon of the piano firm of Raynard y Maseras in Barcelona, declaring that he gave his audience "truly delicious moments."

143. *La Ilustración Musical* 1/3 (April 21, 1883), 4. In Spanish.

Caricature of Albéniz as a slightly paunchy, moustached young fellow in a top hat and tails with the caption: "As a person, a boy; as a pianist, a giant."

144. *LCM* 3/127 (June 7, 1883), 4. In Spanish.

Announces his engagement to a "beautiful and rich" señorita from Barcelona.

145. *LCM* 3/130 (June 29, 1883), 5. In Spanish.

Reports his marriage to the "pretty and discreet" Rosina Jordana in Barcelona (on June 23).

146. *LCM* 3/143 (September 27, 1883), 6. In Spanish.

Favorable report on Albéniz's participation in three concerts by Enrique Fernández Arbós's sextet in La Coruña (on the 20th).

147. *LCM* 3/144 (October 4, 1883), 7. In Spanish.

Albéniz and Arbós's sextet make a successful appearance in Santiago de Compostela.

148. *LCM* 3/147 (October 25, 1883), 6. In Spanish.

Albéniz is passing through Madrid on his way back to Barcelona (where he is now living with his new bride), after a successful tour of the northwest provinces with Arbós's sextet (in truth, the tour was not a success).

149. *LCM* 5/249 (October 8, 1885), 5. In Spanish.

States that Albéniz has played for the royal family in Madrid (where he is now living), giving two concerts at the royal palace. Describes him, without explanation, as the "spoiled child" of Madrid society.

150. *LCM* 5/253 (November 5, 1885), 5. In Spanish.

Albéniz has played again (November 4) at the royal palace at the invitation of the Infanta Doña Isabel. He served up his latest compositions, which she enjoyed.

151. *LCM* 5/259 (December 17, 1885), 6. In Spanish.

Announces that Albéniz is giving private piano instruction at his home at "Plaza de Antón Martin 52, 54 y 56."

152. *LCM* 6/262 (January 7, 1886). In Spanish.

Announcement of his upcoming program at the Salón Romero, listing the ambitious repertoire planned for the evening.

153. *El Liberal* (January 25, 1886), by Miguel Moya. In Spanish.

Fulsome review of his concert at the Salón Romero, praising his "extraordinary facility" and commenting on the public's enthusiastic reception of his program. Contains biographical information extracted from Guerra y Alarcón's contemporary account (B47).

154. *LCM* 6/265 (January 28, 1886), 1-3. In Spanish.

Front-page review of his highly successful recital at the Salón Romero on the 22nd of January. "Albéniz dominates the piano with surpassing ease, and in his hands, the keys reproduce in a marvelous manner the thoughts of the musician and of the poet."

155.   *LCM* 6/266 (February 4, 1886), 6. In Spanish.

Albéniz is receiving numerous invitations to perform from various cities in Spain as a result of his Romero appearance.

156.   *La Ilustración Española y Americana* (February 8, 1886). [Reprinted in Enrique Franco, ed. *Albéniz y su tiempo*, pp. 69-72. Madrid: Fundación Isaac Albéniz, 1990. ISBN 8475063136. ML141.A53 1990. In Spanish.]

Review of the Romero performance, stating that his rendition of a Mayer etude "set off an explosion of thunderous applause." Albéniz is a "passionate and ardent interpreter, who sometimes poeticizes and at others nearly mistreats the piano, and who, in short, carries away and moves his listener."

157.   *LCM* 6/271 (March 11, 1886), 3. In Spanish.

Encomiastic review of his performance with the renowned soprano Adelina Patti at the Teatro de la Zarzuela in Madrid.

158.   *LCM* 6/274 (April 1, 1886), 5. In Spanish.

Favorable review of another performance at the Salón Romero the previous Thursday.

159.   *LCM* 6/275 (April 8, 1886), 6. In Spanish.

Offers condolences to the Albéniz family on the loss of their twenty-month-old daughter Blanca.

160.   *LCM* 6/280 (May 13, 1886), 5. In Spanish.

Reports his return from Málaga, where he garnered applause and money, having had to repeat five or six numbers from a program of no less than twenty-six selections.

161. *LCM* 6/290 (July 22, 1886), 5. In Spanish.

Conveys a review from *El Eco de San Sebastián* of his successful concerts in that city on the 17th and 19th of July.

162. *La Ilustración Musical Española* 1/14 (August 15, 1888), by Felipe Pedrell. [Reprinted in Enrique Franco, ed. *Albéniz y su tiempo*. Madrid: Fundación Isaac Albéniz, 1990, 63-67. ISBN 8475063136. In Spanish.]

In the summer and fall of 1888 Albéniz performed no less than twenty recitals at the Exposición Universal in Barcelona. Pedrell hailed Albéniz's Piano Concerto No. 1 (*Concierto fantástico*) as "without precedent" in Spanish music history, lavished praise on the "poetic calm and inspiration" of his sonatas, and applauded his use of folkloric references in the *Rapsodia española*. In conclusion, Pedrell predicted that "the name of Albéniz is destined to represent a grand personality in the European musical world."

163. *Trade & Finance* (June 19, 1889). In English.

Describes his playing as characterized by "delicate taste, refined reading, dainty execution" and that his "strength lies in the rendering of light, graceful compositions."

164. *Pall Mall Gazette* (June 25, 1889). In English.

"He reminds one of [Anton] Rubinstein in his refined and delicate passages, and of Hans von Bülow in his vigor."

165. *Vanity Fair* (June 25, 1889). In English.

Praises his pianism and comments in particular on his "velvety touch."

166. *Daily Telegraph* (October 24, 1889). In English.

Reports on his performance of works by Handel, Bach, Scarlatti, and Chopin at St. James's Hall, noting the "charming fashion in which he executes works by . . . masters of refinement."

167. *Daily Telegraph* (October 25, 1889). In English.

Announces that Albéniz has "received permission from the Spanish governement to copy, for the purpose of [the upcoming] concert, several important manuscripts in the library of the Escorial." This was probably a fabrication for publicity's sake.

168. *Star* (December 6, 1889), by George Bernard Shaw. In English.

Review of his concert at a *conversazione* of the Wagner Society, where he played excerpts from Wagner's *Ring* arranged by Brassin. "The dead silence produced by his playing, particularly during the second piece ["Ride of the Valkyries"], was the highest compliment he could have desired."

169. *Huddersfield Daily Examiner* (January 10, 1890). In English.

"His pieces are light but remarkably beautiful, thoroughly distinctive, yet all full of the colour of the composer's nationality, and of that graceful individuality which is so strongly characteristic of his playing."

170. *Rochdale Observer* (January 22, 1890). In English.

"The velvety softness of touch—the cadences dying to almost a whisper, yet audible all over the room—must have been the wonder and the admiration—and also the despair—of the amateur pianists present."

171. *Bristol Times & Mirror* (February 6, 1890). In English.

Review of a recent concert, declaring that "his scales are perfect, and his tone shading is remarkable."

172. *Strand Journal* (February 14, 1890). In English.

"He performed lightning-like feats, varied by interludes of sweet, dreamy melody, which none but a past master of his art could hope to rival."

173. *The Times* (June 10, 1890). In English.

Reports on his concert at Steinway Hall, remarking on his "rare power of producing the full tone of his instrument without having recourse to violence of any kind, or ever exceeding the limits of acoustic beauty."

174. *Musical Standard* (June 14, 1890). In English.

Favorable review of his concert at Steinway Hall. Admires his "soft and sympathetic touch."

175. *Dramatic Review* (June 28, 1890). In English.

Glowing review of his concert at Steinway Hall, where he moved "his audience not by astonishing them but by charming them." Compared his "dazzling brightness" and "exquisite delicacy" to the violin playing of his friend Pablo Sarasate, also active in London at this time.

176. *St. James's Gazette* (September 15, 1890). In English.

Review of his concert at Steinway Hall. "Señor Albéniz made as powerful an impression by his composition as by his playing."

177. *Lady* (October 30, 1890). In English.

Biographical account that is loaded with misinformation and outright fabrications. Provides a classic example of Albéniz's penchant for reinventing his past to impress the public, though his career was sufficiently impressive without embellishment.

178. *The Pictorial World* (November 2, 1890). In English.

Review expressing the belief that "there is no distinctive school of musical art belonging to [Spain], and . . . its music is but a pale reflection of French or German thought. It has gone out of use—if it ever was to the fore—with Cordovan leather and liquorice, or Baracco juice."

179. *Figaro* (November 8, 1890). In English.

Negative review of the first orchestral concert he organized at St. James's Hall (November 7, 1890), featuring the Spanish conductor and composer Tomás Bretón, whose conducting passes muster but whose E-flat symphony is deemed nothing but a "bold imitation of Beethoven."

180. *Pall Mall Gazette* (November 8, 1890). In English.

Unflattering report of the first orchestral concert he organized at St. James's Hall, which featured his own works as well as some by his compatriots Ruperto Chapí and Tomás Bretón. Chapí's offerings are rated as "cheap, trashy noise." Albéniz's rendition of the Schumann concerto demonstrated his lack "especially in the left hand of wrist power. There is too little contrast and he would be a much greater pianist if he would consent to let himself go."

181. *Topical Times* (November 8, 1890). In English.

Biographical account that is only slightly less inaccurate than the others that appeared in the London press during his tenure in that city.

182. *Referee* (November 9, 1890). In English.

Negative review of the first of Albéniz's orchestral concerts at St. James's Hall. Harshly dismisses the Chapí offerings as "circus music."

183. *Daily Graphic* (November 10, 1890). In English.

Uncomplimentary assessment of the first of the orchestral concerts at St. James's Hall. Chapí's work was "sheer tea-garden blatancy," while Bretón's conducting lacked "the animation and impetuosity one associates with a Southerner." Albéniz's negotiation of the Schumann concerto displayed insufficient "romance and intellectuality."

184. *World* (November 12, 1890), by George Bernard Shaw. In English.

Pans the recent orchestral concert at St. James's Hall, decrying the "procrustean torturings" of Bretón's symphony, "an ingeniously horrible work."

185. *Footlights* (November 15, 1890). In English.

Negative review of the first orchestral concert at St. James's Hall, complaining that its length "savours of wanton cruelty to tax long suffering [*sic*] humanity so heavily."

186. *Land & Water* (November 15, 1890). In English.

"Nothing can exceed the delicacy and charm of his touch, which seems to show to special advantage when he is giving us one of his own little Spanish dissertations." Hopes for a repetition of "these pleasing trifles" at his next concert.

187. *Modern Society* (November 15, 1890). In English.

Claims that "it is said the clever pianist [Albéniz] is being exploited by an enthusiastic capitalist [probably Henry Lowenfeld, his manager], and the statement is credible."

188. *Queen* (November 15, 1890). In English.

Contrary to all other reviews of the first orchestral concert at St. James's Hall, reports that Chapí's work (a "Moorish Fantasy") "met with a favourable reception, the third movement—the serenade—having to be repeated."

189. *Star* (November 18, 1890). In English.

Biographical portrait of Albéniz. Dispenses claims contradictory to those that appeared in other periodicals of this time in London, including that he is an "opera conductor at Granada, Seville, et al.," and that he has written twelve piano sonatas (he wrote at most seven). The following observation suggests that the information was gained during an interview with him: "Personally, he is very agreeable, overflowing with a cheerful and inspiring humour."

190. *Daily Chronicle* (November 22, 1890). In English.

Glowing review of the second orchestral program at St. James's Hall (November 21, 1890), which led the critic to speculate that Spain enjoyed greater importance in the realm of "high-class music" than commonly supposed, and that it was "quite possible that other nations have been wilfully [*sic*] blind as well as deaf to the labours of Spanish musicians."

191. *New York Herald* (November 22, 1890). In English.

Enthusiastic review of the second orchestral concert at St. James's Hall. Albéniz's pieces demonstrated an "originality colored by national feeling which should . . . be shown by composers born and bred in countries with a musical history."

192. *Pall Mall Gazette* (November 22, 1890). In English.

Favorable review of the second orchestral concert at St. James's Hall, in which Albéniz performed some solos: "Senor Albeñiz is an undemonstrative pianist, with but few mannerisms, but much technical ability."

193. *Standard* (November 22, 1890). In English.

Generally favorable review of the second orchestral concert at St. James's Hall. Albéniz's Piano Concerto No. 1 was "clearly written and easy to follow," though the first movement was "monotonous" and the finale "not very dignified." Albéniz's orchestral works on the program were reminiscent of French ballet music rather than Spain. His solo piano works "were the greatest success of the evening" and "so much applauded that the pianist-composer had to throw in another piece."

194. *Musical Standard* (November 29, 1890). In English.

Reports that Albéniz's "Cuban Rhapsody in G" at the second orchestral concert at St. James's Hall "failed to satisfy strict *connoisseurs.*"

195. *Country Gentleman* (November 29, 1890). In English.

Favorable review of the second orchestral concert at St. James's Hall. States that Bretón "has all the proverbial solemnity of his race [and] may now be considered an established favorite, both as a conductor and composer."

196. *Vanity Fair* (November 29, 1890). In English.

States that Albéniz has won over the public in a remarkably short time: "Señor Albéniz may well inscribe upon his escutcheon the words, 'veni, vidi, vici'; and I am sure that everyone will be glad to hear that he has elected to make London his home."

197. *Leeds Mercury* (January 14, 1891). In English.

Concerning his Leeds concert, states that he possesses a "full, singing touch, facile command of the keyboard, and a masterly adaptation and management of the pedals. He also attaches due importance to . . . the thorough assimilation of what he has to expound, so that . . . he appears to be virtually improvising."

198. *Yorkshire Post* (January 14, 1891). In English.

Review of a concert Albéniz gave in Leeds, assessing his own compositions as "drawing-room music of the daintiest, most polished, and artistic description . . . brilliant and effective, as well as charmingly melodious."

199. *Pall Mall Gazette* (January 30, 1891), "Señor Albéniz at Home: An Interview with the Spanish Pianist." In English.

In this interview, Albéniz gives a brief account of his life in which he declares that he first ran away from home at age eight and a half. Later, after spending three years touring in South America, he received a stipend from the Spanish king with which to study in Leipzig, beginning in 1874. After studying for three years in that city, he spent a year in Italy with Liszt. Here is an account of his life that conforms neither to the historical record nor to the version he provided to Guerra y Alarcón (B47).

200.   *England* (February 4, 1891). In English.

Albéniz possesses an "exquisitely delicate and tender style of playing [that] is peculiar to himself."

201.   *Dramatic Review* (February 14, 1891). In English.

States that Albéniz is writing a light patriotic opera set in Spain at the beginning of the War of Independence (1808); the hero is a reformed brigand converted into a guerilla chief. Nothing ever came of this plan.

202.   *Bazaar* (February 16, 1891). In English.

Of his performance at St. James's Hall, this reviewer perceives that "his great excellence lies in the power to play softly. . . . He can preserve a special shade of tone for a very long period without the slightest fluctuation or variety." He "produces tones which resemble the ripple of water, and which charm the ear by their delicate softness."

203.   *Daily Telegraph* (February 27, 1891). In English.

A qualified assessment of his playing that states, "The Spanish artist is far happier in his moments of subdued neatness and delicacy when all the finest qualities of a peculiarly feathery touch become evident." Applauds the innovations Albéniz has made in his concert series at St. James's Hall beginning on January 17, 1891. These include moderate length, free cloak room and programs, inexpensive tickets, and the opportunity to begin a subscription with any concert in the series.

204.   *Pall Mall Gazette* (February 27, 1891). In English.

Favorable review of his concert at St. James's Hall. "Albéniz represents . . . a reaction against the slap-bang-and-hack school which the genius of Liszt invented. . . . Albéniz possesses the rare Thalbergian art of making the piano sing." Describes Spaniards as a "people implacable alike in love and war, and ready to languish at one moment and stab the next."

205. *Queen* (February 28, 1891). In English.

> Reports that the libretto of his new opera will be written by H. Sutherland Edwards. No such work was written, however.

206. *Mistress & Maid* (March 4, 1891). In English.

> A mildly critical assessment of his pianism, stating that he "lacks strength . . . not delicacy."

207. *World* (March 4, 1891). In English.

> Review of an Albéniz piano recital pronouncing him "one of the pleasantest, most musical, and most original of pianists" and "a man of superior character."

208. *Woman* (March 5, 1891). In English.

> Declares that he is "more charming . . . in delicate and fanciful music than in the more severe school."

209. *Gentlewoman* (March 28, 1891). In English.

> Reports that Albéniz's new opera (which was never written) is set in Salamanca in 1808.

210. *Queen* (April 11, 1891). In English.

> More autobiographical fiction, claiming eight months of study with Liszt in Italy and subsequent directorship of an Italian opera company in Spain.

211. *Deutschen Reiches Anzeiger* (March 2, 1892). In German.

> Encomiastic report of his concert at the Singakademie in Berlin on March 1, 1892. Praises his rendering of Beethoven's "Moonlight" Sonata, with the exception of the last movement in which he used the pedal too much. Chopin was the highlight of the evening, and Albéniz's own pieces exhibited "grace and lively expression."

212. *Vossischen Zeitung* (March 2, 1892). In German.

Praises his "marvelous technical feats," refinement, and taste. Public reacted to his interpretations with "lively and well-deserved applause."

213. *Berliner Tageblatt* (March 3, 1892). In German.

States that he made a favorable impression at the Singakademie but that he should leave aside Beethoven and Bach, because his rapid tempos reveal much practice but a superficial rapport with the music. His rendering of Chopin, however, was excellent, especially in the clarity of his technique and tone control.

214. *National Zeitung* (March 3, 1892). In German.

Praises both the sensitivity and strength in his playing, stating that his Beethoven interpretation revealed both a profound understanding of the music and a well-developed technique.

215. *Berliner Börsen-Zeitung* (March 4, 1892). In German.

Finds his Beethoven (the "Moonlight" Sonata) lacking in sensitivity, a necessary "dream-like character," and altogether too "conventional and coldly correct." States that his own pieces make a pleasant impression but are basically bagatelles in salon clothing and rather superficial.

216. *Berliner Zeitung* (March 4, 1892). In German.

"A pianist of the first order . . . technically and musically well-trained and elegant."

217. *Die Post* (March 4, 1892). In German.

Lauds his well-developed, clean technique and pure (though small) tone.

218. *Nordeutschen Allgemeinen Zeitung* (March 4, 1892). In German.

Praises his tone and general facility but faults his lack of dynamic contrast, "rhythmic sharpness," and clarity in his runs and arpeggios.

219. *Stadtburger Zeitung* (March 4, 1892). In German.

Applauds his "artful phrasing," beautiful tone, and clean technique. Describes the Bach as "lacking energy" and states that "he did not capture the spirit of Beethoven." But he praises Albéniz's handling of pieces by Chopin and Liszt.

220. *Volks-Zeitung* (March 4, 1892). In German.

Equivocal review of his concert at the Singakademie. Finds Albéniz's compositions polished and flowing but remarkable in their lack of any "trace of the fiery blood that one really ought to expect from a Southerner."

221. *Heraldo de Madrid* (August 26, 1894), by Louis Bonafoux. In Spanish.

Summary of an interview with Albéniz that offers the following explanation for his choosing to live outside Spain: "Albéniz is more Spanish than Pelayo, but for Albéniz Spanishness does not consist in writing pages of music at five francs a page, nor in resigning himself, as a consequence, to eating cold food in a garret. Albéniz lives in Paris and in London because there he can eat and sleep. He is not a bullfighter, and therefore he cannot live well in Spain."

222. *La Correspondencia de España* (September 17, 1894). In Spanish.

Report on his concert in San Sebastián for the family of the Grand Duke of Wladimiro and other notables at the Miramar Palace on September 13. Describes him as the "emulator of [Anton] Rubinstein" and states that the Steinway piano "responded in docile fashion to his mastery" in "moments of great inspiration."

II. Reviews of the stage works and *Iberia*. Compositions are in chronological order, reviews in alphabetical order. See the Catalogue of Works in Chapter Three for premiere dates and locations.

Cuanto más viejo

223. *LCM* 2/58 (February 8, 1882), 8. In Spanish.

>   States that Albéniz is completing a zarzuela that will be premiered that week in Bilbao.

224. *LCM* 2/60 (February 21, 1882), 6. In Spanish.

>   Review of the premiere at the Coliseo. States that the "performance has been good and the success gratifying for its authors, especially for the composer Sr. Albéniz."

Catalanes de Gracia

225. *El Liberal* (March 29, 1882), 4. In Spanish.

>   Describes the zarzuela as a comic-lyric "skit" and reports a favorable public reaction to the characters' high jinx.

226. *LCM* 2/64 (March 22, 1882), 7. In Spanish.

>   Announces the premiere of the zarzuela the following Saturday at the Teatro Salón Eslava, with music by the "distinguished" concert artist Don Isaac Albéniz.

227. *LCM* 2/65 (March 29, 1882), 7. In Spanish.

>   States that the "little work" has accomplished its objective, describing the music as "pleasant" and the drama as "amusing." The performance of the singers was warmly applauded, as were the authors themselves.

228. *LCM* 2/67 (April 12, 1882), 7. In Spanish.

>   States that the zarzuela is continuing to draw large audiences at the Eslava.

The Magic Opal

229. *Athenaeum* (January 28, 1893), 131. In English.

"The melodies are for the most part fresh and piquant, and there is no sense of incongruity in the Spanish rhythms which are conspicuous at times. . . . The part-writing for the voices is excellent, and the orchestration is at once refined and picturesque." The writer further characterized it as "the most artistic of the many pieces of the same nature upon which theatrical managers have pinned their faith—unwisely, as it would seem, for the most part—during the current season."

230. *Era* (January 21, 1893), 9. In English.

In addition to praising the libretto (a minority view, to be sure), it declares that "those who can appreciate anything better than the thinly-orchestrated jingle of the ordinary comic opera composer will revel in the refinement and grace of Señor Albéniz's work. The music . . . is sure to improve upon acquaintance, and is decidedly of the sort which will bear to be heard again and again."

231. *Figaro* (Febuary 23, 1893). In English.

Ascribes the failure of *The Magic Opal* to the "popular leaning towards the 'Ta-ra-ra' and 'The Man who Broke the Bank at Monte Carlo' style of melodies."

232. *Graphic* (January 28, 1893). In English.

A laudatory review that nonetheless faults the obvious traces of French *opéra comique* in the score.

233. *Lady* (February 9, 1893). In English.

Expresses skepticism about Albéniz's eclectic approach: "It is called, with equal justness, either light opera or comic opera. As a matter of fact, the composer has chosen to attempt a compromise between both styles, and, moreover, has made several departures into the field of grand opera. Whether such a course is exactly a wise one is doubtful. The plain and simple methods of Offenbach, Lecocq, and other composers of the palmy days of comic opera, have been discarded of late by most composers."

234. *Manchester Examiner* (March 14, 1893). In English.

Remarks on the early demise of the operettta, noting its auspicious opening but failure to continue to hold the public's interest. Along with many other critics, he considers this "a pity."

235. *Music Trades Review* (February 20, 1893). In English.

Favorable review that cites as "gems" in Act I the serenade of the bandit chief Trabucos, "a pretty song for the heroine in waltz time," and Candida's Spanish-style dance in Act II. Express some doubts about Albéniz's eclectic approach, however, finding that many songs were reminiscent of the style of Sir Arthur Sullivan.

236. *Saturday Review* (January 28, 1893), 97-98. In English.

"The cardinal point about it is the extremely bright and pretty music . . . [though the book] is not very robust." Has high praise for the costumes and sets and especially for Candida's dance in Act II.

237. *Sheffield Telegraph* (March 21, 1893). In English.

"Albéniz proves himself capable of good work, excelling in his instrumentation, which is often novel, and always effective."

238. *Sketch* (February 8, 1893), 95. In English.

Positive critique that nonetheless faults Albéniz for not having "chosen to write music that shows off the voice." Provides a detailed description of Candida's dance in Act II, which has a "strange flavour of mystery." Ascribes to the production the power to "do something to raise the tone of comic opera, which been sinking a good deal of late years."

239. *Sportsman* (March 3, 1893). In English.

After the failure of *The Magic Opal*, the critic worries about "what a strange, inexplicable, incomprehensible people [Albéniz] must by now think that we English are." Asserts that Albéniz "has the capacity to do something which must win him fame far exceeding any that even the phenomenal success of 'The Magic Opal' would have brought in its train."

240. *Stage* (January 26, 1893), 12. In English.

"There will be no necessity to bemoan the fate of comic opera while Señor Albéniz continues to write for the stage. . . . There is much originality in [his] music, and a freshness of treatment that is very acceptable is apparent throughout the score."

241. *Sunday Chronicle* (Manchester) (March 13, 1893). In English.

Reports that the number "Lovey Dovey Rosey Posey" was "rapturously encored." Otherwise mocks the production's director, Horace Sedger, with the following little poem: "Dear O-pal, costly O-pal / Dear O-pal, costly O-pal / Making for Sedger / a hole in the ledger / Give us one better than dear Opal."

242. *Theatre* (March 1, 1893), 154-55. In English.

Praises Albéniz's music as "distinguished by a melody, a force, and an eloquence rare indeed in compositions for the comic opera stage." He even had praise for the libretto (a rare occurrence with Albéniz's operas), which he describes as "full of happy humour, dramatic vigour, and pretty sentiment."

243. *The Times* (January 20, 1893), 6. In English.

Lauds the music as "bright, tuneful, and original," and goes on to say: "No inexperience is to be traced . . . in the construction of the many effective numbers, or in the vocal and instrumental writing. The orchestral scoring is, indeed, remarkably interesting and refined, and the ideas throughout original and most characteristic."

244. *Truth* (February 23, 1893), "The Decline of Comic Opera." In English.

An article dealing with the early demise of Albéniz's operetta *The Magic Opal*, which received generally excellent notices but nonetheless ran less than two months. The popularity of music halls has cut into the operetta market; ticket prices are too high, along with production costs. The expenses of *The Magic Opal* exceeded £720 a week. The Lyric Theatre could hold enough to bring in £1,800 if only half full every night, but the production still lost money and closed after seven weeks.

245. *Weekly Sun* (March 12, 1893). In English.

Positive review that states that Miss May Yohe (an American) received an ovation for her singing in the second act.

246. *World* (January 25, 1893), George Bernard Shaw. In English.

"The Magic Opal, at the Lyric, is a copious example of that excessive fluency in composition of which Señor Albéniz has already given us sufficient proofs. His music is pretty, shapely, unstinted, lively, goodnatured, and far too romantic and refined for the stuff which Mr Arthur Law has given him to set. But Albéniz has the faults as well as the qualities of his happy and uncritical disposition; and the grace and spirit of his strains are of rather too obvious a kind to make a very deep impression. And he does not write well for the singers. It is not that the phrases are unvocal, or that the notes lie badly for the voice, but that he does not set the words from the comedian's point of view, his double disability as a pianist and a foreigner handicapping him in this department."

247. Additional reviews in the Bc, M987 (all in English):

Anglo-American Times (February 25, 1893); *Bazaar* (January 25, 1893); *Clarion* (January 28, 1893); *Court Circular* (January 21, 1893); *City Press* (April 15, 1893); *Daily Graphic* (January 20, 1893); *Dramatic Review* (January 28, 1893); *Eastern Morning News* (Hull) (May 3, 1893); *Encore* (February 3, 1893); *Evening Post* (York) (April 22, 1893); *Figaro* (January

26, 1893); *Financial World* (January 20, 1893); *Glasgow Evening Citizen* (February 14, 1893); *Glasgow Evening Times* (February 14, 1893); *Glasgow Herald* (February 14, 1893); *Globe* (January 20, 1893); *Hawk* (January 24, 1893); *Illustrated & Dramatic News* (January 28, 1893); *Lady* (February 9, 1893); *Lady's Pictorial* (January 28, 1893); *Leeds Evening Express* (April 26, 1893); *Liverpool Post* (April 11, 1893); *Man of the World* (January 25, 1893); *Manchester City News* (March 18, 1893); *Manchester Courier* (March 14, 1893); *Manchester Evening Mail* (April 12, 1893); *Manchester Weekly Times* (March 17, 1893); *Morning* (January 16, 1893); *Morning Post* (February 20, 1893); *Musical Times* (February 3, 1893); *Newcastle Journal* (April 25, 1893); *Pelican* (January 28, 1893); *People* (January 22, 1893); *Piccadilly* (January 25, 1893); *Pick Me Up* (February 18, 1893); *Pioneer Allahabad* (February 16, 1893); *Princess* (February 4, 1893); *Queen* (January 28, 1893); *Scotsman* (Edinburgh) (February 21, 1893); *Scotsman* and *Scottish Leader* (Glasgow) (February 14, 1893); *Smart Society* (January 25, 1893); *Society* (January 28, 1893); *Sporting Dramatic News* (January 28, 1893); *Sportsman* (January 20, 1893); *Sussex Daily News* (April 4, 1893); *Truth* (January 26, 1893); *Weekly Scotsman* (Edinburgh) (February 25, 1893).

The Magic Ring (Revision of *The Magic Opal*)

248. *The Times* (April 13, 1893), 13. In English.

States unequivocally that the revision is "far superior, musically speaking, to the average comic opera of the day." Though it describes the comic interest of the first version as "meagre," it extols the "distinct improvements" that have been made in the second, especially the addition of an "extremely effective duet for Lolika and Trabucos."

249. *Era* (April 15, 1893), 11. In English.

Compliments the changes made to the libretto and states that "unreserved praise may be given" to the score. He finds not only the influence of *opéra comique* but ascribes its charm to its "Spanish character, which harmonizes perfectly with the subject.

The melodies, always full of grace, sometimes combine a fascinating vein of sentiment with sparkling effects."

250.   *Stage* (April 15, 1893), 11. In English.

Considers that Albéniz's music for *The Magic Opal* was of "too high an order of merit to be finally shelved after a few performances only." Expresses doubts, however, about the merits of the libretto, even in its revision.

251.   *World* (April 19, 1893), George Bernard Shaw. In English.

Describes the new production as an "attempt . . . to rescue Senor Albéniz's score of The Magic Opal from sinking under the weight of its libretto." He concedes, however, that "the revised version of the opera leaves [Albéniz] easily ahead of the best of his rivals."

252.   *Theatre* (May 1, 1893), 294, by Percy Notcutt. In English.

Does not view the new version as an improvement over the old. States that, in spite of revisions in the text and restructuring of the cast, the libretto remains "lamentably weak." Albéniz's score, however, is "really excellent throughout . . . being musicianly and artistic in the extreme."

253.   Additional reviews in Bc, M987 (all in English):

Court Journal (April 15, 1893); *Fashions of Today* (May 1893); *Morning Leader* (April 13, 1893); *Telegraph* (April 15, 1893); *Umpire* (April 16, 1893); *Westminster Gazette* (April 12, 1893).

La sortija (Spanish revision of *The Magic Opal*)

254.   *El Correo Español* (November 24, 1894), 2, by "Pipí." In Spanish.

Declares that neither the book nor the music is suited to the Spanish taste, despite its success in London, and that the performance was not good. His conclusion is that "Albéniz and Sierra are too *foreignized.*"

255. *El Heraldo de Madrid* (November 24, 1894), 3. In Spanish.

   "Those scenes of bandits, those falsified Andalusians, that amulet ring, and those mishandled love interests could not interest anybody or inspire a musician [of Albéniz's stature]."

256. *El Imparcial* (November 24, 1894), 2-3, by "J. de L." In Spanish.

   Albéniz "has nothing to learn; on the contrary, he has much to forget."

257. *El Liberal* (November 24, 1894), 3, by "J. A." In Spanish.

   States that the music was too good for the simple and uninteresting story. "The audience was cold and reserved and did not accord *La sortija* . . . the general applause that decides the success of a premiere in favor of the author."

258. *El Nacional* (November 24, 1894), 3. In Spanish.

   Criticizes the libretto's lack of dramatic interest and the superabundance of musical numbers, more than many three-act zarzuelas contain. Does, however, praise Albéniz's instrumentation.

259. *El Resumen* (November 24, 1894), 2, by E. Contreras y Camargo. In Spanish.

   "The numbers follow one another without interruption, without allowing time for the ear to rest. Moreover, the numbers are so long that they constitute an invasion of oppressive notes. Twenty-some numbers in two acts! . . . Choruses and more choruses, romances, duets, trios."

260. *La Correspondencia de España* (November 24, 1894), 1, by "El Abate de Pirracas," entitled "Telones y Bambalinas." In Spanish.

   "Albéniz, as a composer, is one of those eternal talkers . . . who spout words and words and words without pause and without saying anything." He further avers that "the music of *La Sortija does not sound*. And I will add that it is *hollow* and lacks color, sonority, grace, freshness, and the *stamp* of that which is inspired and spontaneous. . . . Therefore, the music of Sr. Albéniz is opaque and cold. The notes fall on the ear and remain in the ear, accumulating to form an offensive noise."

261. *La Época* (November 24, 1894), 3, by "Z." In Spanish.

"Intelligent people say that the music is very *learned*. But logarithmic tables are also learned, and I do not believe there is a spectator capable of enduring a recital of them for two and a half hours. The public, despite giving evidence of the patience of Job, manifested, at various times, its disgust."

262. *La Justicia* (November 24, 1894), 2, by "Don Cualquiera." In Spanish.

"Perhaps, within the melodic mania that obsesses him, the cognoscenti will find no musical defect in the whole score. But the public, the anonymous masses, are extremely bored."

Poor Jonathan

263. *Daily Graphic* (June 19, 1893). In English.

"The additions to the score for which the Spanish composer is responsible are in nearly every instance superior in construction, charm, and elegance to the work of the original composer [Karl Millöcker]."

264. *Era* (June 17, 1893). In English.

Positive critique describing Albéniz's numbers as "charming in style and admirably scored for the orchestra."

265. *Morning Leader* (May 16, 1893). In English.

Complimentary assessment of Albéniz's contributions as composer, describing his music as "nearly always delightfully charming and graceful, and more than once he gives us some real comedy in his orchestration."

266. *Standard* (May 16, 1893). In English.

Generally favorable review of the several numbers composed by Albéniz for the production of Millöcker's operetta. Albéniz capably conducted the performance at the Prince of Wales's Theatre.

267. *Telegraphe* (May 15, 1893). In English.

"Albéniz, skilled and graceful composer that he is, flounders hopelessly in his struggles to write the light and lilting tunes which alone could make such a piece acceptable."

268. *The Times* (June 17, 1893). In English.

Declares it "a decided success," calling it a "variety entertainment" on an "elevated level."

269. *Topical Times* (June 17, 1893). In English.

"Speeches are too long, the songs are too long, and the action is too slow."

270. *World* (June 21, 1893), George Bernard Shaw. In English.

Complains that Albéniz's numbers (and those by others) "have made the work more pretentious; but they have also . . . weakened it by making it far too long." In a more sympathetic vein, however, he states that Albéniz's "management is an example to London in point of artistic aim and liberal spirit" (Albéniz conducted the production).

San Antonio de la Florida

Madrid Production (1894):

271. *El Correo Español* (October 27, 1894), 3, by "Pipí." In Spanish.

Rare positive estimation of the work ("a lot of good music") that gives insight into the audience's reaction: "The hall was completely full, the intelligent element predominating, who applauded all the numbers with enthusiasm, especially the prelude, the serenade, and some of the choruses."

272. *El Heraldo de Madrid* (October 27, 1894), 3. In Spanish.

Reports that Albéniz "forcefully aroused the interest and curiosity" of the public with his new zarzuela. Concurs with the other critics, however, that the music was too good, too sophisticated for the type of work it was (light zarzuela) and for the audience and venue.

273. *El Imparcial* (October 27, 1894), 3, by "A." In Spanish.

Acerbic denunciation that accuses Albéniz of having "taken the work as a pretext for demonstrating that he is a musician of great talents. Has he demonstrated that? To excess, in my judgment, insofar as the enormous quantity of music, though of the highest quality, is too great for so diminutive a book. The public received Albéniz with genuine affection . . . and requested the repetition of three or four truly beautiful numbers, at the end calling Isaac Albéniz and the author of the text, D. Eusebio Sierra, to the stage."

274. *El Liberal* (October 27, 1894), 3, by "J. A." In Spanish.

Expresses reservations about the zarzuela, for though "it abounds in melody, and the instrumental parts are handled admirably," Albéniz "sometimes ascends in flight to altitudes in which the exigencies of the genre are lost from view, lacking the sobriety necessary in order to contain himself in the limits the poet has set for him in the poem he has placed at his service."

275. *El Nacional* (October 27, 1894), 3, by "Blas." In Spanish.

Generally favorable review but faults the music as "too learned" for such a light work. Describes the premiere as "un succès d'estime an plus haut degré."

276. *El Resumen* (October 27, 1894), 2. In Spanish.

With lighter, more appropriate music, the work might have been effective, but Albéniz's score was too operatic and unsuited to the performers, theater, and audience.

277. *La Correspondencia de España* (October 27, 1894), 3. In Spanish.

Reports that "the public of the Apolo, despite being accustomed to popular music—inspired and playful—applauded extraordinarily last night the [music] of Sr. Albéniz, demanding a repetition of the introductory chorus, the duet in the first scene, and the prelude of the second [Intermedio]."

278. *La Correspondencia de España* (December 30, 1894), 1, by Conde Guillermo Morphy, entitled "Porvenir de los compositores españoles." In Spanish.

Declares that though the critics accused it of breaking established molds and of being "dangerously innovative," the public reacted well enough to the freshness of his stage works. In response to a critic who had accused Albéniz of "using a frigate to cross a river," he replied that a "simple raft" could only appear like a frigate to someone accustomed to crossing rivers, like the Africans, "on an inflated hide." He let fly another shaft in the direction of the notorious "Zeda" (B279), who had accused Albéniz of abusing truffles by putting them in everything: "Could it not be closer to the truth to affirm that in the *género chico* the garlic and the onion have been so abused that the tired palate does not know how to distinguish the potato from the truffle?" He lamented the lack of national musical theater on a grand scale (that is, with several acts, serious, elevated subjects and style), and encouraged the public and critics to support young composers like Albéniz (who was only thirty-four at this time) who were attempting to do something new and out of the ordinary.

279. *La Época* (October 27, 1894), 2, by "Zeda." In Spanish.

"The lyrical comedy premiered last night at the Teatro de Apolo belongs to the *boring* genre. . . . The text is made up of a series of drab scenes, without interest, without grace, without types, with neither customs, nor comic situations, nor jokes, nor originality, nor anything." Though he offers praise for the introduction and the finale of the first scene, his conclusion is that "Sr. Albéniz has incurred the defect of the character in *Los pavos reales*, who wanted to put truffles in everything. . . . He has abused the truffles."

280. *La Justicia* (October 27, 1894), 4, by "Don Cualquiera." In Spanish.

States that "from the first note to the last there dominates a taste and an elegance in the composition, and [in] the intermedio between the first and second scenes a brilliant melody is developed with enchanting simplicity." But "when the public goes to see a little piece of a popular kind, it does not request excellence of composition or lofty harmonic effects; it is content with something light that the ear can enjoy." Finds that the "text of *San Antonio de la Florida* is poor, and what is more than poor, insubstantial and lacking in verisimilitude."

Barcelona Production (1895):

281. *El Correo Catalán* (November 7, 1895), 2. In Spanish.

Declares that the work was well received and that the duet had to be repeated. However, "the libretto has no literary value" and possesses "many scenic deficiencies."

282. *La Dinastía* (November 7, 1895), 3. In Spanish.

Favorable estimation of the work, whose music "conforms to the diverse situations of the argument, which has a lot of movement." The orchestra was well directed by Albéniz.

283. *La Renaixensa: Diari de Catalunya* (November 8, 1895), 6267. In Catalan.

"Sr. Albéniz has attempted to perform the miracle of imparting interest with his inspired music to a libretto that possesses absolutely nothing to recommend it . . . but as it is impossible to raise the dead, so here all the charming melody the music breathes is lost in futility. It is a genuine pity that the composer finds himself in a labor that under other circumstances would reward him with glory and profit."

284. *La Vanguardia* (November 7, 1895), 3, by "V." In Spanish.

Praises the music, particularly the Preludio, but finds that the libretto produced fatigue and heaviness, the result of "repetition of situations," "lack of popular atmosphere," "dimensions disproportionate to a few scenes," and "lack of novelty and interest in the plot and the text." However, he credits it with "initiating a new current in this genre of works."

285. *Lo Teatro Català* (*El Teatro Catalán*) 6/252 (November 9, 1895), 2, by Armando de la Florida. In Catalan.

"The work of Sr. Sierra is a disgrace. . . The music is . . . a calamity."

Brussels Production (in French, retitled *L'Hermitage fleuri*) (1905):

286. *Le Courrier Musical* 8-3 (February 1, 1905), 76-78, by Octave Maus. In French.

Lauds the "delicious humor" and local color of the zarzuela, though he overstates the case for its popularity in Spain, where it never found a regular place on the stage.

287. *Le Patriote* (January 5, 1905). In French.

Describes it as a "gay satire" and lauds its rhythmic vitality, "at once studied and natural." As with all the other reviews, claims it was received with affectionate enthusiasm by the public.

288. *Le Peuple* (January 5, 1905), 2, by "Labarbe." In French.

Contrasts the zarzuela to *Pepita Jiménez*, praising the former's elegant comedy and popular melody. It was no less a success than the opera, which was a triumph.

289. *Le Soir* (January 5, 1905), 2, by "L. S." In French.

Finds it reminiscent of Italian *commedia dell'arte*, *opera buffa*, and French *opéra comique*. Its "piquant form and abundant melody" reflect Spanish "gaiety and spirit." Despite its apparent simplicity, it is not easy to sing, and the performers acquitted themselves admirably.

Madrid Production (1954):

290. *ABC* (November 20, 1954), 51, by Antonio Fernández-Cid. In Spanish.

Though the score was lost during the Civil War, Pablo Sorozábal rendered a new orchestration and directed the production at the Teatro Fuencarral. Fernández-Cid finds the music worthy of the composer but faults the weakness of Sierra's libretto.

291. *Informaciones* (November 20, 1954), 9, by "A. P." In Spanish.

The audience responded warmly to Albéniz's score, but the drama fails to match the quality of the music.

292. *YA* (November 20, 1954), by "N. G. R." In Spanish.

Praises the production and the freshness and verve of the music but finds that the story does not possess dramatic merit or interest.

Henry Clifford

293. *Diario de Barcelona* (May 10, 1895), 5561-63, by F. Suárez Bravo. In Spanish.

Admires the "mastery demonstrated in the instrumentation—full, picturesque, and of an extreme fineness. Albéniz does not subject himself to the rigorous theory of the *Leitmotiv* . . . but neither does he absolutely scorn it. There are a few characteristic themes that, handled with skill, underline situations and characters."

294. *El Correo Catalán* (May 9, 1895), 3. In Spanish.

Praises the opera because "*Henry Clifford*, in reality, does not belong to any school: it bears the stamp of originality of all the works of its author."

295. *El Diluvio* (May 12, 1895), 11-12, by "Fray Veritas," entitled "Una oleada de música." In Spanish.

Credits Albéniz with helping initiate a "regeneration of Spanish lyric art." Heaps special praise on the second act, but has the usual reservations about the text: "The day that Albéniz works with a libretto that is fashioned to his manner of being and feeling, Albéniz the composer will rival Albéniz the pianist."

296. *La Dinastía* (May 10, 1895), 2, by Joaquín Homs y Parellada. In Spanish.

Offers warm praise for Albéniz's opera, citing the public's enjoyment of several numbers in the first two acts and enthusiastic reception of the authors on stage.

297. *La Ilustración Artística* 14/698 (May 13, 1895), 346. In Spanish.

Reports that Albéniz's work was received by the public with "genuine enthusiasm." The first two acts contained many fine numbers, though "deficiencies in the execution" of the third act prevented this critic from appreciating its "beauties."

298. *La Publicidad* (May 9, 1895), 2. In Spanish.

The opera was an "imcomparable success," and the audience "listened in religious silence, manifesting great interest in the work," which now establishes Albéniz among the "foremost modern composers."

299. *La Renaixensa. Diari de Catalunya* (May 16, 1895), 2763-65, by Enrich [*sic*] Morera, entitled "Carta Oberta á Don Isaac Albéniz." In Catalan.

An open letter from the composer Enric Morera to his friend Albéniz praising the "musical conception, melodic richness, and correct orchestration" of the work. Finds in it the "sincerity, exuberance, richness, and genial originality" characteristic of the composer. Expresses support for the development of national theater, particularly with a Catalan orientation.

300.   *La Vanguardia* (May 9, 1895), 5-6. In Spanish.

"Applause, acclamations, and shouts of enthusiasm still
sound in our ears, mixed and confused with the capital themes
[of the opera]." In particular he cites the funeral chorale in the
first act (sung for Lord Clifford), saying that it was received
amidst bravos and clapping and had to be repeated. The second
act, which all critics agreed was the best, received a "genuine
ovation" from the public at its conclusion, with Albéniz, Money-
Coutts (in Barcelona for the premiere), and the singers appearing
on stage to receive the applause. The third act was a
disappointment, a fact ascribed to an inferior performance.

301.   *La Vanguardia* (May 12, 1895), 4, by J. Roca y Roca, entitled
"La Semana en Barcelona." In Spanish.

Describes the difficult genesis of the production. Declares
that "Albéniz triumphed over everything: over the distrust of
certain unimaginative spirits ill-disposed to recognize the
superior merits of a composer who has excelled as an
outstanding concert pianist; he has triumphed over the suspicions
and fears of a theater management that gives every aid to works
like *L'amico Fritz* and *I pagliacci*, for no other reason than the
nationality of a powerful Italian publisher, and then sits back
when the work of a compatriot is tried; Albéniz, finally, has
succeeded in becoming a prophet in his own country."

302.   *Lo Teatro Català* (*El Teatro Catalán*) 6/226 (May 11, 1895), 4,
by Armando de la Florida. In Catalan.

Ascribes "the exuberant sonority of the new work" to the
high tessitura of the voice parts. Criticizes Albéniz as an
"enthusiast of the modern school who prefers the orchestra and
relegates the voices to a secondary role. . . . His characters
within the musical drama possess complete uniformity in their
manner of being, feeling, and thinking."

303.   *Lo Teatro Català* (*El Teatro Catalán*) 6/230 (June 8, 1895). In
Catalan.

Reports on the performance of the dances from *Henry Clifford* at the Tívoli. States that they were warmly recevied by the public and that they were "the best numbers of the opera."

Pepita Jiménez

Barcelona Production (1896):

304. *Diario de Barcelona* (January 7, 1896), 247-48, by F. Suárez Bravo. In Spanish.

States that Spanish "audiences . . . are in the worst position to appreciate works of this kind, because it deals with a drama in which there is no development of important events and external movement is practically nonexistent; therefore, everything depends on that which is said . . . the beauties [of the music] can be grasped only after two or three hearings." He observes that Money-Coutts had to pull out what action there was in order to "weave the fabric of the libretto," and concludes that "the drama, such as has remained, is sufficiently complete." It required "a few more days of study and rehearsals."

305. *El Correo Catalán* (January 8, 1896), 5-6. In Spanish.

Praises the orchestration as possessing "originality and great richness," though this may have worked against the voices in the soprano-tenor duet, causing them to appear "languid and much less expressive." The libretto itself is deemed to make little more than a "general allusion" to Valera's work, but it did possess the virtue of not presenting any scene or expression that was "objectionable from a moral point of view." The duet between Pepita and Don Luis had to be repeated at the audience's insistence. Albéniz was subsequently called to the stage to receive the accolades of the public, something that occurred after other "fragments" of the work as well as at its conclusion.

306. *La Renaixensa. Diari de Catalunya* (January 6, 1896), 134-35. In Catalan.

"As a result of the libretto, the characters have roles of little substance, which is a real problem for the composer to solve.

Only an imagination like Albéniz's could succeed, and this he has done. For, in the few musical situations provided him, he has conquered the applause of the intelligentsia."

307. *La Vanguardia* (January 6, 1896), 5, by Amadeu Vives. In Spanish.

"In truth and justice we can proclaim that our art is coming to life and that already blood is flowing in its veins, blood regenerated and vivified, whose power and force all feel and experience." Regarding the use of leitmotif, Vives declares it was "applied in a magisterial fashion."

308. *Lo Teatro Català (El Teatro Catalán)* 7/263 (January 25, 1896), 1, by Armando de la Florida. In Catalan.

Deals more with critics and criticism than with the opera itself, finding that most critics do not have the musical training necessary to judge such a work. The general current of praise for the new opera reflects this, and he states that the work lacked sufficient rehearsal and was not a success.

309. *Lo Teatro Regional* 5/205 (January 11, 1896), 15. In Catalan.

The opera has obtained an "extraordinary success" and its score's "many beauties" are proof of the young maestro's talent.

310. *The Musical Times* 59 (March 1, 1918), 116-17, by Herman Klein. In English.

Regarding the libretto, the most controversial aspect, he avers that "an undercurrent of deep passion compensates for lack of dramatic climax . . . its rare poetic feeling and truth to life, made it exactly *en rapport* with the temperament and imaginative qualities of the musician." Compares it favorably to Mascagni's *L'amico Fritz* and further deems Albéniz to have been as "up-to-date" as Verdi in *Falstaff*, and his use of leading motives "more ingenious, more skilful than the rather obvious method affected by Puccini, and consequently more interesting."

311. *The Sunday Times* (January 5, 1896), 6, by Herman Klein. In English.

> Praises Albéniz's handling of the thematic material and his treatment of the voices, saying he writes with great "consideration and melodic freedom." Lauds Albéniz's avoidance of direct quotation of folk melodies, and compares his work favorably to other operas of the 1890's, including those by Verdi, Puccini, and Bretón. Klein also has kind words for the librettist, citing "the infinite tact and skill with which he has evolved from [the novel] a lyric comedy full of deep human interest, and combining pathos and passion with abundant contrast in the shape of characteristic humour and strong local colour." Praises the libretto's condensing of the scant dramatic material in the novel to maintain the "three unities."

Prague Production (1897):

312. *Beilage zu Bohemia* (June 24, 1897), 3, by "K." In German.

> "The libretto does not contain any exciting event and exercises no arousing effect.... A deliberate and thought-out method of composition prevails in the work, so that not infrequently profundity has as a consequence heaviness and lack of melodic grace in the voice." Expresses the opinion that the outcome of Don Luis's "spiritual struggle" was too much delayed in the opera as opposed to the novel.

313. *Deutsches Abendblatt* (June 23, 1897), 2. In German.

> Praises Albéniz's training and ability. He especially appreciates his handling of the orchestra, though he concedes that it often overwhelmed the singers. He also comments on the predominance of triple meter and complains about Albéniz's predilection for double accidentals and the difficulties they posed to reading. But he concludes by declaring that "through its rich polyphony and wealth of ideas it will arouse the interest of the musician, though it may otherwise be caviar for the public."

314. *Neue freie Presse Abendblatt* (June 24, 1897). In German.

Lauds Albéniz's opera for its color and rhythm and reports that the audience received it with enthusiasm. Expresses reservations about the dramatic merits of the libretto and finds Albéniz's vocal writing lacking in impact.

315.   *Prager Tageblatt* (June 23, 1897), 10, by "Dr. A. G." In German.

Favorable assessment of the opera that reports it "engaged the lively interest of the audience. The premiere of the interesting work was a success. The composer was repeatedly called [to the stage] and received more laurels."

316.   *Prager Tageblatt* (June 24, 1897), 7, by "Dr. A. G." In German.

Provides a relatively detailed plot summary and praises Albéniz's originality and avoidance of "banal eclecticism." Finds the "subdued tone" that dominates most of the opera and its "sweet and dreamlike" lyricism appropriate to the drama. Though the rhythm verges on the monotonous at times, it is rescued by "energetic accents" that preserve its effect. Praises Albéniz's masterful orchestration and "passages of rich polyphony."

317.   *Prager Zeitung* (June 24, 1897), 2. In German.

"The plot offers no event with which the music can direct itself toward external effect. . . . He composes what only he, the great virtuoso, can play at the piano [and it is] altogether music out of which the bloom of piano virtuosity opens to the full. In the theater, however, before the orchestra and the stage, many a musical Moravian might shake his clever head with great circumspection."

318.   *Prager Zeitung* (June 24, 1897), 3, by Julius Steinberg. In German.

"The composer demands of his public that they follow him through labyrinthine ways of musical speculation, and to listen more with reason than with the ear. . . . All kinds of baroque figurations emerge and disturb the organic relationship of the individual parts to the overall structure and break up the plasticity of the architecture through the tangle of details."

Madrid Audition (1902):

319. *El Evangelio* 2/118 (August 7, 1902), 2, by López Muguiro. In Spanish.

"When we heard the presentation of *Pepita Jiménez*, we felt pleasure and pain, pride and discouragement. We knew that here was a purely Spanish opera, replete with beautiful ideas, fresh, inspired, with an irreproachable form."

320. *La Correspondencia de España* (August 7, 1902), 1. In Spanish.

Praises the melodious character of the work and cites several numbers as highlights, especially Pepita's famous "Romance" and the closing duet. Views it as the composer's "major triumph."

321. *La Época* (August 6, 1902), 3. In Spanish.

Reports that Albéniz was the "object of sincere and enthusiastic congratulations on the part of those who were fortunate to hear the music of *Pepita Jiménez*.

Brussels Production (1905):

322. *Le Courrier Musical* 8/3 (February 1, 1905), 76-78, by Octave Maus. In French.

"In the place of banal and artificial exoticism, conventional picturesqueness, he has substituted a color more discreet but more truthful, which marvelously evokes the places, customs, and distinctive characters of Spain. The music becomes impetuous, vehemently oppressed. It possesses spirit and warmth."

323. *Le Patriote* (January 5, 1905). In French.

Places Albéniz "among the colorists, possessing innate melody and musical thought." Unfortunately, "there prevails in the dialogue of Pepita a vague scorn for religious matters, an atmosphere of Voltaire-style libertinism, which accentuates the intervention of a vicar, a moralist in the manner of Count Des Grieux in *Manon*. But with an attitude less noble, less sympathetic, so that he does not deliver the appropriate discourse." Still, he regards the work as a "revelation," and "there reigns from one end to the other a discreet emotion and an inimitable something called sincerity, [and the second] act is delicious to listen to."

324. *Le Peuple* (January 5, 1905), 2, by "Labarbe." In French.

"Two roles dominate the entire work, that of Pepita and that of Don Luis, and the rest remain in the shade. Fatally, the situations are repeated without providing much variety. This fault is common in all works inspired by short stories or novels, and very exceptional are those that conserve in their adaptation to the stage all their interest and that which creates their charm." Nonetheless, he judges *Pepita Jiménez* "a very expressive, coherent work, of an absolute sincerity and beautiful lyric flight, which is worthy of gaining and retaining attention."

325. *Le Soir* (January 5, 1905), 2, by "L. S." In French.

Describes the opera as "the revelation of a composer at last original, bringing with him the color, the movement, the warmth of his nationality, of which he wants to convey the atmosphere and express the feelings."

326. *Le Temps* (Paris) (April 11, 1905), by Pierre Lalo. In French.

Views the libretto as the major weakness of the work but attributes "charming qualities" to the music, praising its handling of leitmotiv, transformation of themes, and symphonic development. Nonetheless, he regards the work as redolent not of Bayreuth but of Spain and its "fragrance, flavor, and color." He declares that Albéniz is "one of the greatest inventors of rhythms in the entire universe" and describes the music as "sensual and melancholy, sad and passionate, ardent and fine." "And to add to his subtle eloquence, M. Albéniz has the most lively, the most suple, the most brilliant orchestra, an orchestra in ceaseless movement, changing, glistening, an orchestra that flows . . . like a stream."

327. Additional reviews (all in French):

La Chronique (January 4, 1905), 3, by "J. D'A."; *La Gazette* (January 4, 1905), 2, by "Edm. C."; *Le Matin* (January 11, 1905), 3; *Le Petit Bleu du Matin* (January 4, 1905), 2, by "R. V."

Paris Production (1923):

328. *Comœdia* (June 18, 1923), 1-2, by Raymond Charpentier and Georges Linor. In French.

Finds a "regrettable" Italian influence in the opera and labels it a kind of "Cavalleria Iberica." Describes it as a "flagrant mélange of French romanticism—viewed through Schumann— of Italian verismo, and of hispanism." The overture to the second act, which was repeated, demonstrated a resemblance to the "exaggerated flights" of Puccini. Derides the music as "composed principally of locutions borrowed from the decadence of romanticism."

329. *La France* (June 25, 1923), 1-2, by André Fijan. In French.

"This music of Albéniz, so seductive on the piano, loses, like that of Granados, a great many of its qualites in the orchestra . . . the instrumentation is implacable and heavy [and] consists of always doubling the strings with woodwinds or with brass. One can possess the most beautiful qualities as a musician and compromise the career of a dramatic work by neglecting to submit to that law that is the supremacy of the human voice over the symphony or, if you prefer, over the hundred voices of the orchestra. . . . Nevertheless, the lyric comedy of Albéniz pleases [and] envelops us, despite all, in a perfectly warm and intoxicating atmosphere."

330. *L'Evenement* (June 19, 1923), 1, by Maurice Bouisson. In French.

Praises the music's picturesque use of folk rhythms and local color, particularly in the instrumental writing, as well as its suggestion of "divine aspiration."

331. *L'Echo de Paris* (June 18, 1923), 5, by "Le Capitaine Fracasse." In French.

Compares Albéniz's style of writing to that of Chopin, particularly the latter's sonatas. He also invokes Liszt, Wagner, and Chabrier as prototypes. Albéniz's ideas are "gushing, spontaneous, fresh, abundant, lyrical." These and other elements of his style are "unified, vivified, transfigured by an interior happiness, a joy in inventing melodies."

332. *Le Figaro* (June 19, 1923), 6, by André Messager. In French.

Reveals his unfavorable feelings, perhaps explaining why the opera never made it to Covent Garden, where he was director: "The style is rather hybrid and inclines too often towards Italianism of the verist school. The heavy orchestration does not allow a large enough part to the declamation."

333. *Le Quotidien* (July 5, 1923), 6, by Paul Dukas. In French.

"[The music] is animated by all the life lacking in the play. It breaks the bonds of the little story and sings by itself the most evocative song of Spain, the most sparkling [song] of popular verve, or the most poetical languor of delicate melancholy one can hear. Without pause, without any trifle entering to break its flight, it is elevated in the orchestra, quivering on wings of rhythm, and spreads in charming caprices across each scene . . . so alive, so spontaneous, so delicious."

334. *Le Siècle* (June 18, 1923), 1. In French.

"The local color is less marked in his *Pepita Jiménez*, but one finds in this score a vaporous poetry, of ideas happily created and developed with a . . . delicate art. One listened to it with lively pleasure."

335. *Le Temps* (June 20, 1923), 3, by Henry Malherbe. In French.

Expresses reservations about the work: "But, decidedly, despite the engrossing music of Albéniz, the plot appeared too simple and too naive. It is the music that, alone, is vital and of an agile animalism, hardy and inflamed. It shudders like a beast of prey, it shimmers like a fleece. Languid and ardent, chaste and passionate, it blends mysticism and voluptuousness, the sacred scents of incense and candles with the odors of wet and whirling dancers. The rhythmic frenzy of the composer suffices to our pleasure."

336. *Lyrica* 2/17 (July 1923), 102-04, by "Mercutio." In French.

Derides it as a "banal love story that oscillates between Joscelyn and Desgrieux without the charm of the former and the passion of the latter." Finds Pepita's character unconvincing dramatically and musically, and the work as a whole exhibits a cloying sentimentality. The opera's lack of dramatic impact is unrelieved by the richness of the instrumentation and Albéniz's lyric fecundity.

337. *Revue des Deux Mondes* (July 1, 1923), 226-27, by Camille Bellaigue. In French.

Introduces the work as a colloboration between the "exquisite" musician Albéniz and the "mediocre" poet Money-Coutts. Describes the music as "charming, lively, melodic, and also symphonic." Though it is of a decidedly Spanish character, it does not conform so strictly to national forms that it lacks a wider appeal.

Barcelona Production (1926):

338. *La Noche* (January 15, 1926), 1. In Spanish.

"*Pepita Jiménez* exhibits all the characteristics of the music of Albéniz. The spontaneity, the melodic flight, the winged rhythm of the *Iberia* suite, all are there with the identical freshness and melodic grace. The parallel inspiration and technique proceed in so sympathetic a manner that the melodic line never decays, maintained without deformations, in a vivid expression of the Andalusian soul. In the romance, the second-act duet, and in the dances the orchestra achieves "a supreme brilliance and grace."

339.   Additional reviews (all in Spanish, unless otherwise noted):

Diario de Barcelona (January 15, 1926), 32, by "A. M." ; *El Diluvio* (January 15, 1926), 29, by "Alard"; *El Noticero Universal* (January 15, 1926), 456, by Alfredo Romea; *Las Noticias* (January 16, 1926), 2, by "Salvatore"; *La Vanguardia* (January 15, 1926), 14; *La Veu de Catalunya* (January 15, 1926), 6, by "J. Ll." (in Catalan).

Madrid Production (revision by Pablo Sorozábal) (1964):

340.   *ABC* (June 7, 1964), 109, by Federico Sopeña. In Spanish.

Objects to the plot change, describing it as "irritating" in view of the wide currency of the novel. He calls for a new arrangement of the opera with a restoration of the original ending.

341.   *ABC* (July 5, 1964), by A. Laborda, entitled "Unas cartas de Albéniz sobre el estreno de 'Pepita Jiménez' in Prague." In Spanish.

Excerpts from Albéniz's letters to his wife during the spring of 1897 as he fretted over the rehearsals of the opera and exulted in its eventual, though short-lived, triumph.

342.   *Arriba* (June 6, 1964), 23, by Pablo Sorozábal. In Spanish.

Explains the rationale and method of his revision of the opera. The changes included 1) alteration of the declamatory style of the vocal writing to make it more lyrical, 2) adaptation of the libretto from French to Spanish, 3) reinstrumentation where appropriate, and 4) alteration of the drama itself, giving it a tragic character. Sorozábal was a successful zarzuela composer whose motives were correct but whose procedures were questionable and final product regrettable.

343. *Informaciones* (June 8, 1964), 7, by Antonio Fernández-Cid. In Spanish.

   Ventures to say, as someone familiar with all of Sorozábal's work, that he (Sorozábal) "has placed at the service of his work love, care, mastery, and noble renunciation of all personal ambition. If in other cases—in *San Antonio de la Florida* above all—it was fitting to point out many moments where the adapter intruded in the line of the creation itself, here no. That is the foremost virtue."

Merlin

344. *Diario de Barcelona* (December 20, 1950), 23, by A. Catalá. In Spanish.

   Gives a brief background of the work and of Albéniz as an opera composer. Praises the performance (listing the cast) and reports that the audience received it warmly. No discussion of the music itself.

345. *El Noticiero Universal* (December 19, 1950), 8, by Alfredo Romea. In Spanish.

   Notes the influence of Wagner, particularly in "the robustness with which the orchestral commentary is handled." Though the first and third acts offered "much that was spectacular," the second was "frankly boring."

346. *La Vanguardia Española* (December 20, 1950), 14, by U. F. Zanni. In Spanish.

   Heaps praise on the opera, stating that "the writing is noble, frank, and intelligently adapted to the inspiring themes. The orchestration reveals a firm and skilled hand in the conception of instrumental combinations . . . it is a very worthy opera."

347. *La Vie Musicale* (December-January, 1951-52), 8-9, by M. Casamada. In French.

Favorable though not enthusiastic review. Presents a useful summary of the dramatic and musical development of the opera, illustrated with various leading motives.

Iberia

(Spanish premieres by Joaquim Malats during Albéniz's lifetime)

348. *El Liberal* (December 15, 1906), 2. In Spanish.

Concerning Malats's performance at the Teatro de la Comedia in Madrid: "The very beautiful 'Triana' had to be repeated after a clamorous salvo of applause."

349. *El Noticiero Universal* (November 6, 1906), 3. In Spanish.

"Triana" reveals Albéniz's "inspiration and talent as well as his profound knowledge of music." Had to be repeated at the insistence of the audience at the Teatre Principal in Barcelona.

350. *El Noticiero Universal* (March 25, 1907), 3. In Spanish.

The Barcelona public enthused over the "poetry and Spanish popular flavor" of "El puerto."

351. *La Época* (December 17, 1906), 43, Cecilio Roda. In Spanish.

"Triana" was "truly delicious and of enchanting novelty." It possesses remarkable "freshness and character," and in its intricate rhythms, modern harmony, and virtuosity it is a model worthy of imitation.

352. *La Vanguardia* (November 6, 1906), 9, by "M. J. B." In Spanish.

Malats's "magisterial interpretation" of "Triana" was compensation to Albéniz for the "collective ingratitude" shown him by his homeland.

353. *La Vanguardia* (March 24, 1907), 8-9. In Spanish.

Describes "El puerto" as a "poem of admirable naturalness and freshness," praising its "Spanish ambience."

CHAPTER THREE

Catalogue of Works

The following compilation is greatly indebted to the work of Jacinto
Torres Mulas, *Die Musik in Geschichte und Gegenwart* (new edition,
Personenteil), s.v. "Albéniz" (works list), which in turn is based on his
*Catálogo sistemático descriptivo de las obras musicales de Isaac
Albéniz* (unpublished). In addition to the author's own work, the
catalogue below borrows from Baytelman (B19), Bevan (B20), Falces
Sierra (B35), and Laplane (B60). When it is finally available, Frances
Barulich's *Researches into the Life of Isaac Albéniz* (Ph.D. dissertation,
New York University, in progress) will provide welcome additional
information in English on his works.

Chronology is particularly difficult to determine. Establishing the
order by date of composition is problematic because we retain only a
few of the original manuscripts and are thus dependent on references in
correspondence, concert reviews, and editorial data (first editions and
plates) for information on their genesis. Ordering his music by date of
publication is even less satisfactory because some of his works
remained unpublished or did not appear in print until long after they
were composed. Unfortunately, Albéniz and his publishers carelessly
assigned opus numbers, and these have little or no validity.
Consequently, they do not appear here. The works are simply given
first by medium and then in chronological order by composition date
(as best as can be determined). Where the dates are identical, the works
are listed alphabetically (unless the sequence of their composition in
that year is known). This catalogue includes published works,
manuscripts, and works that are now lost. Alternate titles (from later
editions) appear after the main title. The location of any extant
manuscripts appears in brackets at the end of the entry.

PIANO WORKS

1. *Marcha militar*. Composed 1869. Published Madrid: Calcografía de B. Eslava, 1869.

2. *Rapsodia cubana*. Composed 1881. Published Madrid: Antonio Romero,1886.

3. *Pavana-capricho* [*Pavane espagnole*]. Composed 1882. Published Madrid: Benito Zozaya, c.1885.

4. *Serenata napolitana*. Composed 1882. Lost.

5. *Fantasía sobre motivos de la jota*. Composed in or before 1883. Lost. (Possibly an improvisation.)

6. *Barcarola* [*Barcarolle catalane*]. Composed in or before 1884. Published Barcelona: Valentín de Haas, 1884.

7. *Seis pequeños valses*. Composed in or before 1884. Published Barcelona: R. Guardia, 1884.

8. Sonata No. 1. Scherzo only. Composed in or before 1884. Published Barcelona: R. Guardia(?), 1884.

9. *Deseo. Estudio de concierto*. Composed in or before 1885. Published Madrid: Antonio Romero, 1886.

10. *Dos caprichos andaluces*. Composed in or before 1885. Lost. (Possibly the first numbers of *Suite española No. 1*.)

11. *Dos grandes estudios de concierto*. Composed in or before 1885. Lost. (Possibly *Deseo* and *Estudio impromptu*.)

12. *Estudio impromptu*. Composed in or before 1885. Published Madrid: Antonio Romero, 1886.

13. First Mazurka, Second Mazurka. Composed in or before 1885. Published London: Stanley Lucas, Weber & Co., 1890. (Same as Nos. 1 and 2 from *Seis mazurkas de salón*.)

14. *Marcha nupcial*. Composed in or before 1885. Lost.

15. *Seis mazurkas de salón*. Composed in or before 1885. Published Madrid: Antonio Romero, 1886. (Nos. 1 and 2 same as First and Second Mazurkas.)

   1. "Isabel"
   2. "Casilda"
   3. "Aurora"
   4. "Sofía"
   5. "Christa"
   6. "María"

16. *Serenata árabe*. Composed in or before 1885. Published Madrid: Antonio Romero, 1886.

17. *Suite ancienne No. 1*. Composed in or before 1885. Published Madrid: Antonio Romero, 1886.

   1. "Gavota"
   2. "Minuetto"

18. *Suite morisca*. Composed in or before 1885. Lost.

   1. "Marcha de la caravana"
   2. "La noche"
   3. "Danza de las esclavas"
   4. "Zambra"

19. *Siete estudios en los tonos naturales mayores*. Composed in or before 1886. Published Madrid: Antonio Romero, 1886.

20. *Suite española No. 1*. The original suite consisted of all eight titles but only four scores, for Nos. 1, 2, 3, and 8 (No. 3 composed before 1886; Nos. 1, 2, and 8 composed in 1886). These were published separately in Madrid by Benito Zozaya (Nos. 1 and 3 in 1886, Nos. 2 and 8 in 1892). The other numbers were added later, by Hofmeister in 1911 and Unión Musical Española in 1913, and had originally appeared under the titles in brackets.

   1. "Granada (Serenata)"
   2. "Cataluña (Curranda)" [Mc]
   3. "Sevilla (Sevillanas)"
   4. "Cádiz (subtitled variously Saeta, Canción, or Serenata)" [same as *Serenata española*]
   5. "Asturias (Leyenda)" [same as No. 1 from *Chants d'Espagne*]

      6. "Aragón (Fantasía)" [same as No. 1 from *Deux Morceaux caractéristiques*]

      7. "Castilla (Seguidillas)" [same as No. 5 from *Chants d'Espagne*]

      8. "Cuba (Capricho or Nocturno)" [Mc]

21. *Angustia: Romanza sin palabras*. Composed 1886. Published Madrid: Antonio Romero, 1886.

22. *Balbina valverde (Polka brillante)*. Composed 1886. Published Madrid: Antonio Romero, 1886 (under the pseudonym Príncipe Weisse Vogel).

23. *Diva sin par (Mazurka-capricho)*. Composed 1886. Published Madrid: Antonio Romero, 1886 (under the pseudonym Príncipe Weisse Vogel).

24. Minuetto No. 3. Composed 1886. Published Madrid: Antonio Romero, 1886.

25. Sonata No. 2. Composed 1886. Lost.

26. *Suite ancienne No. 2*. Composed 1886. Published Madrid: Antonio Romero, 1886.

      1. "Sarabande"
      2. "Chacona"

27. *Suite ancienne No. 3*. Composed 1886. Published Madrid: Antonio Romero, 1887.

      1. "Minuetto"
      2. "Gavota"

28. *Andalucía (Bolero)*. Composed 1886-7. Published London: Joseph Williams, 1899. (Same as No. 5 from *Recuerdos de viaje*.)

29. *On the Water (Barcarole)*. Composed 1886-7. Published London: Stanley Lucas, Weber & Co., c.1892. (Same as No. 1 from *Recuerdos de viaje*.)

30. *Recuerdos de viaje*. Composed 1886-7. Published Madrid: Antonio Romero, 1886-7.

      1. "En el mar (Barcarola)" [same as *On the Water*]

    2. "Leyenda (Barcarola)"
    3. "Alborada"
    4. "En la Alhambra"
    5. "Puerta de tierra (Bolero)" [same as *Andalucía (Bolero)*]
    6. "Rumores de la caleta (Malagueña)"
    7. "En la playa"

31. *Mazurka de salón.* Composed in or before 1887. Published Barcelona: Juan Ayné, 1887.

32. Menuet (G Minor). Composed in or before 1887. Published Paris: Alphonse Leduc, 1922 (in *Dix Pièces en un recueil*).

33. *Rapsodia española* (solo-piano version). Composed in or before 1887. Published Madrid: Antonio Romero, 1887.

34. *Recuerdos (Mazurka).* Composed in or before 1887. Published Barcelona: Juan Ayné, 1887.

35. *Cotillón. Album de danzas de salón.* Composed 1887. Published Madrid: Antonio Romero, 1887.

    1. "Champagne (Carte Blanche), vals de salón" [also known as the *Champagne vals* or *Cotillon valse*]

36. *Pavana fácil para manos pequeñas.* Composed 1887. Published Madrid: Antonio Romero, 1887.

37. *Seis danzas españolas.* Composed 1887. Published Madrid: Antonio Romero, 1887.

38. Sonata No. 3. Composed 1887. Published Madrid: Antonio Romero, 1887.

    1. Allegretto
    2. Andante
    3. Allegro assai

39. Sonata No. 4. Composed 1887. Published Madrid: Antonio Romero, 1887.

    1. Allegro
    2. "Scherzino" (Allegro)
    3. "Minuetto" (Andantino)
    4. "Rondó" (Allegro)

40. Sonata No. 5. Composed 1887. Published Madrid: Antonio Romero, 1887.

    1. Allegro non troppo
    2. "Minuetto del gallo" (Allegro assai)
    3. "Rêverie" (Andante)
    4. Allegro

41. Sonata No. 6. Composed in or before 1888(?). Lost.

42. Sonata No. 7. Minuetto only. Composition date unknown, but probably in or before 1888. Published Madrid: Unión Musical Española, 1962.

43. *Dos mazurkas de salón.* Composed 1888. Published Madrid: Benito Zozaya, 1892.

    1. "Amalia"
    2. "Ricordatti"

44. *Douze Pièces caractéristiques* [*Doce piezas características*]. Composed 1888. Published Madrid: Antonio Romero, 1888-89.

    1. "Gavotte"
    2. "Minuetto a Silvia"
    3. "Barcarolle (Ciel sans nuages)" ["Barcarola (Cielo sin nubes)"]
    4. "Prière" ["Plegaria"]
    5. "Conchita (Polka)"
    6. "Pilar (Valse)"
    7. "Zambra"
    8. "Pavana"
    9. "Polonesa"
    10. "Mazurka"
    11. "Staccato (Capricho)"
    12. "Torre Bermeja (Serenata)"

45. *La fiesta de aldea.* Composed 1888. Published Madrid: Unión Musical Española, 1973. (Piano score for the first movement of *Escenas sinfónicas catalanas.*) [Lc]

46. *Deux Morceaux caractéristiques* [*Deux Dances espagnoles*, *Dos danzas españolas*, and *Spanish National Songs*]. Composed in or

before 1889. Published London: Stanley Lucas, Weber & Co. 1889; Paris: Max Eschig, 1889.

    1. "Jota aragonesa" [same as No. 6 from *Suite española No. 1*]

    2. "Tango"

47. *Suite española No. 2* [*Seconde Suite espagnole*]. Composed in or before 1889. Published Madrid: Antonio Romero, 1889.

    1. "Zaragoza (Capricho)"

    2. "Sevilla (Capricho)"

48. *Cádiz-gaditana*. Composed in or before 1890. Published London: Joseph Williams(?), 1890(?).

49. *Serenata española* [*Célèbre sérénade espagnole*]. Composed in or before 1890. Published Barcelona: Juan Bautista Pujol y Cía., 1890. (Same as No. 4 from the *Suite española No. 1*.)

50. *España: Six Feuilles d'album* [*España: Seis hojas de album*]. Composed 1890. Published London: Pitts & Hatzfield, 1890.

    1. "Prélude"

    2. "Tango"

    3. "Malagueña"

    4. "Serenata"

    5. "Capricho catalán"

    6. "Zortzico"

51. *L'Automne (Valse)*. Composed 1890. Published Barcelona: Juan Bautista Pujol y Cía., 1890.

52. *Mallorca (Barcarola)*. Composed 1890. Published London: Stanley Lucas, Weber & Co., 1891.

53. *Rêves* [*Sueños*]. Composed 1890-91. Published London: Stanley Lucas, Weber & Co., c.1891.

    1. "Berceuse"

    2. "Scherzino"

    3. "Chant d'amour" ["Canto de amor"]

54. *Zambra granadina (Danse orientale)*. Composed in or before 1891. Published London: Carlo Ducci & Co., c.1891.

55. *Zortzico*. Composed in or before 1891. Published Paris: Édition Mutuelle, c. 1911.

56. *Album of Miniatures* [*Les Saisons*]. Composed 1892. Published London: Chappell & Co., 1892.

    1. "Spring" ["Le Printemps"]
    2. "Summer" ["L'Été"]
    3. "Autumn" ["L'Automne"]
    4. "Winter" ["L'Hiver"]

57. *Chants d'Espagne* [*Cantos de España*]. Composed 1891-4. Published Barcelona: Juan Bautista Pujol y Cía, 1892 (Nos. 1-3) and 1897 (Nos. 4-5).

    1. "Prélude" [same as No. 5 from *Suite española No. 1*]
    2. "Orientale"
    3. "Sous le palmier (Danse espagnole)" [beginning resembles No. 8 from *Suite española No. 1*]
    4. "Córdoba"
    5. "Seguidillas" [same as No. 7 from *Suite española No. 1*]

58. *Espagne: Souvenirs*. Composed 1896-97. Published Barcelona: Universo Musical, 1897.

    1. "Prélude"
    2. "Asturias"

59. *The Alhambra: Suite pour le piano*. Composed 1897. Published San Sebastián: A. Díaz y Cía, 1908. Premiered by José Vianna da Motta, Société Nationale de Musique, Paris, January 21, 1899. [Bc]

    1. "La vega" [same as the MS in the Mm entitled *Fantasie espagnole pour le piano* (1898)]

60. *Iberia: 12 nouvelles "impressions" en quatre cahiers*. Composed 1905-08. Published Paris: Édition Mutuelle, 1906-08.

1er Cahier (composed 1905; premiered by Blanche Selva, Salle Pleyel, Paris, May 9, 1906):
    1. "Evocación" [Prélude] [Bc]
    2. "El puerto" [Lc]
    3. "Fête-Dieu à Séville" ["El Corpus en Sevilla"] [Oc]

2e Cahier (composed 1906; premiered by Blanche Selva, St. Jean de Luz, France, September 11, 1907):

    4. "Rondeña" [Oc]

    5. "Almería" [Oc]

    6. "Triana" [Oc]

3e Cahier (composed 1906; premiered by Blanche Selva, Salon of Mme. Armand de Polignac, Paris, January 2, 1908):

    7. "El Albaicín" [Bc]

    8. "El polo" [Oc]

    9. "Lavapiés" [Mm]

4e Cahier (composed 1907-08; premiered by Blanche Selva, Salon d'Automne, Paris, February 9, 1909):

    10. "Málaga" [Bc]

    11. "Jerez" [Bc]

    12. "Eritaña" [Bc]

61.   *Yvonne en visite!* Composed in or before 1908. Published Paris: Rouart, Lerolle et Cie, 1909.

    1. "La Révérence"

    2. "Joyeuse Rencontre, et quelques penibles événements"

62.   *Azulejos.* Left unfinished in 1909 and completed by Enric Granados. Published Paris: Édition Mutuelle, 1911.

    1. "Preludio"

63.   *Navarra.* Left unfinished in 1909 and completed by Déodat de Séverac. Published Paris: Édition Mutuelle, 1912.

STAGE WORKS

64.   *Cuanto más viejo.* Zarzuela in 1 act with a libretto by Sr. Zapino. Composed in or before 1882 and premiered Bilbao, Coliseo, February 1882. Lost.

65.   *Catalanes de gracia.* Zarzuela in 1 act with a libretto by Leopoldo Palomino de Guzmán. Composed 1882 and premiered Madrid, Teatro Salón Eslava, March 28, 1882. Lost.

66.   *El canto de salvación.* Composed 1882(?). Zarzuela in 2 acts. Lost.

67.	*Poèmes d'amour.* Incidental music to poems by Paul-Armand Sylvestre. Composed 1892 and premiered Barnes, Lyric Club, June 20, 1892. [Bc, Mm]

68.	"Oh! Horror! Horror!" Finale to Act 2 of *Incognita* (original *Le Coeur et la main* by Charles Lecocq) with a text by Harry Greenbank. Composed 1892 and premiered London, Lyric Theatre, October 6, 1892. Vocal score published London: Hopwood & Crew, 1892.

69.	*The Magic Opal.* Lyric comedy in 2 acts with a libretto by Arthur Law. Composed 1892 and premiered London, Lyric Theatre, January 19, 1893. Vocal score published London: Joseph Williams, 1893. Revised and retitled as *The Magic Ring* and premiered London, Prince of Wales's Theatre, April 11, 1893. Translated into Spanish by Eusebio Sierra and premiered Madrid, Teatro de la Zarzuela, November 23, 1894, under title *La sortija.* [Bc]

70.	*Poor Jonathan* (original *Der arme Jonathan* by Karl Millöcker). Operetta in 2 acts to texts by H. Wittmann, J. Bauer, and Harry Greenbank. Albéniz contributed several (16?) additional numbers, composed 1893 and premiered London, Prince of Wales's Theatre, June 19, 1893. [Bc]

71.	*San Antonio de la Florida.* Zarzuela in 1 act with a libretto by Eusebio Sierra. Composed 1894 and premiered Madrid, Teatro de Apolo, October 26, 1894. Vocal score published Barcelona: Juan Bautista Pujol y Cía., 1894. Libretto published Madrid: R. Velasco, 1894. Translated into French by Lucien Solvay and Robert Sand and produced Brussels, Théâtre Royale de la Monnaie, January 3, 1905, under title *L'Ermitage fleuri.* Libretto published Brussels: Th. Lombaerts, 1904. Reorchestrated (MS full score lost during Spanish Civil War) by Pablo Sorozábal and produced Madrid, Teatro Fuencarral, November 18, 1954. [Bc, Mm, Oc, Se]

72.	*Henry Clifford.* Opera in 3 acts with a libretto by Francis B. Money-Coutts ("Mountjoy"). Composed 1893-95 and premiered Barcelona, Gran Teatre del Liceu, May 8, 1895, in Italian translation by Giuseppe María Arteaga Pereira under title *Enrico*

Clifford. Vocal score published Barcelona: Juan Bautista Pujol y Cía., 1895. Italian libretto published Barcelona: Imprenta Gutenberg, 1895. [Bc, Mm, Oc]

73. *Pepita Jiménez*. Lyric comedy in 2 acts with a libretto by Francis B. Money-Coutts (after a novel by Juan Valera). First version as an opera in 1 act composed 1895 and premiered Barcelona, Gran Teatre del Liceu, January 5, 1896, in Italian translation by Angelo Bignotti. Second version as an opera in 2 acts composed 1896. Vocal and full scores published Leipzig: Breitkopf und Härtel, 1896 (in German, Italian, French, and German). Produced Prague, Neues Deutsches Landestheater, June 22, 1897, in German translation by Oskar Berggruen. Reorchestration of 1899-1902 published Leipzig: Breitkopf und Härtel, 1904. Translated into French by Maurice Kufferath and produced Brussels, Théâtre de la Monnaie, January 3, 1905. Libretto published Leipzig: Breitkopf und Härtel, 1905. Produced Paris, Opéra-Comique, June 18, 1923, in new French translation by Joseph de Marliave. Piano-vocal score published Paris: Max Eschig, 1923 (in French translation by Marliave and Italian translation by Carlo M. A. Galateri). Produced Barcelona, Gran Teatro del Liceu, January 14, 1926, in the Italian translation by Galateri. [Bc, Mm, Am, Archivo Manuel de Falla; copy of proofs of 1904 reorchestration with corrections in Albéniz's own hand at firm of Max Eschig in Paris.] Translated into Spanish and revised as an opera in 3 acts by Pablo Sorozábal and premiered Madrid, Teatro de la Zarzuela, June 6, 1964. [Bn, Se]

74. *Mar y cel*. Opera based on a play by Àngel Guimerà. Begun 1897. Incomplete. [Bc]

75. *King Arthur*. Operatic trilogy with librettos by Francis B. Money-Coutts. Librettos published London: John Lane, 1897. *Merlin*. Opera in 3 acts. Composed 1897-1902 and performed in a concert version at the home of M. Tassel in Brussels, February 13, 1905 (Prelude to Act I premiered Barcelona, 1898). Vocal score in English and French (translation by Maurice Kufferath) published Paris: Édition Mutuelle, 1906. French libretto published Brussels, 1905, for the concert version. Premiered

Barcelona, Gran Teatre del Liceu, December 18, 1950, in a Spanish translation by Manuel Conde. *Launcelot*. Opera in 3 acts. Begun 1902. Incomplete. *Guenevere*. Opera in 4 acts. Never begun. [Bc, Mm]

76. *La Sérénade*. Lyric drama with a libretto by an unknown author. Begun 1899. Incomplete. [Bc, Mm]

77. *La real hembra*. Zarzuela in 3 acts with a libretto by Cristóbal de Castro. Begun 1902. Incomplete. [Bc]

78. *La morena*. Lyric drama in 4 acts with a libretto by Alfred Mortier. Begun 1905. Incomplete. [Bc]

79. *The Song of Songs*. Incidental music to a text by Francis B. Money-Coutts. Begun 1905. Incomplete. [Mm]

VOCAL/CHORAL WORKS

Solo voice:

80. *Cuatro romanzas para mezzo-soprano*. Composed before 1886. Lost.

81. *Tres romanzas catalanas*. Composed before 1886. Lost.

82. *Rimas de Bécquer*. Texts by Gustavo Adolfo Bécquer. Composed c.1886. Published Madrid: Benito Zozaya, 1892.

    1. "Besa el aura."
    2. "Del salón en el ángulo oscuro."
    3. "Me ha herido recatándose en la sombra."
    4. "Cuando sobre el pecho inclinas."
    5. "¿De dónde vengo?"

83. *Seis baladas*. Texts by Marquesa de Bolaños. Composed 1887. Published Madrid: Antonio Romero, c.1889.

    1. "Barcarola."
    2. "La lontananza."
    3. "Una rosa in dono."
    4. "Il tuo sguardo."
    5. "Moriro!!"
    6. "T'ho riveduto in sogno."

84. "Il en est de l'amour." Text by M. Costa de Beauregard. Composed 1892. Published Paris-Baudoux: T. Cée, n.d.

85. *Deux Morceaux de prose de Pierre Loti.* Texts by Pierre Loti. Composed c. 1895. Published San Sebastián: A. Díaz y Cía., 1897.

> 1. "Crépuscule."
> 2. "Tristesse."

86. *To Nellie: Six Songs.* Texts by Francis B. Money-Coutts. Composed 1896. Published Paris: Au Ménestrel-Heugel & Cie., 1896(?).

> 1. "Home."
> 2. "Counsel."
> 3. "May-Day Song."
> 4. "To Nellie."
> 5. "A Song of Consolation."
> 6. "A Song."

87. "Chanson de Barberine." Text by Alfred de Musset. Composed c.1897. Published Madrid: Unión Musical Española, 1972.

88. "The Gifts of the Gods." Text by Francis B. Money-Coutts. Composed c. 1897. Brussels: Dogilbert, 1897.

89. *Six Songs.* Texts by Francis B. Money-Coutts. Composed 1897. Only two extant. Published Madrid: Instituto de Bibliografía Musical, 1997. [Oc]

> 2. "Will You Be Mine?"
> 3. "Separated."

90. "Conseil tenu par les rats." Begun c. 1900. Incomplete. [Bc]

91. "The Caterpillar." Texts by Francis B. Money-Coutts. Composed 1903. Published Paris: Édition Mutuelle, 1913 (with "The Caterpillar," in English and French, translated by Henry Varley, entitled "Les Dons des dieux" and "La Chenille").

92. "Art Thou Gone for Ever, Elaine?" Text by Francis B. Money-Coutts. Composed 1906. Published Madrid: Instituto de Bibliografía Musical, 1997. [Ah]

93.   *Quatre Mélodies*. Texts by Francis B. Money-Coutts. Composed 1908. Published Paris: Rouart, Lerolle et Cie., 1909 (in English and French, translated by M. D. Calvocoressi).

      1. "In Sickness and Health" ("Quand je te vois souffrir").
      2. "Paradise Regained" ("Le Paradis retrouvé").
      3. "The Retreat" ("Le Refuge").
      4. "Amor summa injuria."

Chorus and Orchestra:

94.   *El Cristo*. Oratorio. Composed before 1886. Lost.

95.   *Lo Llacsó*. Symphonic poem for orchestra, chorus, soloists. Text by Apel.les Mestres. Begun 1896. Incomplete. [Bc]

Chorus Alone:

96.   *Salmo VI: Oficio de difuntos*. SATB chorus. Composed 1885. Published Madrid: Instituto de Bibliografía Musical, 1994. [Mc]

ORCHESTRAL WORKS

97.   Concerto No. 1 for Piano and Orchestra in A Minor ("Concierto fantástico"). Composed 1886-87. Two-piano arrangement published Madrid: Unión Musical Española, c.1890. Orchestral version published Madrid: Unión Musical Española, 1975.

98.   *Rapsodia española for Piano and Orchestra*. Composed 1886-87. Two-piano arrangement published Madrid: Antonio Romero, 1887. Original orchestral version (reconstructed by Jacinto Torres) published Madrid: Instituto de Bibliografía Musical, 1997.

99.   *Suite característica*. Orchestrated c. 1887. Lost. (Presumably arrangements of the solo-piano versions.)

      1. "Scherzo"
      2. "En la Alhambra"
      3. "Rapsodia cubana"

100. *Escenas sinfónicas catalanas* [*Scènes symphoniques catalanes*, *Scènes villageoises catalanes*]. Composed 1888-89. [Mm]

      1. "Fête villageoise catalane"
      2. "Idilio"
      3. "Serenata"
      4. "Finale: Baile campestre"

101. *L'Automne (Valse)*. Orchestrated in or before 1890. (Arrangement of the piano work of the same title.) [Oc]

102. *Célèbre sérénade espagnole*. Composed in or before 1891. Published Barcelona: Juan Bautista Pujol y Cía., n.d.

103. Concerto No. 2 for Piano and Orchestra. Begun 1892. Incomplete. [Bc]

104. *La Alhambra.* Begun 1896. Nos. 1 and 3 incomplete, others titles only. [Bc]

      1. "La Vega"
      2. "Lindaraja"
      3. "Generalife"
      4. "Zambra"
      5. "¡Alarme!"
      6. No title

105. *Petite Suite*. Composed 1898. [Oc]

      1: "Sérénade Lorraine."

106. *Rapsodia Almogávar*. Begun 1899. Incomplete. (Initial version of *Catalonia*.) [Bc]

107. *Catalonia. Suite populaire pour orchestre en trois parties.* Composed 1899. Only first number completed (which bears the title of the suite). Published Paris: A. Durand & Fils, 1899. Premiered at a concert of the Société Nationale de Musique, Nouveau-Théâtre, Paris, May 23, 1899. [Bc]

108. *Guajira (Chant populaire cubain)*. Begun 1905. Incomplete. [Bc]

109. *El puerto.* 1907 orchestration of "El puerto" from *Iberia.* [Bc]

CHAMBER WORKS

110.   Concert Suite for Sextet. Composed c. 1883. Lost. (Probably similar to the later *Suite característica*.)

      1. "Scherzo"
      2. "Serenata morisca"
      3. "Capricho cubano"

111.   Trio in F for Piano, Violin, and Cello. Composed in or before 1885. Lost.

112.   Berceuse for Piano, Violin, Cello. Composed 1890. Published London: Stanley Lucas, Weber & Co., c.1892. (Arrangement of "Berceuse" from *Rêves*.)

CHAPTER FOUR

Discography

This is the first attempt at a thorough and complete discography of Albéniz's music since the one that appeared in Gabriel Laplane's 1956 biography. There has, of course, been a considerable increase in recordings since that time, not just in sheer numbers but in available formats, all of which are included here: Compact Disc (CD), Cassette (CS), LP, 45, Reel-to-Reel tape (Reel), and 78. Because this book is not intended primarily as a discography, the entries are as economical and uniform as possible. They include only commerical recordings and are arranged into two principal groups, i.e., original instrumentation and arrangements. The first group is organized in the same order as the catalogue of works. The second group is arranged by medium in alphabetical order, then by work title in the same order as the catalogue of works. Each entry provides the complete title of the work (works that have been published under more than one title appear under the one they bear on the recording and are followed by a cross reference), the artist(s) (and arranger, where known), label, format, and identification number (from the container rather than the recording itself, when a choice was available). Where an artist has made more than one recording of a number, they are arranged by label (in alphabetical order) and then by format (newest to oldest). Identification numbers are separated by commas and are preceded by the format only if it is different from the preceding recordings. The entries do not include the location, date, or title of the recording, or any indication whether a more recent recording is simply a reissue of an earlier recording (in most cases reissue information was not available, but it can often be inferred from the identification number).

This discography is based in part on previous catalogues in the works of Aviñoa (B18), Baytelman (B19), Iglesias (B53), Laplane

(B60), Mast (B70), Raux Deledicque (B83), and Selleck-Harrison (B97). Additional information was available in the Schwann/Opus catalogs, the MUZE database, and the Online Catalog of the Library of Congress (WorldCat). This latter source will be especially helpful to those seeking more details about any particular recording, but the other sources should also be consulted.

It is hoped that this discography will serve 1) to present the most graphic and convincing evidence possible of the enduring popularity of Albéniz's music, 2) to highlight the wide range of transcriptions and arrangements that have been made of his music over the years, 3) to show which artists have been the most active in promoting his music (although the names of Alicia de Larrocha and Andrés Segovia come as no surprise, those of Alexandr Scriabin and Conchita Supervía do. Other notable interpreters include José Iturbi, Alfred Cortot, and Frank Marshall), 4) to offer performers an overview of gaps in the repertoire and what opportunities exist to program and record less frequently heard works (for instance, there are abundant recordings of "Leyenda," but the equally beautiful—though not as characteristic—sonatas have attracted relatively few interpreters), 5) to provide librarians with a resource for assessing their current holdings in this area and possibilities for expansion, and 6) to supply a foundation for future, more comprehensive, discographic efforts.

ORIGINAL INSTRUMENTATION

Piano Works

1. *Marcha militar.*

   Unknown performer: International Piano Library (LP) IPL-5005/6

2. *Rapsodia cubana.*

   Rena Kyriakou: Vox (LP) SVBX-5404

3. *Pavana-capricho.*

   Rena Kyriakou: Vox (LP) SVBX-5403
   Katia and Marielle Labèque: Philips (CD) 438938-2

Alicia de Larrocha: Columbia (LP) ML-6003, MS-6603; Decca
(CS) CS5-6953, (LP) CS-6953; EMI (CD) CMS-7-64504-2,
ZDMB-64504; Erato (LP) STU-70561; Hispavox (CS)
230134, (LP) 130134, CH-249, HH-10-86/7, S-
60.309/10/11; London (CD) 417639-2, 433926-2, (LP) CS-
6953; Musical Heritage Society (LP) MHS-1571/2;
Turnabout (LP) TV-34774; Vox (CS) CT-4774
Antonio Ruiz-Pipó: Zacosa (LP) GML-2036

4. *Barcarola.*

Rena Kyriakou: Vox (LP) SVBX-5405

5. *Seis pequeños valses.*

Rena Kyriakou: Vox (LP) SVBX-5404

6. *Deseo. Estudio de concierto.*

Rena Kyriakou: Vox (LP) SVBX-5405

7. *Estudio impromptu.*

Rena Kyriakou: Vox (LP) SVBX-5405

8. *Seis mazurkas de salón.*

Rena Kyriakou: Vox (LP) SVBX-5405

9. *Serenata arabe.*

Rena Kyriakou: Vox (LP) SVBX-5404

10. *Suite ancienne no. 1.*

Rena Kyriakou: Vox (LP) SVBX-5404

11. *Siete estudios en los tonos naturales mayores.*

Rena Kyriakou: Vox (LP) SVBX-5403
Antonio Ruiz-Pipó: Koch-Schwann (CD) 3-1513-2

12. *Suite española No. 1* (complete).

Genoveva Galve: Columbia (LP) SCLL-14087
Luis Galve: Columbia (LP) SCLL-14987; Ensayo (LP) ENY-78
Pierre Huybregts: Centaur (CD) CRC-2231
Olga Llano Kuehl: Opus (LP) SL-6014
Rena Kyriakou: Vox (LP) SVBX-5405
Alicia de Larrocha: Columbia (LP) ML-6003, MS-6603; EMI
    (CD) CMS-7-64504-2; Erato (LP) STU-70561; GME (CD)
    GME-223; Hispavox (CS) 230134, (LP) 130134, CH-249,
    HH-10-86/7; London (CD) 417639-2, 417887-2, 433923-2;
    Musical Heritage Society (CD) 513460-Y, (CS) 323647-F,
    (LP) 1571/2; Vox (CS) CT-4774
Alma Petchersky: ASV (LP) ALH-949; ASV/Quicksilva (CD)
    QS-6079
Ricardo Requejo: Claves (CD) CD-50-8003/4
Esteban Sánchez: Ensayo (LP) CENY-1007, ENY-7B
Gonzalo Soriano: Boston Records (LP) B-302; Sucretet (LP)
    300-C-031

13.   *Suite española No. 1* (selections).

      Franz-Josef Appelhans: Life (LP) St-341.7647

14.   *Suite española No. 1*, "Granada (Serenata)."

      Joaquín Achúcarro: RCA (LP) RL-31404
      Jean-Joël Barbier: Accord (CD) ACD-200332
      Guillermo Cases (shortened version): Odeon (78) 195127 in
          OM-112
      José Cubiles: RCA (LP) LSC-16354
      José Echániz: Westminster (LP) WL-5382, XWN-18431
      María Garzón: ASV (CD) CD-DCA-798
      Amparo Iturbi: RCA (LP) A-630231, LM-1788
      Ruth Laredo: MCA (CD) MCAD-6265, (CS) MCAC-6265
      Alicia de Larrocha: GME (CD) GME-223; EMI (CD) ZDMB-
          64504; Hispavox (LP) C-30.072, S-20.025, S-30.072, S-
          66.316; Turnabout (CS) CT-4774, (LP) TV-34774; Vox
          (LP) SVBX-5801
      María Panthés: Columbia (78) DFX-169
      Marjan Rawicz and Walter Landauer (arr. for 2 pianos by the
          performers): Columbia (78) DB-2132

Manuela del Río (L. Campolietti, castanets): Gramophone/His
    Master's Voice (78) K-8088
Santiago Rodríguez: Elan (CD) CD-2202
Allan Schiller: ASV (CD) CDQA-6032; ASV/Quicksilva (CD)
    QS-6032
José Tordesillas: Philips (LP) RPF-761/2,3,4
Unknown performer: Moss Music Group (CS) LC-1101
Alejandro Vilalta: Odeon (78) 177265 in OM-63
Ricardo Viñes: EMI (LP) 1731791; Columbia (78) LFX-73

15.   *Suite española No. 1*, "Cataluña (Curranda)."

Alicia de Larrocha: Hispavox (CD) GME-223; Turnabout (CS)
    CT-4774, (LP) TV-34774
Marjan Rawicz and Walter Landauer (arr. for 2 pianos by the
    performers): Columbia (78) DB-2132
Alejandro Vilalta: Odeon (78) 177266 in OM-63

16.   *Suite española No. 1*, "Sevilla (Sevillanas)."

Joaquín Achúcarro: RCA (LP) RL-31404
Ayke Agus: Protone (CD) PRCD-1108, (CS) CSPR-172
Rafael Arroyo: Adès (CD) ADE-13.207-2
Guillermo Cases (shortened version): Odeon (78) 195127
Cor de Groot: Epic (LP) 3175; Philips (LP) A-00131-R
José Echániz: Westminster (LP) WL-5382, XWN-18431
Andor Foldes: Continental (78) M-34
Gérard Gahnassia: Magne (LP) MAG-2018
José Iturbi: Angel (LP) RL-32123, S-35628; EMI (LP) 2C-053-
    12024; Gramophone/His Master's Voice (78) DB-2164;
    Victor (78) 11562
Beatriz Klien: Turnabout (LP) TV-34327; Vox (LP) STPL-
    513.540, VS-3134
Katia and Marielle Labèque: Philips (CD) 438938-2
Ruth Laredo: MCA (CD) MCAD-6265, (CS) MCAC-6265
Alicia de Larrocha: Decca (CS) CS5-6953, (LP) CS-6953; GME
    (CD) GME-223; Hispavox (LP) C-30.072, S-20.078; S-
    30.072; London (CD) 417639-2, 417751-2, 417795-2, (LP)
    CS-6953; Turnabout (CS) CT-4774, (LP) TV-34774; Vox
    (LP) SVBX-5801

Josef Lhevinne: Argo (LP) DA-41; L'Oiseau-Lyre (LP) 414123-1

John Novacek: Ambassador (CD) ARC-1014

Leonard Pennario: Capitol (LP) CTL-7054, P-8190

Leopoldo Querol: Gramophone/His Master's Voice (78) DB-4207

Marjan Rawicz and Walter Landauer (arr. for 2 pianos by the performers): ASV (CD) AJA-5158; Columbia (78) DB-2134

Artur Rubinstein: EMI Electrola (LP) 1C-151-003-244/5-M; Gramophone/His Master's Voice (78) DB-1257; Iron Needle (CD) IN-1310; Odeon (LP) QALP-10363; RCA (CD) 61261, (LP) LM-2181, (78) 7249

Antonio Ruiz-Pipó: Zacosa (LP) GML-2036

Balazs Szokolay: Naxos (CD) 8.550215

Magda Tagliaferro: Pathé (78) PAT-22

José Tordesillas: Philips (LP) RPF-761/2,3,4

Alejandro Vilalta: Odeon (78) 177268 in OM-63

17. *Suite española No. 1,* "Cádiz (Canción)." [See also *Serenata española.*]

Guillermo Cases (shortened version): Odeon (78) 195129

Cor de Groot: Epic (LP) 3175; Philips (LP) A-00131-R

José Echániz: Westminster (LP) WL-5382, XWN-18431

Gérard Gahnassia: Magne (LP) MAG-2018

María Garzón: ASV (CD) CD-DCA-798

José Iturbi: Angel (LP) RL-32123, S-35628; EMI/Angel (CS) 4RL-32123

Beatriz Klien: Turnabout (LP) TV-34327; Vox (LP) STPL-513.540, VS-3134

Katia and Marielle Labèque: Philips (CD) 438938-2

Ruth Laredo: MCA (CD) MCAD-6265, (CS) MCAC-6265

Alicia de Larrocha: GME (CD) GME-223; Turnabout (CS) CT-4774, (LP) TV-34774; Vox (LP) SVBX-5801

Marjan Rawicz and Walter Landauer (arr. for 2 pianos by the performers): ASV (CD) AJA-5158; Columbia (78) DB-2133

Alejandro Vilalta: Odeon (78) 177265 in OM-63

Ricardo Viñes: Gramophone/His Master's Voice (78) DA-4885; RCA (78) 4331

18. *Suite española No. 1*, "Asturias (Leyenda)." [See also the "Prélude" from *Chants d'Espagne*.]

Rafael Arroyo: Decca (LP) FAT-173696; London (LP) TW-91151
Jorge Bolet: Boston (LP) 300
Guillermo Cases (shortened version): Odeon (78) 195128
Gérard Gahnassia: Magne (LP) MAG-2018
María Garzón: ASV (CD) CD-DCA-798
G. Gourevitch: Pathé (78) X-9957
Waleed Howrani: Performer (CD) 3D0-01
José Iturbi: Angel (LP) RL-32123, S-35628; EMI (LP) 2C-053-12024; EMI/Angel (CS) 4RL-32123
Alicia de Larrocha: Hispavox (LP) C-30.072, S-30.072; London (CD) 417795-2
John Novacek: Ambassador (CD) ARC-1014
Marjan Rawicz and Walter Landauer (arr. for 2 pianos by the performers): Columbia (78) DB-2133
Allan Schiller: ASV (CD) CDQA-6032
Raúl Spivak: RCA (78) 11-8075
José Tordesillas: Philips (LP) RPF-761/2,3,4
Alejandro Vilalta: Odeon (78) 177266 in OM-63

19. *Suite española No. 1*, "Aragón (Fantasía)."

Katia and Marielle Labèque: Philips (CD) 438938-2
Ruth Laredo: MCA (CD) MCAD-6265, (CS) MCAC-6265
Alicia de Larrocha: GME (CD) GME-223; Turnabout (CS) CT-4774, (LP) TV-34774
Marjan Rawicz and Walter Landauer (arr. for 2 pianos by the performers): Columbia (78) DB-2134
Alejandro Vilalta: Odeon (78) 177267 in OM-63

20. *Suite española No. 1*, "Castilla (Seguidillas)." [See also "Seguidillas" from *Chants d'Espagne*.]

Alfred Cortot: Gramophone/His Master's Voice (78) DA-1121; Music and Arts (CD) 615; RCA (78) 1581
José Cubiles: RCA (LP) LSC-16354
Cor de Groot: Epic (LP) 3175; Philips (LP) A-00131-R

Andor Foldes: Continental (78) M-34
María Garzón: ASV (CD) CD-DCA-798
Katia and Marielle Labèque: Philips (CD) 438938-2
Alicia de Larrocha: Hispavox (LP) C-30.072, S-30.072
Enrique Luzuriaga (with Mariemma, castanets): Columbia (LP)
    CPS-9757
M. Mirimanowa: Columbia (78) CQX-16447
Marjan Rawicz and Walter Landauer (arr. for 2 pianos by the
    performers): ASV (CD) AJA-5158; Columbia (78) DB-2134
S. Schneevoigt: Ultraphone (78) AP-199
Alejandro Vilalta: Odeon (78) 177267 in OM-63
Ricardo Viñes: Columbia (78) 2659-D, LF-42

21. *Suite española No. 1*, "Cuba (Capricho)."

    Gérard Gahnassia: Magne (LP) MAG-2018
    Alejandro Vilalta: Odeon (78) 177268 in OM-63

22. *Angustia (Romanza sin palabras).*

    Rena Kyriakou: Vox (LP) SVBX-5404

23. Minuetto No. 3.

    Rena Kyriakou: Vox (LP) SVBX-5405

24. *Suite ancienne No. 2.*

    Rena Kyriakou: Vox (LP) SVBX-5404

25. *Suite ancienne No. 3.*

    Rena Kyriakou: Vox (LP) SVBX-5404

26. *Recuerdos de viaje* (complete).

    Rena Kyriakou: Vox (LP) SVBX-5403
    Esteban Sánchez: Ensayo (LP) ENY-209

27. *Recuerdos de viaje*, "Puerta de tierra (Bolero)."

Alicia de Larrocha: Decca (CS) CS5-6953, (LP) CS-6953; EMI
(CD) CMS-7-64504-2, ZDMB-64504; GME (CD) GME-
223; Hispavox (LP) 130135, 530-769612-1, C-30.072, CH-
254, HH-10-86/7, S-20.078, S-30.072, S-60.309/10/11;
London (CD) 417639-2, 433926-2, (LP) CS-6953; Musical
Heritage Society (LP) 1571/2; Turnabout (LP) TV-34775;
Vox (CS) CT-4775

28. *Recuerdos de viaje,* "Rumores de la caleta (Malagueña)."

Anna Antoniades: Polydor (78) 47392
Jean-Joël Barbier: Accord (CD) ACD-200332
Michèle Boegner: Adès (CD) ADE-203742
George Copeland: RCA (78) 1624 in VM-178
Alfred Cortot: Biddulph (CD) LHW-014/15; EMI (LP) HQM-
    1182; Gramophone/His Master's Voice (78) DA-1121;
    Music and Arts (CD) 615; RCA (78) 1581; Seraphim (LP)
    60143
Cor de Groot: Philips (LP) A-00131-R
Evelyne Dubourg: Laserlight (CD) 14-229; Master (CD) 19-404
Lily Dymont: Polydor (78) 21886
José Echániz: Westminster (LP) WL-5382, XWN-18431
José Falgarona: Belter (LP) 70.915
Orazio Frugoni: Pathé-Vox (LP) PL-9420
Luis Galve: Columbia (LP) CCL-32027
Pierre Huybregts: Centaur (CD) CRC-2231
José Iturbi: RCA (LP) 630.339, 3L-16097
Peter Katin: Discourses (LP) ABK-11
Beatriz Klien: Turnabout (LP) TV-34327
Alicia de Larrocha: Decca (CS) CS5-6953, (LP) CS-6953; EMI
    (CD) CDM-7-64523-2, CMS-7-64504-2, ZDMB-64504;
    GME (CD) GME-223; Hispavox (LP) 130135, 530-769612-
    1, CH-254, HH-10-86/7, S-60.309-10-11; London (CD)
    417639-2, 433926-2, (LP) CS-6953; Musical Heritage
    Society (LP) 1571/2; Turnabout (LP) TV-34775; Vox (CS)
    CT-4775
Frank Marshall: Columbia (LP) 4294
Arturo Benedetti Michelangeli: Arkadin (CD) 624; EMI (CD)
    077776449029, CDH-64490; Gramophone/His Master's

Voice (78) DA-5432; Musical Heritage Society (CD) 513996-F

Leo Nadelman: Appian Publications and Recordings (CD) APR-7025

Esteban Sánchez: Ensayo (LP) ENY-206

José Tordesillas: Philips (LP) A-10625-R, RPF-761/2,3,4, S-05922

Unknown performer: Royale (LP) 1244

29. Menuet (G Minor).

Rena Kyriakou: Vox (LP) SVBX-5404

30. *Rapsodia española* (version for piano solo).

Rena Kyriakou: Vox (LP) SVBX-5405

31. *Cotillon (Carte blanche), vals de salón* [*Champagne vals* or *Cotillon valse*].

Rena Kyriakou: Vox (LP) SVBX-5405
Antonio Ruiz-Pipó: Koch-Schwann (CD) 3-1513-2

32. *Pavana fácil para manos pequeñas.*

Rena Kyriakou: Vox (LP) SVBX-5405

33. *Seis danzas españolas.*

Rena Kyriakou: Vox (LP) SVBX-5405

34. Sonata No. 3.

Albert Guinovart: Harmonia Mundi France (CD) HMI-987007
Rena Kyriakou: Vox (LP) SVBX-5403

35. Sonata No. 4.

Albert Guinovart: Harmonia Mundi France (CD) HMI-987007
Rena Kyriakou: Vox (LP) SVBX-5404

36. Sonata No. 5.

Albert Guinovart: Harmonia Mundi France (CD) HMI-987007
Rena Kyriakou: Vox (LP) SVBX-5405
Esteban Sánchez: Ensayo (LP) ENY-710, SENY-1710

37. *Dos mazurkas de salón*, No. 1: "Amalia."

   Rena Kyriakou: Vox (LP) SVBX-5405

38. *Dos mazurkas de salón*, No. 2: "Ricordatti."

   Rena Kyriakou: Vox (LP) SVBX-5404

39. *Douze Pièces caractéristiques pour piano* [*Doce piezas características*] (complete).

   Rena Kyriakou: Vox (LP) SVBX-5404

40. *Douze Pièces caractéristiques pour piano* [*Doce piezas características*], "Gavotte."

   Pierre Huybregts: Centaur (CD) CRC-2231

41. *Douze Pièces caractéristiques pour piano* [*Doce piezas características*], "Pavana."

   Esteban Sánchez: Ensayo (LP) ENY-209

42. *Douze Pièces caractéristiques pour piano* [*Doce piezas características*], "Torre Bermeja (Serenata)."

   Jean-Joël Barbier: Accord (CD) ACD-200332
   Michel Bourgeot: Coronet (LP) LPS-3003
   José Cortés: Spanish Music Center (LP) 501
   Luis Galve: Columbia (LP) CCL-32027
   Pierre Huybregts: Centaur (CD) CRC-2231
   Frank Marshall: Columbia (LP) ML-4294
   Manuela del Río (L. Campolietti, castanets): Gramophone/His
     Master's Voice (78) K-7716
   Esteban Sánchez: Ensayo (LP) ENY-209
   Alejandro Vilalta: Odeon (78) 177269
   Ricardo Viñes: Columbia (78) D-15245; EMI (LP) 1731791

43. *Deux Morceaux caractéristiques* [*Deux Dances espagnoles*], "Tango."

  Jean-Joël Barbier: Accord (CD) ACD-200332
  George Copeland: RCA (78) 15346
  José Echániz: Westminster (LP) WL-5382, XWN-18431
  Eileen Joyce: Decca (LP) DL-9528
  Rena Kyriakou: Vox (LP) SVBX-5405
  Ricardo Viñes: EMI (LP) 1731791; Gramophone/His Master's
  Voice (78) DA-4885; RCA (78) 4331

44. *Suite española No. 2* [*Seconde Suite espagnole*] (complete).

  Rena Kyriakou: Vox (LP) SVBX-5405
  Esteban Sánchez: Ensayo (LP) ENY-710, SENY-1710

45. *Suite española No. 2* [*Seconde Suite espagnole*], "Zaragoza (Capricho)."

  Alicia de Larrocha: EMI (CD) CDM-7-64523-2; Hispavox (LP)
  130135, CH-254, HH-10-86/7, S-60.309/10/11; Musical
  Heritage Society (LP) MHS-1571/2; Turnabout (LP) TV-
  34775; Vox (LP) SVBX-5801

46. *Cádiz-gaditana.*

  Pierre Huybregts: Centaur (CD) CRC-2231

47. *Serenata española.* [See also "Cádiz (Canción)" from the *Suite española No. 1.*]

  José Iturbi: Angel (LP) 35628; EMI (LP) 2C-053-12024
  Santiago Rodríguez: Elan (CD) 2202, (CS) 1204, (LP) 2202
  Ricardo Viñes: EMI (LP) 1731791

48. *España: Six Feuilles d'album* [*España: Seis hojas de album*] (complete).

  Michel Block: IMP (CD) 30367-00042; O.M. (CD) OM-80501
  Pierre Huybregts: Centaur (CD) CRC-2026
  Rena Kyriakou: Vox (LP) SVBX-5405
  William Masselos: MGM (LP) E-3165

Antonio Ruiz-Pipó: Zacosa (LP) GML-2030
Esteban Sánchez: Ensayo (LP) CENY-1006, ENY-6

49. *España: Six Feuilles d'album* [*España: Seis hojas de album*], "Tango."

Joaquín Achúcarro: RCA (LP) RL-31404
Daniel Adni: EMI (CD) CDCFP-4622
Rafael Arroyo: Adès (CD) ADE-13.207-2
Wilhelm Backhaus (L. Godowsky): Gramophone/His Master's Voice (78) DA-1018; His Master's Voice (LP) 29-0345-3; RCA (78) 1445
Jean-Joël Barbier: Accord (CD) ACD-200332
Jorge Bolet (L. Godowsky): London (CS) 417361-4
Victor Borge: Columbia (CD) 484042-2
Michel Bourgeot: Coronet (LP) LPS-3003
Emma Boynet: Pathé-Vox (45) VIP-500
Leonid Brumberg: Melodiya (LP) C10-05795-6
Shura Cherkassky (L. Godowsky): Desmar (LP) DSM-1005; Éditions de l'Oiseau-Lyre (LP) DSLO-7, DSLO-15; London (CD) 433651-2, 433653-2; Telefunken (CS) 4.42610-CH, (LP) 6.42610-AG
George Copeland: MGM (LP) E-87, E-3025; RCA (78) 15346
Sequeira Costa: Camerata (CD) 30MC-369
José Cubiles: RCA (LP) LSC-16354
José Echániz: Columbia (78) 162-M; Westminster (LP) WL-5382, XWN-18431
Philippe Entremont: CBS (LP) MG-35185; Columbia (CS) IT2-6916, (LP) MG-35185
Andor Foldes: Continental (78) M-43
Nelson Freire: Audiofon (CD) CD-72023
Orazio Frugoni: Pathé-Vox (LP) PL-9420
Leopold Godowsky: Appian Publications and Recordings (CD) APR-7011
Marc-André Hamelin (L. Godowsky): Musica Viva (LP) MVCD-1026
José Iturbi: Angel (LP) RL-32123, S-35628; EMI (LP) 2C-053-12024; EMI/Angel (CS) 4RL-32123
Martin Jones: Nimbus (CD) NI-5326

Eileen Joyce: Polydor (78) R-2738

Constance Keene (L. Godowsky): Mercury (LP) MG-10113; Protone (CD) PRCD-1102, (LP) PR-148

Beatriz Klien: Turnabout (LP) TV-34327; Vox (LP) STPL-513.540, VS-3134

Antonin Kubalek: Dorian (CD) DOR-90218

Alicia de Larrocha: Decca (CS) CS5-6953, (LP) CS-6953; EMI (CD) CMS-7-64504-2, ZDMB-64504; GME (CD) GME-223; Hispavox (LP) 130135, 530-769612-1, C-30.072, CH-254, HH-10-86/7, S-20.078, S-30.072, S-60.309/10/11; London (CD) 417639-2, 433926-2, (LP) CS-6953; Musical Heritage Society (LP) 1571/2; Turnabout (LP) TV-34775; Vox (CS) CT-4775

Oscar Levant: Columbia (LP) CL-1134, ML-2018, (78) 17455-D in CM-560

Moura Lympany (L. Godowsky): Angel (LP) S-35995; EMI (CD) 0777-7-67718-2-3, CDZ-62523; Dutton (CD) CDLXT-4000

M. Mirimanowa: Columbia (78) CQ-102

William Murdoch: Decca (78) F-3584

John Novacek: Ambassador (CD) ARC-1014

Guiomar Novaës: Music and Arts (CD) CD-702

Emilio Osta: Allegro (LP) 3151; Pacific (LP) LDA-D-148

Leonard Pennario: Capitol (LP) P-8190

Ida Perrin (L. Godowsky): Pathé (78) X-98153

L. Pouishnoff: Columbia (78) 4830

Esteban Sánchez: Ensayo (LP) ENY-209

André-Sebastien Savoie: Radio Canada International (LP) RCI-418

Allan Schiller: ASV (CD) CDQA-6032; ASV/Quicksilva (CD) QS-6032

Alexandr Scriabin (L. Godowsky): Recorded Treasures (LP) 681

Robert Silverman: Marquis (CD) MAR-201

Anna Maria Stancyzk: Muza-Polskie Nagrania (CD) ECD-060

Edvard Syomin: Melodiya (CD) 33217

Balázs Szokolay: Naxos (CD) 8.550218, 8.550647

50. *España: Six Feuilles d'album* [*España: Seis hojas de album*], "Malagueña."

Joaquín Achúcarro: RCA (LP) RL-31404
Juan Bernal: La Voz de Plata (LP) VP-101
Jorge Bolet: Boston (LP) 300 (may also be "Rumores de la caleta (Malagueña)" from *Recuerdos de viaje*)
Consuelo Colomer: Contemporary Recording Studios (LP) CRS-8634
José Echániz: Westminster (LP) WL-5382, XWN-18431
Luis Galve: Columbia (LP) CCL-32027
José Iturbi: RCA (LP) RL-43636; RCA Victor (LP) LM-1167, (78) DM-1344; Turia (LP) 101-S
Beatriz Klien: Vox (LP) STPL-513.540, VS-3134
Alicia de Larrocha: Decca (CS) CS5-6953, (LP) CS-6953; EMI (CD) CDM-7-64523-2; GME (CD) GME-223; Hispavox (LP) 130135, 530-769612-1, C-30.072, CH-254, HH-10-86/7, S-30.072, S-60.309/10/11; London (CD) 417639-2, 433926-2, (LP) CS-6953; Musical Heritage Society (LP) 1571/2; Turnabout (LP) TV-34775; Vox (CS) CT-4775
Enrique Luzuriaga (with Mariemma, castanets): Columbia (LP) CPS-9757
Moura Lympany: EMI (CD) CDZ-67204
Arturo Benedetti Michelangeli: EMI (CD) 3C-053-17017; Odeon (LP) 3C-163-50104/5/6, QALP-10341
Earl Wild: RCA (LP) CSC-318

51. *España: Six Feuilles d'album* [*España: Seis hojas de album*], "Zortzico."

Antonio Ruiz-Pipó: Zacosa (LP) GML-2036
Helmut Schultes: Colosseum (LP) SM-612

52. *L'Automne (Valse).*

Rena Kyriakou: Vox (LP) SVBX-5405
Antonio Ruiz-Pipó: Koch-Schwann (CD) 3-1513-2

53. *Mallorca (Barcarola).*

Rafael Arroyo: Decca (LP) FAT-173696; London (LP) TW-91151
Jean-Joël Barbier: Accord (CD) ACD-200332

Juan Bernal: La Voz de Plata (LP) VP-101
José Falgarona: Belter (LP) 70.915
Gérard Gahnassia: Magne (LP) MAG-2018
Luis Galve: Columbia (LP) CCL-32027
Pierre Huybregts: Centaur (CD) CRC-2231
Rena Kyriakou: Vox (LP) SVBX-5403
Alicia de Larrocha: EMI (CD) CDM-7-64523-2; GME (CD)
    GME-223; Hispavox (LP) 130135, 530-769612-1, CH-254,
    HH-10-86/7, S-60.309/10/11; Musical Heritage Society
    (LP) MHS-1571/2; Turnabout (LP) TV-34775; Vox (CS)
    CT-4775
Gerhard Oppitz: RCA (CD) 61968
Santiago Rodríguez: Elan (CD) 2202, (CS) 1204, (LP) 2202
Esteban Sánchez: Ensayo (LP) CENY-1007, ENY-7B

54. *Rêves* [*Sueños*] (complete).

Rena Kyriakou: Vox (LP) SVBX-5403
Antonio Ruiz-Pipó: Koch-Schwann (CD) 3-1513-2

55. *Zambra granadina (Danse orientale).*

Rena Kyriakou: Vox (LP) SVBX-5404
Alicia de Larrocha: EMI (CD) CDM-7-64523-2; Hispavox (LP)
    130135, 530-769612-1, CH-254, HH-10-86/7; Musical
    Heritage Society (LP) MHS-1571/2; Turnabout (LP) TV-
    34775; Vox (CS) CT-4775

56. *Album of Miniatures* [*Les Saisons*] (complete).

Rena Kyriakou: Vox (LP) SVBX-5405
Antonio Ruiz-Pipó: Koch-Schwann (CD) 3-1513-2

57. *Album of Miniatures* [*Les Saisons*], "L'Automne."

Albert Guinovart: Harmonia Mundi France (CD) HMI-987007

58. *Chants d'Espagne* [*Cantos de España*] (complete).

Jean-Joël Barbier: Accord (CD) ACD-200332
José Echániz: Westminster (LP) WAL-219, XWN-2217

Orazio Frugoni: Pathé-Vox (LP) PL-9420 (except for No. 2)
Pierre Huybregts: Centaur (CD) CRC-2231
Eva Knardahl: Simax (CD) PSC-1082
Rena Kyriakou: Vox (LP) SVBX-5404
Ruth Laredo: MCA (CD) MCAD-6265, (CS) MCAC-6265
Alicia de Larrocha: Columbia (LP) ML-6003, MS-6603; Decca
    (LP) 6.35093, 6799159.9, CSA-2235, SXL-6586/7; EMI
    (CD) CDM-7-64523-2; Ensayo (LP) ENY-209; GME (CD)
    GME-223; Hispavox (LP) 530-769612-1, CH-254, HH-10-
    86/7; London (CD) 433923-2, (CS) CSA-52235, (Reel)
    LON-K-42235; Musical Heritage Society (LP) 1571/2; The
    Classics Record Library, Book of the Month Club (LP) 10-
    240; Turnabout (LP) TV-34775; Vox (CS) CT-4775
Rafael Orozco: Valois (CD) V-4663
Leonard Pennario: Capitol (LP) P-8319
Marisa Regules: Counterpoint/Esoteric (LP) CPT-3002/ESP-
    3002
Ricardo Requejo: Claves (CD) CD-50-8003/4, D-8504
Gustavo Romero: REM (CD) 311150

59. *Chants d'Espagne* [*Cantos de España*], "Prélude." [See also
    "Asturias (Leyenda)" from the *Suite española No. 1*.]

Jorge Bolet: Boston (LP) 300
Geisa Dutra: Yellow Tail (CD) 4TR-10102, YTC-10102, (CS)
    4TR-10102
Alicia de Larrocha: GME (CD) GME-223; Jubilee (CD) 2LM-
    417795; Vox (LP) SVBX-5801
Frank Marshall: Columbia (LP) ML-4294
Alma Petchertsky: ASV/Quicksilva (CD) QS-6079
Marisa Regules: Esoteric (LP) 3002

60. *Chants d'Espagne* [*Cantos de España*], "Orientale."

Alicia de Larrocha: Hispavox (LP) S-60.309/10/11
Moritz Rosenthal: Argo (LP) DA-42; Editions de L'Oiseau-Lyre
    (CS) 414-098-4, (LP) 414-098-1
Ricardo Viñes: Columbia (78) LF-42, 2659-D; EMI (LP)
    1731791

61. *Chants d'Espagne* [*Cantos de España*], "Sous le palmier (Danse espagnole)."

George Copeland: Constance Wardle (LP) GC-1
Alfred Cortot: Everest Records (LP) Archive of Piano Music
    906; RCA (78) 1275
Geisa Dutra: Yellow Tail (CD) YTC-10102
Suzanne Gyr: Gramophone/His Master's Voice (78) DB-10068
Alicia de Larrocha: Hispavox (LP) S-60.309/10/11
Marcelle Meyer: EMI (CD) CDZF-67405, CZS-7-67405-2; Pearl
    (CD) GEMM-CD-9495
Alejandro Vilalta: Odeon (78) 177269
Janine Weill: Decca (78) M-125

62. *Chants d'Espagne* [*Cantos de España*], "Córdoba."

Rafael Arroyo: Adès (CD) ADE-13.207-2; Decca (LP) FAT-
    173696; London (LP) TW-91151
Dmitri Bashkirov: Erato (CD) 4509-94678-2
Jorge Bolet: Boston (LP) 300
Leonid Brumberg: Melodiya (LP) C10-05795-6
Guillermo Cases: Odeon (78) 195128 in OM-112
George Copeland: MGM (LP) E-87, E-187, E-3025
José Cubiles: RCA (LP) LSC-16354
Geisa Dutra: Yellow Tail (CD) 4TR-10102, YTC-10102, (CS)
    4TR-10102
José Falgarona: Belter (LP) 70.915
Carmen Guilbert: Columbia (78) LFX-607
Suzanne Gyr: Gramophone/His Master's Voice (78) DB-10068
Amparo Iturbi: RCA (LP) A-630231, LM-1788
José Iturbi: Angel (LP) RL-32123, S-35628; EMI (LP) 2C-053-
    12024; EMI/Angel (CS) 4RL-32123; Gramophone/His
    Master's Voice (78) DA-1611; RCA (78) 1844, 4373
Leon Kartun: Odeon (78) 177242
Beatriz Klien: Turnabout (LP) TV-34327; Vox (LP) STPL-
    513.540, VS-3134
Alicia de Larrocha: Vox (LP) SVBX-5801
Josef Lhevinne: L'Oiseau-Lyre (LP) 414123-1
Enrique Luzuriaga (with Mariemma, castanets): Columbia (LP)
    CPS-9757

Cristina Ortiz: EMI (LP) ASD-3716; Price-less (CS) XY-2243
Dmitrii Paperno: Cedille (CD) CDR-90000-007
Menahem Pressler: MGM (LP) E-3129
Marisa Regules: Esoteric (LP) 3002; RCA (78) 11-9417 in VM-
1092
Artur Rubinstein: EMI/His Master's Voice (LP) 1C-027-
1435551; Gramophone/His Master's Voice (78) DB-1266;
RCA (CD) 61261, (LP) LM-2181, (78) 7248
Esteban Sánchez: Ensayo (LP) CENY-1006, ENY-6
Paolo Spagnolo: Decca (LP) LXT-2947; London (LP) LLP-1040

63. *Chants d'Espagne* [*Cantos de España*], "Seguidillas." [See also
"Castilla (Seguidillas)" from the *Suite española No. 1*.]

Emma Boynet: Pathé-Vox (45) VIP-500
Alfred Cortot: Biddulph (CD) LHW-014/15; EMI (LP) HQM-
1182; Seraphim (LP) 60143
Sequeira Costa: Camerata (CD) 30MC-369
Arthur de Greef: Recital Hall (LP) RH-2
Geisa Dutra: Yellow Tail (CD) 4TR-10102, YTC-10102, (CS)
4TR-10102
Alicia de Larrocha: GME (CD) GME-223
Cristina Ortiz: Price-less (CS) XY-2243
Leonard Pennario: Capitol (LP) P-8190
Marisa Regules: Esoteric (LP) 3002
Paolo Spagnolo: London (LP) LLP-1040
Martino Tirimo: Kingdom (CD) KCLCD-2003
Ricardo Viñes: EMI (LP) 1731791

64. *Espagne: Souvenirs* (complete).

Jean-Joël Barbier: Accord (CD) ACD-200332
Rena Kyriakou: Vox (LP) SVBX-5404
Antonio Ruiz-Pipó: Koch-Schwann (CD) 3-1513-2

65. *Espagne: Souvenirs*, "Asturias."

Antonio Ruiz-Pipó: Zacosa (LP) GML-2036

66. *The Alhambra. Suite pour le piano*, "La vega."

Rena Kyriakou: Vox (LP) SVBX-5405
Alicia de Larrocha: EMI (CD) CDM-7-64523-2; Erato (LP)
    STU-70561; Hispavox (CS) 230134, (LP) 130134, CH 249,
    HH-10-86/7; Musical Heritage Society (LP) MHS 1571/2;
    Turnabout (LP) TV-34774; Vox (CS) CT-4774
William Nabore: Trio (LP) PAX-6002
Esteban Sánchez: Ensayo (LP) CENY-1006, ENY-6
Johan Schmidt: EMI (CD) CDC-7-49732-2

67. *Iberia. 12 nouvelles "impressions" en quatre cahiers*
    (complete).

Martha Ärgerich: Erato (CD) RD-01
Francisco Aybar: Connoisseur (LP) CSQ-2601
Pilar Bayona (Nos. 1, 5, 7, 8, 9, 10, 12 only): Lumen (45) LD 1-
    412/13/14/15
Michel Block: Connoisseur (LP) CS-2120/1; EMI (LP) 167-
    053.330/1
Aldo Ciccolini: EMI (CD) CDZB-62889, CZS-7-62889-2;
    Seraphim (LP) S-60, SIB-6091
José Echániz: Westminster (LP) XWN-2217
José Falgarona: Vox (LP) PL-9212; Vox-Pathé (LP) 9212
Jean-François Heisser: Erato (CD) 4509-94807-2, WE-810
Claude Helffer: Musidisc (LP) 30-RC-16017
Hisako Hiseki: Edicions Albert Moreleda (CD) REF-1094-1
Irene Kohler: Concert Artist (LP) LPA-1015/16
Rena Kyriakou: Vox (LP) SVBX-5403
Alicia de Larrocha: Columbia (LP) M2L-268 (recorded in Spain
    by Hispavox); Decca (CD) 417887-2, 448191-2, (LP)
    6.35093, 6799159.9, CSA-2235, SXL-6586/7; EMI (CD)
    CMS-7-64504-2, ZDMB-64504-2; Epic (LP) BSC-158, SC-
    6058; Hispavox (LP) 137003, 546-7696261, HH-10-76/7,
    HH-10-89/90; Hispavox/Clave (LP) 181241/2-S; London
    (CD) 417882-2, 417887-2, 433926-2, (CS) CSA-52235,
    (Reel) LON-K-42235; Musical Heritage Society (CD)
    513460-Y, (CS) 323647-F, (LP) MHS-1307/8; Turnabout
    (LP) TV-34750/1; Vox (CS) CT-4750/1
Rafael Orozco: Valois (CD) V-4663
Leopoldo Querol: Ducretet (LP) DTL-93022-3, LPG-8557-8

Ricardo Requejo: Claves (CD) CD-50-8003/4, D-8003/4, (CS)
D-8003

Rosa Sabater: Decca (LP) SXL-29033/4; Zacosa (LP) GML-
2015/16

Blanca Uribe: Orion (CS) OC-627, (LP) ORS-75202/3

68. *Iberia* (selections).

José Echániz: Musical Heritage Society (LP) MHS-811-S
Artur Rubinstein: Klavier (LP) KD-138/39

69. *Iberia*, "Evocación."

Claudio Arrau: Arlecchino (CD) ARL-168; Columbia (LP) ML-
4194, (78) 72578 in CM-757; Columbia Odyssey (LP) Y-
35229

Michel Bourgeot: Coronet (LP) LPS-3003

Frank Braley: Auvidis (CD) V-4662

José Cubiles: RCA (LP) LSC-16354

José Falgarona: Belter (LP) 70.915

Sidney Foster: IPAM (CD) 1204A/B

Nelson Freire: Alphée (CD) 9502003; Audiofon (CD) 72023

William Kapell: RCA (CS) LM-2588, (LP) LM-2588, (78) 11-
9457; Victor (78) SP-11-8866/7

Dubravko Kovacevic: RTB (LP) 2130475

Alicia de Larrocha: Hispavox (LP) S-60.309/10/11; Turnabout
(LP) TV-34750

Yvonne Loriod: Adès (CD) ACD-14.071-2

Sergio de Los Cobos: Disc Makers (CD) SC-10194 (DIDX-
020198)

Enrique Luzuriaga (with Mariemma, castanets): Columbia (LP)
CPS-9757

Benita Meshulam: Classic Masters (CD) CMCD-1033

Guiomar Novaës: Columbia (78) 71171-D

Roland Pöntinen: BIS·(CD) CD-661

Marisa Regules: RCA (78) 11-9416 in VM-1092

Artur Rubinstein: EMI/His Master's Voice (LP) 1C-027-
1435551; Gramophone/His Master's Voice (78) DB-1266;
RCA (CD) 61261, (78) 7248

70.   *Iberia*, "El puerto."

Ayke Agus: Protone (CD) PRCD-1108
Claudio Arrau: Arlecchino (CD) ARL-168; Columbia (LP) ML-
      4194, (78) 72579-D in CM-757; Columbia Odyssey (LP) Y-
      35229
Michel Bourgeot: Coronet (LP) LPS-3003
Sequeira Costa: Supraphon (LP) 1-11-0850-G
José Cubiles: RCA (LP) LSC-16354
León Kartun: Odeon (78) 171080
Alicia de Larrocha: Hispavox (LP) S-20.078, S-60.309/10/11;
      Turnabout (LP) TV-34750
Sergio de Los Cobos: Disc Makers (CD) SC-10194 (DIDX-
      020198)
Benita Meshulam: Classic Masters (CD) CMCD-1033
William Murdoch: Columbia (78) 9360
Marisa Regules: RCA (78) 11-9415 in VM-1092
Unknown performer: Elektra (CD) PRCD-8971

71.   *Iberia*, "Fête-Dieu à Séville" ["El Corpus en Sevilla"].

Claudio Arrau: Arlecchino (CD) ARL-168; Columbia (LP) ML-
      4194, (78) 72579/80-D in CM-757; Columbia Odyssey (LP)
      Y-35229
Rafael Arroyo: Decca (LP) FAT-173696; London (LP) TW-
      91151
Michel Bourgeot: Coronet (LP) LPS-3003
Alicia de Larrocha: Hispavox (LP) S-60.309/10/11; Turnabout
      (LP) TV-34750
Yvonne Loriod: Adès (CD) ACD-14.071-2
Sergio de Los Cobos: Disc Makers (CD) SC-10194 (DIDX-
      020198)
Benita Meshulam: Classic Masters (CD) CMCD-1033
André-Sebastien Savoie: Radio Canada International (LP) RCI-
      418

72.   *Iberia*, "Rondeña."

Claudio Arrau: Arlecchino (CD) ARL-168; Columbia (LP) ML-4194, (78) 72580/1-D in CM-757; Columbia Odyssey (LP) Y-35229

Rafael Arroyo: Decca (LP) FAT-173696; London (LP) TW-91151

Michel Block: La Voix de Son Maître (EMI/Pathé) (LP) 2C-063.11633

Benita Meshulam: Classic Masters (CD) CMCD-1033

Leopoldo Querol: Telefunken (LP) TLA-20009

Cecilio Tieles: Areito (LP) LD-3559

73. *Iberia*, "Almería."

Claudio Arrau: Arlecchino (CD) ARL-168; Columbia (LP) ML-4194, (78) 72581/2-D in CM-757; Columbia Odyssey (LP) Y-35229

Michel Block: La Voix de Son Maître (EMI/Pathé) (LP) 2C-063.11633

Manuel Carra: RCA (LP) SRL-12040

José Cubiles: RCA (LP) LSC-16354

Dubravko Kovacevic: RTB (LP) 2130475

Yvonne Loriod: Adès (CD) ACD-14.071-2

Benita Meshulam: Classic Masters (CD) CMCD-1033

Leopoldo Querol: Telefunken (LP) TLA-20009

Cecilio Tieles: Areito (LP) LD-3559

74. *Iberia*, "Triana."

Gregory Allen (L. Godowsky): Musical Heritage Society (CD) 512827-W

Claudio Arrau: Columbia (LP) ML-4194, (78) 72582-D in CM-757; Columbia Odyssey (LP) Y-35229

Wilhelm Backhaus: Gramophone/His Master's Voice (78) DB-1123

Michel Block: La Voix de Son Maître (EMI/Pathé) (LP) 2C-063.11633

Leonid Brumberg: Melodiya (LP) C10-05795-6

Alfred Cortot: Biddulph (CD) LHW-014/15

Sequeira Costa: Supraphon (LP) 1-11-0850-G

Jacques Dupont: Pathé (78) X-98177

Nadya and Steven Gordon: Klavier (LP) KS-554
Constance Keene (L. Godowsky): Mercury (LP) MG-10113
Beatriz Klien: Turnabout (LP) TV-34327; Vox (LP) STPL-
513.540, VS-3134
Katia and Marielle Labèque: Philips (CD) 438938-2
Alicia de Larrocha: EMI (CD) ZDMB-64241; Hispavox (LP) C-
30.072, S-20.025, S-30.072, S-60.309/10/11, S-66.316;
London (CD) 417795-2, (CS) CS5-7147, (LP) CS-7147
Yvonne Loriod: Adès (CD) ACD-14.071-2
Benita Meshulam: Classic Masters (CD) CMCD-1033
Guiomar Novaës: Columbia (78) 71171-D
Cristina Ortiz: EMI (LP) ASD-3716; Price-less (CS) XY-2243
Emilio Osta: Allegro (LP) 3151; Pacific (LP) LDA-D-148
Leopoldo Querol: Telefunken (LP) TLA-20009
Marisa Regules: RCA (78) 11-9417 in VM-1092
Moritz Rosenthal: OPAL (LP) 812/13; Parlophone (78) 57063;
Pearl (CD) GEMM-CD-9963
Artur Rubinstein: EMI/His Master's Voice (LP) 1C-027-
1435551; Gramophone/His Master's Voice (78) DB-1762;
Odeon (LP) QALP-10363; RCA (78) 7853
David Saperton (L. Godowsky): RCA (78) 13664; VAI Audio
(CD) VAIA/IPA-1037-2
Abbey Simon (L. Godowsky): Danacord (CD) DACOC-379;
Turnabout (LP) 34783; Vox-Allegretto (CD) ACD-8204
Cyril Smith: Columbia (78) DX-1214
Magda Tagliaferro: Ducretet (45) LAP-1006
Cecilio Tieles: Areito (LP) LD-3559
J. Van Ijzer: Columbia (78) D-17202
Arthur Whittemore and Jack Lowe: Capitol (LP) SP-8500
Earl Wild: RCA (LP) CSC-318

75.   *Iberia*, "El Albaicín."

Rafael Arroyo: Decca (LP) FAT-173696; London (LP) TW-
91151
Michel Block: La Voix de Son Maître (EMI/Pathé) (LP) 2C-
063.11633
José Echániz: Westminster (LP) WAL-219
José Falgarona: Belter (LP) 70.915

José González Alonso: Blue Angel (LP) BA-29001
Alicia de Larrocha: Hispavox (LP) C-30.072, S-30.072; Vox
(CS) CT-4751
Yvonne Loriod: Adès (CD) ACD-14.071-2
Benita Meshulam: Classic Masters (CD) CMCD-1033
Cristina Ortiz: EMI (LP) ASD-3716; Price-less (CS) XY-2243
Leopoldo Querol: Telefunken (LP) TLA-20009
Darío Raucca: Decca (LP) LXT-2969; London (LP) LLP-1033

76. *Iberia*, "El polo."

Michel Block: La Voix de Son Maître (EMI/Pathé) (LP) 2C-
063.11633
José Echániz: Westminster (LP) WAL-219
Alicia de Larrocha: Vox (CS) CT-4751
Yvonne Loriod: Adès (CD) ACD-14.071-2
Leopoldo Querol: Telefunken (LP) TLA-20009

77. *Iberia*, "Lavapiés."

Michel Block: La Voix de Son Maître (EMI/Pathé) (LP) 2C-
063.11633
Frank Braley: Auvidis (CD) V-4662
José Echániz: Westminster (LP) WAL-219
Alicia de Larrocha: Vox (CS) CT-4751
Leopoldo Querol: Telefunken (LP) TLA-20009

78. *Iberia*, "Málaga."

Alexander Borowsky: Polydor (78) 27343, 516613
Sequeira Costa: Supraphon (LP) 1-11-0850-G
Alicia de Larrocha: Vox (CS) CT-4751
Benita Meshulam: Classic Masters (CD) CMCD-1033

79. *Iberia*, "Jerez."

Alicia de Larrocha: Vox (CS) CT-4751
Yvonne Loriod: Adès (CD) ACD-14.071-2

80. *Iberia*, "Eritaña."

Sequeira Costa: Supraphon (LP) 1-11-0850-G
Alicia de Larrocha: Vox (CS) CT-4751
Yvonne Loriod: Adès (CD) ACD-14.071-2

81. *Azulejos*.

Rena Kyriakou: Vox (LP) SVBX-5405
Alicia de Larrocha: EMI (CD) CDM-7-64523-2; Erato (LP)
    STU-70561; GME (CD) GME-223; Hispavox (CS) 230134,
    (LP) 130134, CH 249, HH-10-86/7; Musical Heritage
    Society (LP) MHS-1571/2; Turnabout (LP) TV-34774; Vox
    (CS) CT-4774
Douglas Riva: Centaur (CD) CRC-2043

82. *Navarra*.

Joaquín Achúcarro: RCA (LP) RL-31404
Michel Block: Connoisseur (LP) CS-2120/1
Leonid Brumberg: Melodiya (LP) C10-05795-6
Sequeira Costa and Artur Pizzarro: Collins Classics (CD) COL-
    14662
José Echániz: Westminster (LP) WAL-219, XWN-2217
Nelson Freire: Alphée (CD) 9502003; Audiofon (CD) 72023
Rena Kyriakou: Vox (LP) SVBX-5405
Katia and Marielle Labèque: Philips (CD) 438938-2
Alicia de Larrocha: Decca (CD) 417887-2, (LP) 6799159.9,
    CSA-2235; EMI (CD) CDM-64523, CMS-7-64504-2,
    ZDMB-64504; Epic (LP) BSC-158, SC-6058; Hispavox
    (LP) 137003, 546-7696261, C-30.072, HH-1076/77, HH-10-
    89/90, S-30.072, S-60.309/10/11; Hispavox/Clave (LP)
    181241/2-S; London (CD) 417795-2, 417887-2, 433926-2,
    (CS) CSA-52235, (Reel) LON-K-42235; Musical Heritage
    Society (CD) 513460-Y, (CS) 323647-F, (LP) MHS-1307/8
Marcelle Meyer: EMI (CD) CZS-7-67405-2; EMI/Angel (CD)
    CDZF-67405; Pearl (CD) GEMM-9495
Emilio Osta: Allegro (LP) 3151; Pacific (LP) LDA-D-148
Leopoldo Querol: Ducretet (LP) DTL-93022-3, LPG-8557-8;
    Gramophone/His Master's Voice (78) DB-4207
Artur Rubinstein: EMI Electrola (LP) 1C-151-003-244/5-M;
    Gramophone/His Master's Voice (78) DB-6315; Iron Needle

(CD) IN-1310; Odeon (LP) QALP-10363; Pearl (CD)
GEMM-CD-9464; RCA (CD) 5670-2-RC, 61261, 61445,
(CS) ARK-13850, (LP) 09026-61445-2, ARL-13850, RL-
13850, (78) 7249, 11-8622
Esteban Sánchez: Ensayo (LP) CENY-1006, ENY-6
Edvard Syomin: Melodiya (CD) 33217

83. Untitled Improvisations.

   Isaac Albéniz playing three improvisations in F# minor,
   originally recorded on cylinder in 1903 and transferred to
   compact disc on *The Catalan Piano Tradition*: VAI Audio
   (CD) VAIA/IPA-1001; International Piano Archives (LP)
   IPA-109

Stage Works

84. *Pepita Jiménez* (revision by Pablo Sorozábal).

   Teresa Berganza, Julián Molina, et al. with Pablo Sorozábal
   conducting the Orquesta Sinfónica de Madrid: Alhambra
   (LP) SCE-931/2; Columbia (LP) MCE-821/2, SCE-931/2.

85. *Pepita Jiménez* ("Intermedio" only).

   Enrique Fernández Arbós and the Orquesta Sinfónica de Madrid:
   Columbia (78) 264539, 52068-X, 67820-D, AG-8009
   José María Franco and the Orquesta Sinfónica Española (Pilar
   López, footwork): Capitol (LP) P-18020; La Voz de su Amo
   (LP) LDLP-1011, (45) 7EPL-13028

86. *Pepita Jiménez* (concert suite of selections from the opera).

   Susan Chilcott and Francesc Garrigosa with Josep Pons
   conducting the Orquestra de Cambra Teatre Lliure:
   Harmonia Mundi (CD) HMC-901537

Vocal Works (solo voice and piano)

87. *Rimas de Bécquer*, "Besa el aura."

Montserrat Caballé and Miguel Zanetti: Acanta (LP) 29.394;
Alhambra (LP) SCE-985; London (LP) OS-26617

88.   *Rimas de Bécquer*, "Del salón en el angulo oscuro."

Montserrat Caballé and Miguel Zanetti: Acanta (LP) 29.394;
Alhambra (LP) SCE-985; London (LP) OS-26617

89.   *Seis baladas* (complete).

Victoria de Los Angeles and Geoffrey Parsons: Columbia (CS)
MT-35139, (LP) M-35139

90.   *Seis baladas*, "La lontananza."

Manuel Cid and Felix Lavilla: Fundación Banco Exterior (LP)
IB-33-148

91.   *Seis baladas*, "Una rosa in dono."

Manuel Cid and Felix Lavilla: Fundación Banco Exterior (LP)
IB-33-148

92.   *Seis baladas*, "Moriro!!"

Manuel Cid and Felix Lavilla: Fundación Banco Exterior (LP)
IB-33-148

93.   *Seis baladas*, "T'ho riveduta in sogno."

Manuel Cid and Felix Lavilla: Fundación Banco Exterior (LP)
IB-33-148

Orchestral Works (including concertos)

94.   Concerto No. 1 for Piano and Orchestra in A Minor ("Concierto
fantástico")

Daniel Blumenthal with Alberto Zedda and the Turin Orchestra:
Marfer (LP) M.50242
Felicja Blumental with Alberto Zedda and the Orchestra
Sinfonica della RAI di Torino: Auditorium (LP) AUD-101;

Columbia (LP) M-50-242; Price-less (CS) XY-2261;
Vox/Turnabout (LP) TV-S-34372

Aldo Ciccolini with Enrique Bátiz and the Royal Philharmonic
Orchestra (orch. by Trayter): Angel (CS) 4XS-38038, (LP)
DS-38038; EMI (LP) ASD-1653881; IMG/Pickwick (CD)
IMGCD-1607

Enrique Pérez de Guzmán with Manuel Galduf and the Orquesta
de Valencia: Auvidis Valois (CD) V-4661

95. *Rapsodia española* (for piano and orchestra).

Felicja Blumental with Luigi Toffolo and the Filarmonica
Triestina: Vox (LP) PL-10070

Oscar Esplá with Rafael Frühbeck de Burgos and the Orquesta
Nacional de España: London (LP) CS-6423

Juan Lamote de Grignon and the Banda Municipal de Barcelona
(arr. for band): Gramophone/His Master's Voice (78) AB-
339/40

Alicia de Larrocha with Rafael Frühbeck de Burgos and the
London Philharmonic (orch. by C. Halffter): London (CD)
410289-2, (CS) 410289-4, (LP) 410289-1, R-115410

Alicia de Larrocha with Rafael Frühbeck de Burgos and the
Philharmonia Orchestra (orch. by C. Halffter): London (CD)
433905-2

Gonzalo Soriano with Rafael Frühbeck de Burgos and the
Orquesta Nacional de España (orch. by C. Halffter):
Columbia (LP) CS-8569; London (LP) CM-9423, CS-6423;
Zacosa (LP) GML-2019

96. *Catalonia.*

Igor Markevitch and the Orquesta Sinfónica de la RTV
Española: Classette (CS) 412302-4; Philips (CD) 432-826-2,
(CS) 412-912-4, (LP) 839-775-LY

Enrique Bátiz and Orquesta Filarmónica de la Ciudad de
Mexico: ASV (CD) DCA-735; IMG/Pickwick (CD)
IMGCD-1607

ARRANGEMENTS

Accordion

97.   *España: Six Feuilles d'album* [*España: Seis hojas de album*], "Tango."

Stefan Hussong: Denon (CD) CO-78841

Bassoon and Piano

98.   *España: Six Feuilles d'album* [*España: Seis hojas de album*], "Tango."

Masahito Tanaka and Kazue Kojima: Pavane (CD) ADW-7252, (LP) ADW-7252

Bayan

99.   *Suite española No. 1*, "Asturias (Leyenda)."

Fridrikh Lips: Melodiya (LP) S20-16633/4

100.   *Chants d'Espagne* [*Cantos de España*], "Córdoba."

Fridrikh Lips: Melodiya (LP) S20-16633/4

Brass Ensemble

101.   *Suite española No. 1*, "Sevilla (Sevillanas)."

Empire Brass Quintet: Telarc (CD) CD-80301

102.   *Suite española No. 1*, "Asturias (Leyenda)."

Bowie Brass Quintet: Bowie Brass Quintet Productions (CD) BBQ-101
Stuttgart Brass Quartet: Hanssler (CD) CD-98.952

103.   *Iberia*, "Fête-Dieu à Séville" ["El Corpus en Sevilla"].

Empire Brass Quintet: Telarc (CS) CS-30301

Cello(s)

104. *Suite española No. 1,* "Sevilla (Sevillanas)."

Maria Kliegel and Werner Thomas: Signum (CD) SIG-X12-00

105. *Suite española No. 1,* "Asturias (Leyenda)."

Maria Kliegel and Werner Thomas: Signum (CD) SIG-X12-00

106. *Suite española No. 1,* "Cuba (Capricho)."

Maria Kliegel and Werner Thomas: Signum (CD) SIG-X12-00

Cello and Guitar

107. *Suite española No. 1,* "Granada (Serenata)."

Marek Jerie and Konrad Ragossnig: Bayer (CD) BR-100173-CD
Rolf Petrich and Peter Korbel: FSM (CD) FSM-97745

108. *España: Six Feuilles d'album* [*España: Seis hojas de album*], "Tango."

Michaela Fukacova and Jacob Christensen: Kontrapunkt (CD)
KPT-32044

109. *España: Six Feuilles d'album* [*España: Seis hojas de album*], "Malagueña."

Michaela Fukacova and Jacob Christensen: Kontrapunkt (CD)
KPT-32044

110. *España: Six Feuilles d'album* [*España: Seis hojas de album*], "Capricho catalán."

Michaela Fukacova and Jacob Christensen: Kontrapunkt (CD)
KPT-32044

111. *Chants d'Espagne* [*Cantos de España*], "Córdoba."

Michaela Fukacova and Jacob Christensen: Kontrapunkt (CD)
KPT-32044

Marek Jerie and Konrad Ragossnig: Bayer (CD) BR-100173-
CD; Deutsche Harmonia Mundi (LP) HM-686-D

Cello and Orchestra

112. *Recuerdos de viaje*, "Puerta de tierra (Bolero)."

Julian Lloyd Webber with Nicholas Cleobury and the English
Chamber Orchestra: Musical Heritage Society (LP) MHS-
912226-H; Philips (CD) 412231-2, (CS) 412231-4, (LP)
412231-1

Cello and Piano

113. *Suite española No. 1*, "Cádiz (Canción)."

Gaspar Cassado and Miguel Raucheisen: Telefunken (78) A-
2127
André Navarra and Jacqueline Dussol: Odeon (LP) OD-1014

114. *Recuerdos de viaje*, "Rumores de la caleta (Malagueña)."

Raya Garbousova and Erich Itor-Khan: RCA (78) 11-8871
Janos Starker and Leon Pommers: Contrepoint (LP) MC-20054;
Everest (CS) SDBR-3222; Legacy (CD) CD-412; Period
(LP) 584

115. *España: Six Feuilles d'album* [*España: Seis hojas de album*],
"Tango."

Emanuel Feuermann and Gerald Moore: Columbia (78) 17158-
D; Pearl (CD) GEMM-CD-9446
Milos Sadlo and Alfred Holecek: Supraphon (LP) SUA-ST-
50919

116. *España: Six Feuilles d'album* [*España: Seis hojas de album*],
"Malagueña."

Alexander Baillie and Peter Evans: Unicorn/Kanchana (CD)
UKCD-2017
Josep Bassal and Marta Oncins: Picap (LP) 301183

Albert Catell and Edward Gold: Musical Heritage Society (LP)
MHS-1219

Milos Sadlo and Alfred Holecek: Supraphon (LP) SUA-ST-
50919

Daniel Shafran and Nina Musinian: Melodiya (LP) 028163/4

Janos Starker and Leon Pommers: Everest (LP) SDBR-3222;
Period (LP) SPL-584

Cimbalom

117. *Suite española No. 1*, "Asturias (Leyenda)."

Gyongyi Farkas: Odeon (LP) 1-C-065-30-249

Clarinet(s)

118. *Suite española No. 1*, "Sevilla (Sevillanas)."

Ensemble Clarinesque Köln (arr. for 4 clarinets by H. Karabell):
Signum (CD) SIG-X63-00

Flute and Guitar

119. *Mallorca.*

Rebecca Montoya and Thomas Muller-Pering: Dabringhaus und
Grimm (LP) MD+G-1216

120. *Chants d'Espagne [Cantos de España]*, "Cordoba."

Arthur Lauer and Patrick Ferreri: Realmusic (CD) 1878328093
(ISBN)

Guitar(s)

121. *Pavana-capricho.*

Leif Christensen (F. Tárrega): Paula (CD) PACD-59
Duo Horreaux-Trehard: Calliope (CD) CAL-9222
Hilary Field: Yellow Tail (CD) 4TR-10101, YTC-101

122. *Suite española No. 1* (complete).

Amsterdam Guitar Trio: Fidelio (CD) 8853

Manuel Barrueco (M. Barrueco): EMI (CD) CDC-7-54382-2;
    Vox (CS) CT-2247; Vox/Turnabout (LP) TV-34738
Julian Byzantine: Classics for Pleasure (CD) CFP-4631
[Michael] Newman and [Laura] Oltman Duo: Music Masters
    (CD) 67181
Kurt Schneeweiss: Arte Nova (CD) 37633
Göran Söllscher: Deutsche Grammophon (CD) 2FM-439149

123. *Suite española No. 1* (selections).

Julian Bream: RCA (CD) 09026-61608-2, (CS) 09026-61608-4
Unknown performer: Vox (CD) ACD-8819
Narciso Yepes: Deutsche Grammophon (CS) 413991-4, (LP)
    413991-1

124. *Suite española No. 1*, "Granada (Serenata)."

Christian Aubin: Eko (LP) LG-1
Manuel Barrueco: Vox Box (CD) CD3X-3007
Ernesto Bitteti: EMI (CD) CDM-7-64685-2; Deutsche
    Grammophon (LP) 2530-769; Hispavox (LP) 037-762680-1,
    HHX-10-460; Musical Heritage Society (LP) MHS-3621
Jørgen Bjørslev: Danica (CD) DCD-8146
Vladislav Bláha: PEHY (CD) PY-0003-2231
Miguel Borrull: Gramophone/His Master's Voice (78) AE-2006
Liona Boyd: CBS (LP) 73879 (M-35137)
Ludomir Brabec: Supraphon (CD) 11-0369-2
Julian Bream (A. Segovia): Musical Heritage Society (CD)
    513212-T; RCA (CD) 09026-61594-2, 6798-2RG, 68814,
    RCD-14378, (CS) 09026-61594-4, 6798-4RG, ARE-14378,
    (LP) ARC-14378, LM-2606, LSC-2606, RL-14378, VCS-
    7057
Wim Brioen: Rene Gailly International Productions (CD) CD88-
    008
Julian Byzantine: EMI (CD) CDCFP-4631
Javier Calderón: Centaur (CD) CRC-2179
Mark Davis: North Star (CD) NS-0016
Alirio Díaz (A. Segovia): Vanguard (CD) OVC-5004, SVC-048,
    (LP) SRV-357/8, VRS-1084
Duo Horreaux-Trehard: Calliope (CD) CAL-9222

Michael Erni: Pan Classics (CD) 510086
Eduardo Fernández: London (CD) 448560-2
José Luis Gutiérrez: FSM (CD) FCD-97-750
Nicola Hall: London (CD) 448-560-2
Rafael Iturri: Pavane (CD) ADW-7214
Marcelo Kayath (M. Kayath): IMP (CD) PCD-876, PCD-2037
J. P. del Moral: Regal (78) RS-5514
Georgi Moravsky: Laserlight (CD) 14-299
Jürg Moser and Fredy Rahm (R. Tarragó): Gallo (CD) CD-881
Mozzani: Gramophone/His Master's Voice (78) GW-1754
Santiago Navascues: Eurodisc (LP) 86-853-KK
Annamaría Padilla: Música Mundial (CD) MMP-1
Carlo Pezzimenti: Encore Performance Recordings (CD) EPR-
    9407
Ida Presti: Gramophone/His Master's Voice (78) K-7957
Konrad Ragossnig: Moss Music Group (CD) MWCD-7135; Vox
    (CS) CT-4494; Vox/Allegretto (CD) ACD-8175; Vox Cum
    Laude (CD) PVT-7135; Vox/Turnabout (CS) PCT-7135
Alexander-Sergei Ramírez: Denon (CD) CO-75715
Pepe Romero (Celedonio Romero): Philips (CD) 416384-2,
    434727-2 (CS) 416384-4, (LP) 416384-1
Pepe and Celin Romero (P. Romero): Philips (CD) 411432-2,
    432827-2, (CS) 7337-182, (LP) 6514-182
Miguel Rubio: Gallo (LP) 30-254
Andrés Segovia (A. Segovia): Angel (CD) H-61049; Columbia
    (45) 80004; Decca (LP) 710063, 8022, AXT-233029, DL-
    10.063, (78) 29154 in DM-A-384; Doremi (CD) DHR-7703;
    EMI (CD) CDH-7-61049-2; Enterprise (CD) SO-53002;
    International Music (CD) MAG-48001; MCA (CD) MCAD-
    42069, (CS) MCAC-2528, (LP) M-24.018, MCA-2528, S-
    26.042; Odeon (78) 263770
Göran Söllscher (A. Segovia): Deutsche Grammophon (CD)
    413720-2, (CS) 413720-4, (LP) 413720-1
Tinturin Duo: Cambria Master (CD) CD-1099
Unknown performer: Bellaphon (LP) 6323289; EMI (CD)
    CDCFP-4671; Excelsior (CS) EXL-4-5280; IMP (CD)
    PCDS-23; London (CD) 2LH-448560; Special Music
    Company (CD) SCD-5211; Vox (CD) ACD-8701, ACD-
    8742

Louise Walker: Epic (LP) LC-3055; Philips (LP) N-00640
John Williams (A. Segovia): CBS (CD) MDK-45638, MFK-
    46358, MK-36679, (CS) HMT-36679, IMT-36679, (LP)
    DCX-36679, IM-36679; Columbia (CD) MDK-45648,
    MFK-46358, MK-36679, (CS) IMT-36679, MDT-45648,
    MFT-46358; Sony (CD) SK-36679
Narciso Yepes (A. Segovia): London (CS) 417043-4
John Zaradin: Classics for Pleasure (LP) CFP-40012; Sine Qua
    Non Superba (CS) C-2005, (LP) SA-2005

125. *Suite española No. 1,* "Cataluña (Curranda)."

Manuel Barrueco: Vox Box (CD) CD3X-3007
Julian Bream: RCA (CD) RCD-14378, (CS) ARE-14378, (LP)
    ARC-14378, RL-14378
Edoardo Catemario: Arts Music (CD) 47145-2
Duo Horreaux-Trehard: Calliope (CD) CAL-9222
Susan Grisanti: Blaze of Glory (CS) SG-91291
Susanne Mebes: Leman Classics (CD) LC-44201

126. *Suite española No. 1,* "Sevilla (Sevillanas)."

Nicolas Alfonso: Véga (LP) C-30-S-121
Laurindo Almeida (L. Almeida): Capitol (LP) P-8295, SP-8686
Manuel Barrueco: Vox Box (CD) CD3X-3007
Manuel Barrueco or Konrad Raggosnig: Vox/Turnabout (CS)
    CT-4806
Ernesto Bitteti: Deutsche Grammophon (LP) 2530-769; EMI
    (CD) CDC-7-49973-2, CDM-7-64685-2; Hispavox (LP)
    037-762680-1, HHS-10-365, HHX-10-460; Musical
    Heritage Society (LP) MHS-3621
Vladislav Bláha: PEHY (CD) PY-0003-2231
Julian Bream (J. Bream): RCA (CD) 6206-2-RC, RCD-14378,
    (CS) ARE-14378, (LP) ARC-14378, RL-14378
Javier Calderón: Centaur (CD) CRC-2179
Edoardo Catemario: Arts Music (CD) 47145-2
Mark Davis: North Star (CD) NS-0016
Alirio Díaz (J. de Azpiazu): Vanguard (CD) OVC-5004, SVC-
    048, (LP) SRV-357/8, VRS-1084
Duo Horreaux-Trehard: Calliope (CD) CAL-9222

English Guitar Quartet: Saydisc (CD) CDSDL-399
Michael Erni: Pan Classics (CD) 510086
Vicente Escudero: Columbia (LP) CL-982
Eduardo Fernández: London (CD) 417618-2, (CS) 417618-4
Walter Feybli and Daniel Erni: Orfeo (CD) C-189891-A
Lynne Gangbar: Canadian Broadcasting Corporation (LP) MV-
    1006
Slava Grigoryani: Sony (CD) SK-62627
Susan Grisanti: Blaze of Glory (CS) SG-91291
Paul Henry: Centaur (CD) CRC-2113; Musicmax (CS) 414
Rita Honti: Laserlight (CD) 14-299
Marcelo Kayath (M. Kayath): IMP (CD) PCD-876, PCD-2037
Timo Korhonen: Ondine (CD) ODE-752-2
Norbert Kraft: Chandos (CD) CHAN-8857, (CS) ABTD-1473;
    Fanfare (CS) DFC-6003; Naxos (CD) 8.553999
Alexandre Lagoya (A. Lagoya): Philips (LP) 6599-760
Vincenzo Macaluso: Klavier (CD) KCD-11003
Domenico Martucci: Nuova Era (CD) 7238
Harold Micay: Fleur de Son (CD) 57919
Jürg Moser and Fredy Rahm (R. Tarragó): Gallo (CD) CD-881
Santiago Nebot (bandurria) and Augusto Hita (guitar): RCA
    (LP) 31.16138
Christopher Parkening (A. Segovia): Angel (CD) C-47194, (CS)
    4XS-36020, 4XS-36069
Konrad Ragossnig: Moss Music Group (CD) MWCD-7135;
    Turnabout (LP) TV-S-34494; Vox (CS) CT-4494;
    Vox/Allegretto (CD) ACD-8175; Vox Cum Laude (CD)
    PVT-7135; Vox/Turnabout (CS) PCT-7135
Alexander-Sergei Ramírez: Denon (CD) CO-75715
Angel Romero (A. Romero): Angel (CD) C-47192, (CS) 4XS-
    37312, 4XS-37350, (LP) S-37312, S-37350
Pepe Romero (P. Romero): Philips (CD) 416384-2, 426682-2,
    434727-2, (CS) 416384-4, (LP) 416384-1
Los Romeros: Mercury (CS) MRI-75027, (LP) MG-50295, SR-
    90295, SRI-75027
Turibio Santos: Erato (CD) 2292-45950-2, ECD-55028, (CS)
    MCE-55028; Erato Bonsai (CD) AW-45950; Musical
    Heritage Society (LP) MHS-3629

Andrés Segovia (A. Segovia): Angel (CD) H-61094; Columbia
(45) 80004; Decca (LP) 8022, AXT-233029, (78) 29156 in
DM-A-384; Doremi (CD) DHR-7703; EMI (CD) CDH-7-
61049-2; Enterprise (CD) SO-53002; Ermitage (CD) ERM-
119, ERM-131, ERM-12012, ERM-12013; International
Music (CD) MAG-48001; MCA (CD) MCAD-42069, (LP)
M-24.018, MCA-2533, S-26.037; Odeon (78) 263771
South German Guitar Duo: RBM Musikproduktion Mannheim
(CD) CD-6.3191
Stockholm Guitar Quartet: Opus 3 (CD) CD-7810
Tinturin Duo: Cambria Master (CD) CD-1099
Ishan Turnagoel: Fono (LP) FSM-68205-EB
Unknown performer: EMI (CD) CDCFP-4671; Excelsior (CS)
EXL-4-5280; IMP (CD) PCDS-23; Vox (CD) ACD-8704,
ACD-8742, (CS) CC-1021, CTX-4806
John Williams: CBS (CD) MFK-46358, MK-36679, MK-44794,
MLK-45522, (CS) HMT-36679, IMT-36679, MLK-45522,
(LP) DCX-36679, IM-36679; Columbia (CD) MDK-45648,
MFK-46358, MK-36679, MK-44794, MLK-45522, SBK-
46347, (CS) IMT-36679, (LP) M-32678, MDT-45648,
M3X-32677, SBT-46347; Sony (CD) DIDC-071768, MLK-
66704, SK-36679, SK-53359, SLV-53475, (CS) ST-53359

127. *Suite española No. 1,* "Cádiz (Canción)."

Laurindo Almeida (L. Almeida): Capitol (LP) P-8367
María Luisa Anido: RCA (78) 9676
Manuel Barrueco: Vox Box (CD) CD3X-3007
Manuel Barrueco or Konrad Raggosnig: Vox/Turnabout (CS)
CT-4806
Ernesto Bitteti: Deutsche Grammophon (LP) 2530-769; EMI
(CD) CDM-7-64685-2; Hispavox (LP) 037-762680-1,
HHX-10-460; Musical Heritage Society (LP) MHS-3621
Julian Bream: RCA (CD) 29C-6206, RCD-14378, (CS) ARE-
14378, (LP) ARC-14378, RL-14378
Edoardo Catemario: Arts Music (CD) 47145-2
English Guitar Quartet: Saydisc (CD) CDSDL-399
Michael Erni: Pan Classics (CD) 510086

Eduardo Fernández: London (CD) 414161-2, 448560-2, (CS) 414161-4, (LP) 414161-1
Alexandre Lagoya: Columbia (LP) M-35857
Georgi Moravsky: Laserlight (CD) 14-299
Santiago Nebot (bandurria) and Augusto Hita (guitar): RCA (LP) 31.16138
[Michael] Newman and [Laura] Oltman Duo: Musicmasters (CD) 67181
Walter Ranalli: Bongiovanni (CD) GB-5042
Pepe Romero (P. Romero): Philips (CD) 416384-2, (CS) 416384-4, (LP) 416384-1
Norman Ruiz: Centaur (CD) CRC-2279
John Stover: High Water (LP) 8201
Ishan Turnagoel: Fono (LP) FSM-68205-EB
Unknown performer: London (CD) 2LH-448560; Vox (CD) ACD-8742, (CS) CTX-4806
John Williams (A. Segovia): CBS (CD) MFK-46358, MK-36679, (CS) HMT-36679, IMT-36679, (LP) DCX-36679, IM-36679; Columbia (CD) MFK-46358, MK-36679, (CS) IMT-36679, MFT-46358; Sony (CD) SK-36679

128. *Suite española No. 1,* "Asturias (Leyenda)."

José Manuel Aldana: Odeon (LP) 1J-063-20.139, ASDL-935
Laurindo Almeida (L. Almeida): Capitol (LP) P-8295
Muriel Anderson: CGD Music (CD) CGD-168
María Luisa Anido: Capitol (LP) P-18014
Manuel Barrueco: EMI (CD) CDC-54382; Vox Box (CD) CD3X-3007
René Bartoli: Harmonia Mundi (CD) HMP-390928; (LP) HMU-572
Ernesto Bitteti: Deutsche Grammophone (LP) 2530-769; EMI (CD) CDM-7-64685-2, CDZ-7-67602-2, ZDMB-64241; Hispavox (LP) 037-762680-1, HHS-10-344, HHX-10-460, S-20.078, S-60.135, S-60.157; Musical Heritage Society (LP) MHS-3621
Jørgen Bjørslev: Danica (CD) DCD-8146
Vladislav Bláha: PEHY (CD) PY-0003-2231

Diego Blanco: BIS (CD) CD-233
Liona Boyd: CBS (LP) FM-37248, FM-37788, M-35137, M-36732; Columbia (CS) FMT-37788, (LP) M-35853, M-36675
Julian Bream (J. Bream): Musical Heritage Society (CD) 513212-T; RCA (CD) 09026-61594-2, 61848, (CS) 09026-61594-4, 09026-62663-4, (LP) LM-2606, LSC-2606
David Burgess: Camerata (CS) CRL-8127
Irma Costanzo: EMI (LP) 1-J-063-21010
Alirio Díaz: Everest (LP) SDBR-3155; Laserlight (CD) 14-129; Murray Hill (LP) S-4194; Vanguard (CD) OVC-5006, SVC-049, (LP) VSD-71135
Michel Dintrich: Forlane (CD) FF-010
Arnaud Dumond: Pierre Verany (CD) PV-786103
English Guitar Quartet: Saydisc (CD) CDSDL-399
Michael Erni: Pan Classics (CD) 510086
Eduardo Fernández: London (CD) 417618-2, (CS) 417618-4, (LP) 417618-1
Guillermo Fierens: ASV/Harmonia Mundi (CD) CDDCA-685; ASV/Quicksilva (CD) ASQ-6190
Gerald Garcia: Naxos (CD) 8.550220
Mohino González: Fontana (LP) 6535-003
Eric Hill: Emergo Classics (CD) EC-3386-2; Saga (CD) EC-3386, (LP) 5355
Pedro Ibañez: Planett (CD) PNT-242077
Sharon Isbin (A. Segovia): Sound Environment Recording Corp. (LP) TR-1010; Virgin Classics (CD) 0777-7595912-3, CDC-59591, VC7-91128-2, (CS) VC7-91128-4
Rafael Iturri: Alpha (LP) DB-144-C; Pavane (CD) ADW-7214
Ivan Kalcina: Regency (CS) V-80104 (CMP-2R04)
Siegfried Kobilzer: Preiser (LP) SPR-135017
Norbert Kraft: Fanfare (CS) DFC-6003; Naxos (CD) 8.553999
Alexander Lagoya: Pathé (45) ED-2, EMD-10004; Philips (LP) 6833-159
Sylvia Lagoya: Philips (CD) 446002
Rey de La Torre: Epic (LP) LC-3564; Nonesuch (CS) 71233-4-SR, (LP) H-71233
Wolfgang Lendle: Teldec (CD) 8.44142, 9031-75864-2, 94523, AW-75864

Leo León: Leo (LP) EMCA-87225
Celia Linde: Bluebell (LP) Bell-202
David Lorenz: Laserlight (CD) 14-299
Luis Maravilla: Ducretet (LP) LPG-8495; Westminster (LP)
5194
Julio J. Martínez Oyanguren: RCA (78) 10-1066
González Mohino: Fontana (LP) 6535-003
Erik Mollerstrom: Artemis (LP) ARTE-7116
J. P. del Moral: Regal (78) RS-5023
Santiago Navascues: Eurodisc (LP) 89-427-KK
Santiago Nebot (bandurria) and Augusto Hita (guitar): RCA
(LP) 31.16138
William Orbaugh: Classic Records (CD) CSV-0237
Annamaría Padilla: Música Mundial (CD) MMP-1
Christopher Parkening (A. Segovia): Angel (CS) 4XS-36069,
(LP) S-36020, S-36069; EMI (CD) CDC-547194
Carlo Pezzimenti: Encore Performance Recordings (CD) EPR-
9407
Randy Pile (P. Romero): RP Recordings (CD) 1193
Konrad Ragossnig: Claves (CD) CD-50-0806, (LP) P-806;
Supraphon (LP) 1-11-1040
Alexander-Sergei Ramírez: Denon (CD) CO-75357
Angel Romero (A. Romero): Angel (CD) C-47192, (CS) 4XS-
37312, 4XS-37350, (LP) S-37312, S-37350; Telarc (CD)
CD-80213, (CS) CS-30213
Celedonio Romero: Delos (LP) DEL-25441, D/QA-25441
Pepe Romero (P. Romero): Philips (CD) 411033-2, 416288-2,
426682-2, 434727-2, (CS) 7337-381, (LP) 6514-381, 9500-
295; Telarc (CD) 80213, (CS) 30213
Sherri Rottersman: Auric (CD) CDC-8-23446-2
Turibio Santos: Erato (CD) 2292-45950-2, 4509-92134-2,
95568, AW-92134, ECD–55028, (CS) MCE-55028;
Musical Heritage Society (LP) MHS-3629; Erato Bonsai
(CD) AW-45950
Andrés Segovia (A. Segovia): MCA (CD) MCAD-42069, (LP)
M-26.037, MCA-2533, (CS) MCAC-2533; Time-Life (CS)
4TL-P08, (LP) TL-P08
Antonio Francisco Serra: Barclay (LP) 86014
Luis Suelves: Mace (LP) M-9019

Ishan Turnagoel: Fono (LP) FSM-68205-EB
Unknown performer: Bellaphon (LP) 6323289
Carl Volk: Chiron (CD) AR-4853
John Williams: CBS (CD) MDK-45648, MFK-46358, MK-
36679, MK-44794, MLK-45522, (CS) HMT-36679, IMT-
36679, (LP) DCX-36679, IM-36679, MT-30057; Columbia
(CD) MDK-45648, MFK-46358, MK-36679, MK-44794,
MLK-45522, SBK-46347, (CS) MDT-45648, MFT-46358,
MT-30057, MT-31407, MT-36679, SBT-47347, (LP) M-
31407, M-32680, M3X-32677; Sony (CD) DIDC-071768,
MLK-66704, SK-36679, SK-53359, (CS) ST-53359
Narciso Yepes: Accord (CD) 139225; Deutsche Grammophon
(CD) 435843-2, 439171-2, D-100063, (LP) 2530-159;
Everest (LP) SD-3274; London (CS) 417043-4, (LP) STS-
15224

129. *Suite española No. 1,* "Aragón (Fantasía)."

De Falla Trio: Concord Concerto (CD) CCD-42011, (CS) CC-
2011-C, (LP) CC-2011
Duo Horreaux-Trehard: Calliope (CD) CAL-9222

130. *Suite española No. 1,* "Castilla (Seguidillas)." [See also
"Seguidillas" from *Chants d'Espagne.*]

Julian Bream and John Williams (M. Llobet): RCA (CD) RD-
89645, (LP) RL-03090
Duo Horreaux-Trehard: Calliope (CD) CAL-9222
Groningen Guitar Duo (Remco de Haan and Erik Westerhof; arr.
by performers): Ottavo (CD) OTR-C48710
Norwegian Guitar Duo (Sven Lundestad and Geir-Otto Nilsson):
VEPS (CD) 022-88
Jürgen and Monika Röst: Capriccio (CD) 10174; Laserlight
(CD) 15-602, (CS) 79-602

131. *Suite española No. 1,* "Cuba (Capricho)."

Manuel Barrueco: Vox Box (CD) CD3X-3007
Michael Erni: Pan Classics (CD) 510086
Georgi Moravsky: Laserlight (CD) 14-299

Santiago Nebot (bandurria) and Augusto Hita (guitar): RCA (LP) 31.16138

132. *Recuerdos de viaje* (complete).

Julian Byzantine: Classics for Pleasure (CD) CFP-4631

133. *Recuerdos de viaje* (selections).

Narciso Yepes: Deutsche Grammophon (CS) 413991-4, (LP) 413991-1

134. *Recuerdos de viaje*, "Leyenda (Barcarola)," transcribed by Andrés Segovia.

Julian Bream: RCA (CD) ZRG-6798
Rafael Iturri: Pavane (CD) ADW-7214
Rey de La Torre: Philarmonia (LP) 106
Christopher Parkening: EMI (CD) ZDCB-54905
Angel Romero: Telarc (CD) CD-80213
Andrés Segovia: Brunswick (LP) AXTL-1005; CID (LP) UMT-273.141; Decca (LP) DL-9633; MCA (CD) MCAD-11124, MCAD-42069
Unknown performer: RCA (CD) 68586, (CS) 68586
Narciso Yepes: Accord (CD) ACD-222032; Decca (LP) FST-133076, LXT-2974; London (LP) LLP-1042
Gustavo Zepoll: Sound of Our Times (LP) 1024; Supraphon (LP) SLPY-142

135. *Recuerdos de viaje*, "Alborada."

Unknown performer: EMI (CD) CDCFP-4671

136. *Recuerdos de viaje*, "Rumores de la caleta (Malagueña)."

Laurindo Almeida (L. Almeida): Capitol (LP) P-8367
René Bartoli: Harmonia Mundi (CD) HMP-390928, (LP) HM-583
Ernesto Bitteti: EMI (CD) CDZ-7-67602-2; Musical Heritage Society (LP) MHS-1274

Luis Campos (accompanied by various instruments): Black Gold
  (CD) BG-126-D
Alirio Díaz: Laserlight (CD) 14-129
Kimbal Dykes: Music West (LP) MWLP-140
Michael Erni: Pan Classics (CD) 510086
Eduardo Fernández: London (CD) 414161-2, (CS) 414161-4,
  (LP) 414161-1
Hilary Field: Yellow Tail (CD) 4TR-10101, YTC-101
Edward Flower and David McLellan: Music Minus One (LP)
  MMO-5044
Bob Hardaway: Guitar-Czar (LP) KM-5483
Eric Hill: Emergo Classics (CD) EC-3386-2; Saga (CD) EC-
  3386, (LP) 5355
Pedro Ibañez: Planett (CD) PNT-242046
Klaus Jäckle: Bayer (CD) 100122
Machiko Kikuchi: Camerata (45) CMT-1019
Santiago Navascues: Eurodisc (LP) 86-853-KK
[Michael] Newman and [Laura] Oltman Duo: Musicmasters
  (CD) 67181
Christopher Parkening: Angel (CS) 4XS-36021, 4XS-36069,
  (LP) S-36021, SFO-36021, SNP-7; EMI (CD) ZDCB-54905
Randy Pile (P. Romero): RP Recordings (CD) 1193
Ida Presti: Columbia (78) X-4924; Gramophone/His Master's
  Voice (78) K-7957
Alexander-Sergei Ramírez: Denon (CD) CO-75715
Pepe Romero (P. Romero): Philips (CD) 416384-2, (CS)
  416384-4, (LP) 416384-1
Pepe and Celin Romero (P. Romero): Philips (CD) 411432-2,
  432827-2, 434727-2, (CS) 7337-182, (LP) 6514-182
Norman Ruiz: Centaur (CD) CRC-2279
Turibio Santos: Erato (CD) 4509-92134-2, AW-92134, ECD-
  55028, (CS) MCE-55028; Erato Bonsai (CD) 45950
Simeon Simov: Laserlight (CD) 14-299
John Svoboda: Classic Production (CD) ACPCD-002
Renata Tarragó: Columbia (LP) CS-8567
Trio Albéniz (bandurria, lute, guitar): Hispavox (LP) HH-1401
Unknown performer: Digitel (CD) DGT-91A100
Narciso Yepes (N. Yepes): Accord (CD) ACD-222032; Decca
  (LP) FST-133076, LXT-2974; Deutsche Grammophon (CD)

435843-2, 439171-2, D-100063, (LP) 2530-159; Everest
(LP) SD-3274; London (LP) LLP-1042, STS-15224;
Murray Hill (LP) S-4194

137. *Recuerdos de viaje*, "En la playa."

Duo Horreaux-Trehard: Calliope (CD) CAL-9222
Norman Ruiz: Centaur (CD) CRC-2279
Unknown performer: EMI (CD) CDCFP-4671

138. Menuet (G Minor).

Duo Horreaux-Trehard: Calliope (CD) CAL-9222

139. *Douze Pièces caractéristiques pour piano* [*Doce piezas características*], "Pavana."

Duo Horreaux-Trehard: Calliope (CD) CAL-9222

140. *Douze Pièces caractéristiques pour piano* [*Doce piezas características*], "Staccato-Capricho."

Duo Horreaux-Trehard: Calliope (CD) CAL-9222

141. *Douze Pièces caractéristiques pour piano* [*Doce piezas características*], "Torre Bermeja (Serenata)."

Lalyta Almirón: Odeon (78) 183249
Ernesto Bitteti: Deutsche Grammophon (LP) 2530-769; EMI
(CD) CDM-7-64685-2; Hispavox (LP) 037-762680-1, HHS-
10-344, HHX-10-460; Musical Heritage Society (LP) MHS-
3621
Javier Calderón: Centaur (CD) CRC-2179
Alirio Díaz (A. Lonzano): Vanguard (CD) OVC-5004, SVC-
048, (LP) SRV-357/8, VRS-1084
Michael Erni: Pan Classics (CD) 510086
Eduardo Fernández: London (CD) 414161-2, (CS) 414161-4,
(LP) 414161-1
Slava Grigoryani: Sony (CD) SK-62627
Norbert Kraft: Chandos (CD) CHAN-8857, (CS) ABTD-1473;
Fanfare (CS) DFC-6003

Rey de La Torre: Epic (LP) LC-3564; Nonesuch (CS) 71233-4-
    SR, (LP) H-71233; Philarmonia (LP) 106
David Lorenz: Laserlight (CD) 14-299
Roland Mueller: Bayer (CD) 100134
Michael Newman (F. Tárrega/M. Llobet): Sheffield Lab (CD)
    SLS-504, (LP) SL-36
Christopher Parkening (P. Russ): EMI/Angel (CD) CDC-49404,
    (CS) 4DS-49404
Konrad Ragossnig: Claves (CD) CD-50-0806, (LP) P-806
Pepe Romero: Philips (CD) 442150-2, G2-42150
Andrés Segovia: Decca (LP) AXT-233029, DL-8022, (78)
    29155 in DM-A-384; Doremi (CD) DHR-7703; Ermitage
    (CD) ERM-119, ERM-131, ERM-12012, ERM-12013;
    Fonomusic (CD) CD-1010; Intercord (LP) INT-160.815;
    MCA (LP) M-24.018; Odeon (78) 263771; RCA (LP) ARL-
    10485
John Stover: High Water (LP) 8201
John Svoboda: Classic Production (CD) ACPCD-002
Ishan Turnagoel: Fono (LP) FSM-68205-EB
Trio Albéniz (bandurria, lute, guitar): Hispavox (LP) HH-1402
Unknown performer: Bellaphon (LP) 6323289
John Williams: CBS (CD) MK-36679 (CS) HMT-36679, IMT-
    36679, (LP) DCX-36679, IM-36679; Columbia (CD) MK-
    36679; Everest (LP) SDBR-3195; London (CD) 2LC-
    421165, (LP) STS-15549; Murray Hill (LP) S-4194; Sony
    (CD) SK-36679
Narciso Yepes: Deutsche Grammophon (CD) 435843-2, 439171-
    2, D-100063, (LP) 2530-159; Everest (LP) SD-3274

142. *Deux morceaux caractéristiques [Deux dances espagnoles]*,
    "Tango."

    [Joanne] Castellani-[Michael] Andriaccio Duo: Fleur de Son
        (CD) FDS-57918-2
    Tamara Kropat and Theo Krumeich: Channel Classics/Canal
        Grande (CD) CG-9103
    Jürg Moser and Fredy Rahm (R. Tarragó): Gallo (CD) CD-881

143. *España: Six Feuilles d'album* (complete).

Peter and Zoltán Katona: Channel Classics (CD) CCS-10397

144. *España: Six Feuilles d'album* [*España: Seis hojas de album*], "Prélude."

Simeon Simov: Laserlight (CD) 14-299

145. *España: Six Feuilles d'album* [*España: Seis hojas de album*], "Tango."

Laurindo Almeida (L. Almeida): Capitol (LP) P-8367, SP-8686
Ernesto Bitteti: Deutsche Grammophon (LP) 2530-769; EMI
(CD) CDM-7-64685-2; Hispavox (LP) 037-762680-1,
HHX-10-460, HIS-160076; Musical Heritage Society (LP)
MHS-3621
Michael Erni: Pan Classics (CD) 510086
Eduardo Fernández: London (CD) 417618-2, 448560-2
Groningen Guitar Duo (Remco de Haan and Erik Westerhof; arr.
by performers): Ottavo (CD) OTR-C48710
Lars Klevstrand and Eric Stenstadvold: Fugitive (LP) ALP-
11001
Tamara Kropat and Theo Krumeich: Channel Classics/Canal
Grande (CD) CG-9103
Rey de La Torre: Epic (LP) BC-1073, LC-3674
Jürg Moser and Fredy Rahm (E. Pujol): Gallo (CD) CD-881
Santiago Nebot (bandurria) and Augusto Hita (guitar): RCA
(LP) 3L-16138
[Michael] Newman and [Laura] Oltman Duo: Musicmasters
(CD) 67181
Ida Presti and Alexandre Lagoya: Mercury (LP) MG-50427;
Philips (LP) 6730-009, 6768-657
Angel Romero (A. Romero): Angel (CS) 4XS-36094, (LP) S-
36094
Pepe Romero (P. Romero): Philips (CD) 426682-2, 6514182
Pepe and Celin Romero (P. Romero): (CD) 432827-2, 434727-2,
(CS) 7337-182, (LP) 6514-182
Turibio Santos and Oscar Casares: Erato (LP) STU-71092
John Williams: CBS (CD) MK-36679, MK-44794, MLK-45542,
(CS) HMT-36679, IMT-36679, MT-30057, (LP) DCX-
36679, IM-36679; Columbia (CD) MK-36679, (LP) M-

31407, M-32680, M3X-32677; Sony (CD) MLK-66704,
SK-36679
Narciso Yepes: Deutsche Grammophon (LP) SLPM-139366

146. *España: Six Feuilles d'album* [*España: Seis hojas de album*],
"Malagueña."

Nicolas and Ilse Alfonso: Rene Gailly (CD) CD-86-005
Ernesto Bitteti: Hispavox (LP) 130-299, HHS-10-365; Musical
Heritage Society (LP) OR-322
Rafael Iturri: Pavane (CD) ADW-7214
Pepe and Celin Romero (P. Romero): Philips (CD) 432827-2,
(CS) 7337-182, (LP) 6514-182
Renata Tarragó: Philips (LP) RPF-761/2,3,4
Narciso Yepes: Decca (LP) LXT-2974; Deutsche Grammophon
(CD) 423699-2, 439149, (LP) SLPM-139365

147. *España: Six Feuilles d'album* [*España: Seis hojas de album*],
"Capricho catalán."

Bob Hardaway: Guitar-Czar (LP) KM-5483
Timo Korhonen: Ondine (CD) ODE-752-2
Susanne Mebes: Leman Classics (CD) LC-44201
Marc Regnier (A. Segovia): Musical Heritage Society (CD)
513008-M, (CS) 313008
Andrés Segovia (M. Lorimer): RCA (LP) ARL-11323

148. *España: Six Feuilles d'album* [*España: Seis hojas de album*],
"Zortzico."

Mark Davis: North Star (CD) NS-0016

149. *Mallorca (Barcarola).*

Ernesto Bitetti (A. Segovia): EMI (CD) CDC-7-49973-2, CDZ-
7-67602-2; Hispavox (LP) 130-299, HHS-0-365, S-60.157;
Musical Heritage Society (LP) OR-322
Liona Boyd (L. Boyd): CBS (CS) IMT-39031, (LP) IM-39031
Julian Bream: RCA (CD) 09026-61608-2, RCD-14378, (CS)
09026-61608-4, ARE-14378, (LP) ARC-14378, RL-14378
Michael Erni: Pan Classics (CD) 510086

Paul Henry: Centaur (CD) CRC-2113; Musicmax (CS) 414
Sharon Isbin (A. Segovia): Sound Environment Recording Corp.
(LP) TR-1010; Virgin (CD) 0777-7595912-3, VC7-91128-2
Peter and Zoltán Katona: Channel Classics (CD) CCS-10397
Marcelo Kayath (A. Segovia): IMP (CD) PCD-876, PCD-2037
Machiko Kikuchi: Denon (CD) CO-8100
Norbert Kraft: Chandos (CD) CHAN-8857, (CS) ABTD-1473;
Naxos (CD) 8.553999
Wolfgang Lendle: Teldec (CD) 9031-75864-2
David Lorenz: Laserlight (CD) 14-299
Michael Lucarelli: LMS (CD) LMS-1002-CD, (CS) LMS-1002-
C
Roland Mueller: Bayer (CD) 100134
Carlo Pezzimenti: Elba (CD) 2, (LP) JSS-80-106
Walter Ranalli: Bongiovanni (CD) GB-5042
Marc Regnier (A. Segovia): Musical Heritage Society (CD)
513008-M, (CS) 313008
Pepe Romero (M. Switzer): Philips (CD) 416384-2, 434727-2,
(CS) 416384-4, (LP) 416384-1
Norman Ruiz: Centaur (CD) CRC-2279
Turibio Santos: Erato (CD) 4509-92134-2, (CS) MCE-55028
Andrés Segovia (A. Segovia): MCA (CS) MCAC-2501, (LP)
MCA-2501, S-26.041
Unknown performer: Laserlight (CD) 14-299
John Williams: CBS (CD) MFK-46358, MK-36679, (CS) HMT-
36679, IMT-36679, (LP) DCX-36679, IM-36679; Columbia
(CD) MDK-45648, MK-36679, (CS) MDT-45648; Sony
(CD) SK-36679

150. *Rêves [Sueños]*, "Berceuse."

Duo Horreaux-Trehard: Calliope (CD) CAL-9222

151. *Zambra granadina (Danse orientale).*

Laurindo Almeida (L. Almeida): Capitol (LP) P-8367
Ernesto Bitteti: Deutsche Grammophon (LP) 2530-769; EMI
(CD) CDM-7-64685-2; Hispavox (LP) 037-762680-1,
HHX-10-460; Musical Heritage Society (LP) MHS-3621

Wim Brioen: Rene Gailly International Productions (CD) CD88-008

Alirio Díaz (A. Segovia): Vanguard (CD) OVC-5004, SVC-048, (LP) SRV-357/8, VRS-1084

Marcelo Kayath (A. Segovia): IMP (CD) PCD-876, PCD-2037

Machiko Kikuchi: Camerata (45) CMT-1019

Norbert Kraft: Naxos (CD) 8.553999

Michael Lorimer: Dancing Cat (CD) DD-3002

Akinobu Matsuda (A. Segovia): Argo (LP) ZDA-205

Roland Mueller: Bayer (CD) 100134

[Michael] Newman and [Laura] Oltman Duo: Musicmasters (CD) 67181

Carlo Pezzimenti: Elba (LP) JSS-80-106

Konrad Ragossnig: Claves (CD) CD-50-0806, (LP) P-806

Norman Ruiz: Centaur (CD) CRC-2279

Andrés Segovia: Decca (LP) DL7-10039, (Reel) ST7-10039; Ermitage (CD) ERM-131, ERM-12013; MCA (CD) MCAD-42069, (LP) MCA-2524, S-26.032

John Williams: CBS (CD) MFK-46358, MK-36679, (CS) HMT-36679, IMT-36679, (LP) DCX-36679, IM-36679; Columbia (CD) MK-36679; Sony (CD) SK-36679

152. *Chants d'Espagne* [*Cantos de España*] (complete).

[Michael] Newman and [Laura] Oltman Duo: Musicmasters (CD) 67181

Pro Arte Guitar Trio: ASV (CD) CD-WHL-2061

153. *Chants d'Espagne* [*Cantos de España*], "Orientale."

Laurindo Almeida (L. Almeida): Capitol (LP) P-8295

Ernesto Bitteti: Deutsche Grammophon (LP) 2530-769; EMI (CD) CDM-7-64685-2; Hispavox (LP) 037-762680-1, HHX-10-460; Musical Heritage Society (LP) MHS-3621

Norman Ruiz: Centaur (CD) CRC-2279

154. *Chants d'Espagne* [*Cantos de España*], "Sous le palmier (Danse espagnole)."

Julian Bream and John Williams: BMG (CS) 09026-614524; RCA (CD) 09026-61452-2, RD-80456, (CS) ARK-10456, (LP) ARL-10456

[Joanne] Castellani-[Michael] Andriaccio Duo: Fleur de Son (CD) FDS-57918-2; Icarus (LP) 1002

Groningen Guitar Duo (Remco de Haan and Erik Westerhof; arr. by performers): Ottavo (CD) OTR-C48710

Unknown performer: BMG (CD) 09026-68161-2; RCA (CD) 68161, (CS) 68161

155. *Chants d'Espagne* [*Cantos de España*], "Córdoba."

Ernesto Bitteti: Deutsche Grammophon (LP) 2530-769; EMI (CD) CDM-7-64685-2; Hispavox (LP) 037-762680-1, HHX-10-460; Musical Heritage Society (LP) MHS-3621

Julian Bream: RCA (CD) 09026-61608-2, RCD-14378, (CS) 09026-61608-4, ARE-14378, (LP) ARC-14378, LSC-3257, RL-14378

Julian Bream and John Williams: Musical Heritage Society (CD) 523791-H, (CS) 523791-M; RCA (CD) 09026-61450-2, (CS) 09026-61450-4, RK-42233, (LP) 2641118, LSC-3257

David Burgess: Camerata (CS) CRL-8127

[Joanne] Castellani-[Michael] Andriaccio Duo: Fleur De Son (CD) FDS-57918-2; Icarus (LP) 1002

Duo Horreaux-Trehard: Calliope (CD) CAL-9222

Vicente Escudero: Columbia (LP) CL-982

Walter Feybli and Daniel Erni: Orfeo (CD) C-189891-A

Klaus Jäckle: Bayer (CD) 100122

Timo Korhonen: Ondine (CD) ODE-752-2

Tamara Kropat and Theo Krumeich: Channel Classics/Canal Grande (CD) CG-9103

Rey de La Torre: Epic (LP) BC-1073, LC-3674

Julio J. Martínez Oyanguren: RCA (78) 10-1067

Netherlands Guitar Trio: Globe (CD) GLO-5014

Angel Romero (A. Romero): Angel (CS) 4XS-36094, (LP) S-36094

Pepe Romero: Philips (CD) 416384-2, (CS) 416384-4, (LP) 416384-1

South German Guitar Duo: RBM Musikproduktion Mannheim
(CD) CD-6.3191
Unknown performer: BMG (CD) 09026-68161-2; Digitel (CD)
DGT-91A100; RCA (CD) 68161, (CS) 68161
Ware-Patterson Duo: Sugo (CD) SR-9308, (CS) SR-9308
John Williams: CBS (CD) MDK-45648, MFK-46358, MK-
36679, MK-44794, (CS) IMT-36679, MT-30057, (LP)
DCX-36679, IM-36679; Columbia (CD) MDK-45648, MK-
36679, (CS) MDT-45648, (LP) M-32680; Sony (CD) SK-
36679

156. *Chants d'Espange* [*Cantos de España*], "Seguidillas." [See also
"Castilla (Seguidillas)" from the *Suite española No. 1.*]

Nicolas Alfonso: Rene Gailly (CD) CD-86-005
English Guitar Quartet: Saydisc (C D) CDSDL-399
Tamara Kropat and Theo Krumeich: Channel Classics/Canal
Grande (CD) CG-9103
Jürgen Röst: Laserlight (CD) 15-671
South German Guitar Duo: RBM Musikproduktion Mannheim
(CD) CD-6.3191

157. *Espagne: Souvenirs*, "Asturias."

[Michael] Newman and [Laura] Oltman Duo: Musicmasters
(CD) 67181

158. *Catalonia.*

South German Guitar Duo: RBM Musikproduktion Mannheim
(CD) CD-6.3191

159. *Iberia* (complete).

Peter and Zoltán Katona: Channel Classics (CD) CCS-10397
Paco de Lucia, José M. Bandera, Juan Manuel Cañizares (P. de
Lucia): Verve (CD) 314-510-301-2

160. *Iberia* (selections).

Amsterdam Guitar Trio: Fidelio (CD) 8853

Julian Bream and John Williams: Musical Heritage Society (LP)
923791-W

161. *Iberia*, "Evocación."

Sérgio and Eduardo Abreu (S. Abreu): Columbia (LP) M-30575
María Luisa Anido and Miguel Llobet: Chanterelle (CD) CHR-
001; Decca (78) 20369; El Maestro (LP) EM-8003; Odeon
(78) 196521
Julian Bream and John Williams: BMG (CS) 09026-614524;
RCA (CD) 09026-61452-2, RD-80456, (CS) ARK-10456,
(LP) ARL-10456

162. *Iberia*, "El puerto."

[Joanne] Castellani-[Michael] Andriaccio Duo: Fleur De Son
(CD) FDS-57918-2
Netherlands Guitar Trio: Globe (CD) GLO-5014

Guitar and Orchestra

163. *Suite española No. 1*, "Granada (Serenata)."

Konrad Ragossnig with Paul Angerer and the Southwest German
Chamber Orchestra: Special Music Company (CD) SCD-
5189; Vox (CD) ACD-8795

164. *Suite española No. 1*, "Sevilla (Sevillanas)."

Konrad Ragossnig with Paul Angerer and the Southwest German
Chamber Orchestra: Special Music Company (CD) SCD-
5189; Vox (CD) ACD-8795

165. *Suite española No. 1*, "Asturias (Leyenda)."

Ernesto Bitetti with Enrique García Asensio and the Orquesta de
Conciertos de Madrid (F. Moreno Torroba): Hispavox (LP)
S-60157
Ernesto Bitetti with Enrique García Asensio and the Orquesta
Sinfónica de la RTV Española (F. Moreno Torroba):
Hispavox (LP) HHS-10-420

Gerald Garcia with Peter Breiner and the Slovak State
Philharmonic Orchestra (P. Breiner): Lydian (CD) LYD-
18139; Naxos (CD) 8.550220

Enrico Macias with an orchestra conducted by Jean Claudric:
Philips (LP) 6311003

166. *Mallorca (Barcarola).*

Ernesto Bitetti with Enrique García Asensio and the Orquesta de
Conciertos de Madrid (F. Moreno Torroba): Hispavox (LP)
S-60157

Ernesto Bitetti with Enrique García Asensio and the Orquesta
Sinfónica de la RTV Española (F. Moreno Torroba):
Hispavox (LP) HHS-10-420

167. *Zambra granadina (Danse orientale).*

Gerald Garcia with Peter Breiner and the Slovak State
Philharmonic Orchestra (P. Breiner): Lydian (CD) LYD-
18139; Naxos (CD) 8.550220

168. *Iberia* ("Rondeña," "Triana," "El Albaicín" only)

John Williams with Paul Daniel and the London Symphony
Orchestra (S. Gray): Sony (CD) SK-48480, (CS) ST-48480

Hammered Dulcimer and Guitar

169. *Recuerdos de viaje*, "Rumores de la caleta (Malagueña)."

Rudi Zapf and Ingrid Westermeier: PAN (CD) OV-75007, (LP)
OV-30120

Handbells

170. *Suite española No. 1*, "Asturias (Leyenda)."

Sonos Handbell Ensemble: Well-Tempered Productions (CD)
WTP-5170

Harmonica and Piano

171. *Suite española No. 1*, "Sevilla (Sevillanas)."

Larry Adler and Lee Colin: Concert Hall Society (LP) CHS-1168; Mercury (LP) MLP-7026
Larry Logan and James Roberts: Bon-Tim (LP) 101

Harp(s)

172. *Suite española No. 1*, "Granada (Serenata)."

Victoria Drake: Well-Tempered Productions (CD) WTP-5179
Sylvia Kowalczuk: Hungaroton (CD) HCD-31577
Aristid von Würtzler and the New York Harp Ensemble:
Hungaroton (CD) HCD-31295
Nicanor Zabaleta: Deutsche Grammophon (LP) 2530-230

173. *Suite española No. 1*, "Asturias (Leyenda)."

Victoria Drake: Well-Tempered Productions (CD) WTP-5179
Eva Marton with the New York Harp Ensemble: Hungaroton
(CD) HCD-12939
Nicanor Zabaleta: Deutsche Grammophon (LP) 2530-230

174. *Suite española No. 1*, "Castilla (Seguidillas)" (arr. for 4 harps).

M. L. Casadesus, M. T. Jacquot, M. Couée, and S. Tribier :
Gramophone/His Master's Voice (78) K-5984

175. *Recuerdos de viaje*, "Rumores de la caleta (Malagueña)."

Maria Rosa Carlo-Manzano: ARLV Discos (CD) AD-002
Sylvia Kowalczuk: Hungaroton (CD) HCD-31577
Susann McDonald: Delos (CD) DE-3005, (LP) DMS-3005
Marisa Robles: Argo (LP) ZRG-5457; Hispavox (LP) HH-1026;
London (CD) 436293

176. *Douze Pièces caractéristiques pour piano* [*Doce piezas características*], "Torre Bermeja (Serenata)."

Victoria Drake: Well-Tempered Productions (CD) WTP-5179
Marcel Grandjany: Capitol (LP) P-8473
Marisa Robles (G. Bruno): Argo (LP) ZRG-5457; Boston
Skyline (CD) BSD-119; London (CD) 433938-2, 436293

177. *Suite española No. 2* [*Seconde Suite espagnole*], "Zaragoza (Capricho)."

Naoko Yoshino (S. McDonald, L. Wood): CBS/Sony (CD) 32DC-5002
Nicanor Zabaleta: Deutsche Grammophon (LP) 2530-230

178. *España: Six Feuilles d'album* [*España: Seis hojas de album*], "Tango."

Nicanor Zabaleta: Deutsche Grammophon (LP) 2530-230

179. *España: Six Feuilles d'album* [*España: Seis hojas de album*], "Malagueña."

Sylvia Kowalczuk: Hungaroton (CD) HCD-31577
Emilia Moskvitina: Westminster (LP) WG-8363
Anna-Maria Ravnopolska: Gega New (CD) GR-24
Nicanor Zabaleta: Deutsche Grammophon (LP) LPM-18890;
Period (LP) PRST-745, SPL-745

180. *Mallorca.*

Nicanor Zabaleta: Deutsche Grammophon (LP) 2530-230

181. *Chants d'Espagne* [*Cantos de España*], "Córdoba."

Anne Adams: Two Harps As One (CD) AAPH-95

Harp and Bassoon

182. *España: Six Feuilles d'album* [*España: Seis hojas de album*], "Tango."

Werner Karlinger and Isamu Magome: Camerata (CD) 30CM-355

183. *Rêves* [*Sueños*], "Berceuse."

Werner Karlinger and Isamu Magome: Camerata (CD) 30CM-355

Harp and Piano

184. *España: Six Feuilles d'album* [*España: Seis hojas de album*], "Malagueña."

    Brigitte Langnickel-Kohler and Reinhard Langnickel: Aulos
    (CD) AUL-66017

Mandolin(s)

185. *Suite española No. 1,* "Asturias (Leyenda)."

    Ikuko Takeuchi and the Tokyo Mandolin Ensemble conducted
    by Seiichi Mitsuishi: Toshiba (LP) TA-72119

Marimba

186. *Suite española No. 1,* "Asturias (Leyenda)."

    Kai Stensgaard: Danacord (CD) DACOCD-309

Orchestra or Symphonic Band

187. *Pavana-capricho.*

    Germán Lago and the Orquesta Ibérica de Madrid (orchestra of
    guitars and lutes) (G. Lago): Odeon (78) 203256

188. *Suite española No. 1,* orchestrated by Rafael Frühbeck de Burgos
    (all except "Cuba").

    Enrique Bátiz and the Orquesta Sinfónica del Estado de México:
    ASV (CD) ASV-888
    Rafael Frühbeck de Burgos and the New Philharmonia
    Orchestra: Alhambra (LP) SCLL-14081; Columbia (LP)
    SCLL-14081; Decca (LP) LXT-6355; London (CD)
    417786-2, 448601-2, (CS) 417786-4; Zacosa (LP) GML-
    2002
    Rafael Frühbeck de Burgos and the Philharmonia Orchestra:
    London (CD) 433905-2, (LP) CS-6581

189. *Suite española No. 1* (two unspecified selections).

Enrique Jordá and the Orchestre du Conservatoire de Paris (O.
Esplà): Hispavox (LP) 10-209, 260068-160068

190. *Suite española No. 1*, "Granada (Serenata)."

Capdevila and the Odeon Orchestra: Odeon (78) 194853, 203460
Rafael Frühbeck de Burgos and the London Symphony
Orchestra: IMP (CD) PCD-924; MCA (CD) MCAD-25887
Gelabert and the Gramophone Symphony Orchestra:
Gramophone/His Master's Voice (78) AF-184
Harry Horlick and the Decca Concert Orchestra (E. F. Arbós):
Decca (LP) DL-5070, (78) 18087 in DM-A-150
Enrique Jordá and the Orquesta de Conciertos de Madrid (O.
Esplà): Hispavox (LP) 10-209, CT-69-2
Koninklijke Militaire Kapel (arr. for band by Juan Vicente Mas
Quiles): Molenaar's Muziekcentrale N.V. (CD) MBS-17,
MBS-31.0017.65
José Olmedo and the Orquesta Lírica "Audio Museum" de
Madrid: Telefunken (LP) 270-TC-023, 65029, LGM-65029,
TC-8027, TLD-10022
Orchestra Locatelli: Columbia (78) DF-2043
Orquesta Nebreo: Ultraphone (78) AP-133
Regino Sáinz de la Maza and the Orquesta Lírica: Movieplay
(LP) M-18040
Viebig and the Berlin Philharmonic Orchestra (J. Nemeti):
Ultraphone (78) EP-521
Ricardo Villa and the Banda Municipal de Madrid: Odeon (78)
121028, 177228

191. *Suite española No. 1*, "Cataluña (Curranda)."

Enrique Jordá and the Orquesta de Conciertos de Madrid (O.
Esplà): Hispavox (LP) 10-209, CT-69-2, S-60.309/10/11
Koninklijke Militaire Kapel (arr. for band by Juan Vicente Mas
Quiles): Molenaar's Muziekcentrale N.V. (CD) MBS-17,
MBS-31.0017.65
Viebig and the Berlin Philharmonic Orchestra (J. Nemeti):
Ultraphone (78) EP-521

192. *Suite española No. 1*, "Sevilla (Sevillanas)."

Guillermo Cases and the Orquesta de Conciertos de Buenos
   Aires: Tempo (LP) 2256
José María Franco and the Orquesta Sinfónica Española (Pilar
   López, footwork): Capitol (LP) P-18020; La Voz de su Amo
   (LP) LDLP-1011, (45) 7EPL-13028
Gelabert and the Gramophone Symphony Orchestra:
   Gramophone/His Master's Voice (78) DB-1277
Harry Horlick and the Decca Concert Orchestra (E. F. Arbós):
   Decca (LP) DL-5070, (78) 18089 in DM-A-150
Koninklijke Militaire Kapel (arr. for band by Juan Vicente Mas
   Quiles): Molenaar's Muziekcentrale N.V. (CD) MBS-17,
   MBS-31.0017.65
"La Argentinita" (arr. for orchestra and castanets):
   Gramophone/His Master's Voice (78) K-5497
Rafael Martínez and the Orquesta Sinfónica Española:
   Hispavox/Montilla (LP) FM-16; Montilla (LP) 29007
Antonia Mercé ("La Argentina") (arr. for orchestra and
   castanets): Odeon (LP) OD-1023, (78) 188755
José Olmedo and the Orquesta Lírica "Audio Museum" de
   Madrid: Telefunken (LP) 270-TC-023, 65029, LGM-65029,
   TC-8027, TLD-10022
Roberti y Típica Sevilla: Odeon (78) 173503
Regino Sáinz de la Maza and the Orquesta Lírica: Movieplay
   (LP) M-18040
Ricardo Villa and the Banda Municipal de Madrid: Odeon (78)
   177047, 177228

193. *Suite española No. 1*, "Cádiz (Canción)."

Guillermo Cases and the Orquesta de Conciertos de Buenos
   Aires: Tempo (LP) 2256
José María Franco and the Orquesta Sinfónica Española (Pilar
   López, footwork): Capitol (LP) P-18020; La Voz de su Amo
   (LP) LDLP-1011, (45) 7EPL-13029
Harry Horlick and the Decca Concert Orchestra (E. F. Arbós):
   Decca (LP) DL-5070, (78) 18089 in DM-A-150
Enrique Jordá and the Orquesta de Conciertos de Madrid:
   Hispavox (LP) S-60.309/10/11

"La Argentinita" (arr. for orchestra and castanets):
Gramophone/His Master's Voice (78) GY-344, K-5497
Germán Lago and the Orquesta Ibérica de Madrid (orchestra of
guitars and lutes) (G. Lago): Odeon (78) 194270, 203323
Teodoro Murua and the Banda Municipal de Irún: Columbia (45)
SCGE-80042
José Olmedo and the Orquesta Lírica "Audio Museum" de
Madrid: Telefunken (LP) 270-TC-023, 65029, LGM-65029,
TC-8027, TLD-10022
Orchestra Locatelli: Columbia (78) DF-2000
Regino Sáinz de la Maza and the Orquesta Lírica: Movieplay
(LP) M-18040
Vladimir Spivakov and the Moscow Virtuosi (R. Frühbeck de
Burgos): RCA (CD) 09026-68185-2

194. *Suite española No. 1*, "Asturias (Leyenda)."

Enrique Fernández Arbós and the Orquesta Sinfónica de Madrid
(E. F. Arbós): Columbia (78) AG-7005
Enrique Jordá and the Orquesta de Conciertos de Madrid (O.
Esplà): Hispavox (LP) 10-209, CT-69-2
Germán Lago and the Orquesta Ibérica de Madrid (orchestra of
guitars and lutes) (G. Lago): Regal (LP) 33-LC-1013
J. L. Lloret and the Orquesta Cámara de Madrid: Montilla (LP)
29003, FM-22

195. *Suite española No. 1*, "Aragón (Fantasía)."

Enrique Jordá and the Orquesta de Conciertos de Madrid (O.
Esplà): Hispavox (LP) 10-209, CT-69-2, S-60.309/10/11
José Olmedo and the Orquesta Lírica "Audio Museum" de
Madrid: Telefunken (LP) 270-TC-023, 65029, LGM-65029,
TC-8027, TLD-10022
Roberti y Típica Sevilla: Odeon (78) 183981, 194924, 203600
Regino Sáinz de la Maza and the Orquesta Lírica: Movieplay
(LP) M-18040

196. *Suite española No. 1*, "Castilla (Seguidillas)."

Guillermo Cases and the Orquesta de Conciertos de Buenos
   Aires: Tempo (LP) 2256
Indalecio Cisneros and the Gran Orquesta Sinfónica (with R.
   Córdoba, footwork, and C. Mora, clapping): Columbia (45)
   SCGE-80059
José María Franco and the Orquesta de Conciertos de Madrid
   (Oscar Esplà): Hispavox (LP) S-20.098
Harry Horlick and the Decca Concert Orchestra (E. F. Arbós):
   Decca (78) 18088 in DM-A-150
Enrique Jordá and the Orquesta de Conciertos de Madrid (O.
   Esplà): Hispavox (LP) 10-209, CT-69-2, S-60.309/10/11
José Olmedo and the Orquesta Lírica "Audio Museum" de
   Madrid: Telefunken (LP) 270-TC-023, 65029, LGM-65029,
   TC-8027, TLD-10022
Regino Sáinz de la Maza and the Orquesta Lírica: Movieplay
   (LP) M-18040

197. *Recuerdos de viaje*, "Puerta de tierra (Bolero)."

Guillermo Cases and the Orquesta Teatro Colón de Buenos
   Aires: Odeon (LP) OD-1018
José María Franco and the Orquesta de Conciertos de Madrid (O.
   Esplà): Hispavox (LP) S-20.098
J. L. Lloret and the Orquesta Cámara de Madrid: Montilla (LP)
   29003, FM-22
José Olmedo and the Orquesta Lírica "Audio Museum" de
   Madrid: Telefunken (LP) 270-TC-023, 65029, LGM-65029,
   TC-8027, TLD-10022
Roberti y Típica Sevilla: Odeon (78) 183981, 194924, 203615
Regino Sáinz de la Maza and the Orquesta Lírica: Movieplay
   (LP) M-18040

198. *Recuerdos de viaje*, "Rumores de la caleta (Malagueña)."

Rafael Ferrer and the Orquesta Sinfónica Española: Angel (LP)
   65008; Regal (LP) 33-LCX-104, (45) SEDL-108
Harry Horlick and the Decca Concert Orchestra: Decca (LP) DL-
   5070, (78) 18086 in DM-A-150

Federico Moreno Torroba and the Orquesta Teatro de la
    Zarzuela de Madrid: Columbia (LP) CCL-35028; Decca
    (LP) DL-9789
José Olmedo and the Orquesta Lírica "Audio Museum" de
    Madrid: Telefunken (LP) 270-TC-023, 65029, LGM-65029,
    TC-8027, TLD-10022
Regino Sáinz de la Maza and the Orquesta Lírica: Movieplay
    (LP) M-18040

199. *Douze Pièces caractéristiques pour piano* [*Doce piezas
      características*], "Torre Bermeja (Serenata)."

      Rafael Ferrer and the Orquesta Sinfónica Española: Angel (LP)
          65008; Cetra (LP) 70.008; Regal (LP) 33-LCX-104, (45)
          SEDL-108
      Federico Moreno Torroba and the Orquesta Teatro de la
          Zarzuela de Madrid: Columbia (LP) CCL-350222; Decca
          (LP) DL-9763
      José Olmedo and the Orquesta Lírica "Audio Museum" de
          Madrid: Telefunken (LP) 270-TC-023, 65029, LGM-65029,
          TC-8027, TLD-10022
      Roberti y Típica Sevilla: Odeon (78) 173503, 177686, 214503
      Regino Sáinz de la Maza and the Orquesta Lírica: Movieplay
          (LP) M-18040

200. *España: Six Feuilles d'album* [*España: Seis hojas de album*],
      "Tango."

      Lars Almgren and the Palm Court Orchestra of the Stockholm
          Philharmonic: Bluebell (CD) ABCD-007
      Stanley Black and the Mantovani Orchestra: Bainbridge (CD)
          BBR-6296
      Evgueni Bushkov and the Moscow Concertina: Discover
          International (CD) DICD-920129
      Carmen Dragon and the Hollywood Bowl Orchestra: Capitol
          (LP) P-8314
      Barnabas von Geczi Orchestra: Gramophone/His Master's Voice
          (78) DA-4353
      William Harrison and the Stuttgart Festival Band: Music Minus
          One (LP) 7043

Harry Horlick and the Decca Concert Orchestra: Decca (LP) DL-5070, (78) 18086 in DM-A-150
Claude Lazzaro Orchestra: Musical Heritage Society (CS) MHC-6908-T, (LP) MHS-4098-M
Mantovani and His Orchestra: London (LP) LL-3269, PS-269
Orchestra José Albéniz: Columbia (LP) CCL-35030; Decca (LP) 8265
Original Salon-Ensemble Prima Carezza: Tudor (CD) 766
Franck Pourcel and His Orchestra (F. Pourcel): Angel (LP) DS-37751
Albert Semperi (arr. for piano and orchestra): Capitol (LP) T-10144
Lucero Teno (castanets) with Miguel Ramos conducting a chamber orchestra (M. Ramos): Musical Heritage Society (LP) MHS-972

201. *Mallorca (Barcarola)*.

J. L. Lloret and the Orquesta Teatro de la Zarzuela de Madrid: Montilla (LP) 29003, FM-22
Roberti y Típica Sevilla: Odeon (78) 177686, 214503
Sexteto Eduardo Toldrá: Pathé (78) 54556

202. *Chants d'Espagne [Cantos de España]*, "Orientale."

Roberti y Típica Sevilla: Odeon (78) 194654, 203600

203. *Chants d'Espagne [Cantos de España]*, "Sous le palmier."

Roberti y Típica Sevilla: Odeon (78) 194654, 194881, 203615

204. *Chants d'Espagne [Cantos de España]*, "Córdoba."

Enrique Bátiz and the Orquesta Sinfónica del Estado de México (R. Frühbeck de Burgos): ASV (CD) CDA-888
Capdevila and the Odeon Orchestra: Odeon (78) 194853, 203460
José María Franco and the Orquesta Sinfónica Española (Pilar López, footwork): Capitol (LP) P-18020; La Voz de su Amo (LP) LDLP-1011, (45) 7EPL-13029

Rafael Frühbeck de Burgos and the New Philharmonia Orchestra
   (R. Frühbeck de Burgos): Alhambra (LP) SCLL-14081;
   Zacosa (LP) GML-2002
Rafael Frühbeck de Burgos and the Philharmonia Orchestra (R.
   Frühbeck de Burgos): London (CD) 433905-2, (LP) CS-
   6581
Gelabert and the Gramophone Symphony Orchestra:
   Gramophone/His Master's Voice (78) AF-184
Harry Horlick and the Decca Concert Orchestra: Decca (LP) DL-
   5070, (78) 18087 in DM A-150
Enrique Jordá and the Orquesta de Conciertos de Madrid:
   Hispavox (LP) S-20.078, S-60.309/10/11
André Kostelanetz and His Orchestra: Columbia (LP) CL-943;
   Sony (CD) SFK-47279, (CS) SFT-47279
"La Argentinita" (arr. for orchestra and castanets):
   Gramophone/His Master's Voice (78) K-5640
Germán Lago and the Orquesta Ibérica de Madrid (orchestra of
   guitars and lutes) (G. Lago): Regal (LP) 33-LC-1013
J. L. Lloret and the Orquesta Cámara de Madrid: Montilla (LP)
   29003, FM-22
Rager Machado and the Orquesta Teatro de la Zarzuela de
   Madrid, with the José Greco Dance Co.: Columbia (LP)
   CCL-35002; Decca (LP) DL-9757
Antonia Mercé ("La Argentina") (arr. for orchestra and
   castanets): Odeon (LP) OD-1023
Charles O'Connell and the Victor Symphony Orchestra (C.
   O'Connell): RCA (78) 36318
Orquestra Toldrá: Pathé (78) 54628
Ricardo Villa and the Banda Municipal de Madrid: Odeon (78)
   121045, 177052

205. *Chants d'Espagne* [*Cantos de España*], "Seguidillas."

Indalecio Cisneros and the Gran Orquesta Sinfónica (with R.
   Córdoba, footwork, and C. Mora, clapping): Columbia (LP)
   CCL-32005
Carmen Dragon and the Hollywood Bowl Orchestra: Capitol
   (LP) P-8314

Harry Horlick and the Decca Concert Orchestra: Decca (LP) DL-5070

206. *Iberia*, orchestrated by Enrique Fernández Arbós ("Evocación," "El puerto," "Fête-Dieu à Séville," "Triana," "El Albaicín" only; see also under those individual titles).

Ernest Ansermet and the Orchestre de la Suisse Romande: Ace of Diamonds (LP) SDD-180; Decca (LP) 6594116.9, SDD-180; London (CD) 433905-2, (CS) STS5-15374, (LP) CM-9263, CS-6194, STS-15374

Enrique Fernández Arbós and the Orquesta Sinfónica de Madrid: InSyc (CS) 4141; VAI Audio (CD) VAIA-1046-F

Ataúlfo Argenta and the Orchestre de la Société des Concerts du Conservatoire de Paris: Columbia (LP) C-7562, CCL-3200; Decca (LP) LXT-2889; Everest (LP) 3325, SDBR-3325; London (LP) LL-921

Daniel Barenboim and the Orchestre de Paris: Erato (CD) 2292-45266-2, D-103121, ECD 88255, ZK-45266, (CS) 2292-45266-4, MCE-75316, (LP) NUM-75316

Enrique Bátiz and the London Symphony Orchestra: Angel (LP) S-37878; EMI (CD) CDC-7-49405-2; EMI/Angel (CS) 4XS-37878; IMG/Pickwick (CD) IMGCD-1607

Enrique Bátiz and the Orquesta Sinfónica del Estado de México: ASV (CD) DCA-888

Herbert L. Carter and the East Carolina Symphonic Band (L. Caillet): Silver Crest (LP) CBD-69-8

Antal Doráti and the Minneapolis Symphony Orchestra: Mercury (CD) 434-388, (LP) MG-50146, SR-90007, SRI-75101; Mercury Wing (LP) SRW-18085, WC-18063

Anatole Fistoulari and the London Symphony Orchestra: Parlophon (LP) PMC-1006

Jean Fournet and the Orchestre des Concerts Lamoureux: Epic (LP) LC-3068

Manuel Galduf and the Orquesta de Valencia: Audivis Valois (CD) V-4661

Eugene Goosens and the Philharmonia Orchestra: Capitol (LP) G-7129; His Master's Voice (LP) ALP-1470

Kenneth Jean and the Slovak Radio Symphony Orchestra (all
except "El puerto"): Naxos (CD) 8.550174

Eduardo Mata and the Dallas Symphony Orchestra: Pro-Arte
(CD) CDS-581

Charles Munch and the Orchestre National de France: Concert
Hall (LP) 171218/6; Nonesuch (LP) H-71189

Eugene Ormandy and the Philadelphia Orchestra: Columbia (LP)
CL-921

Gaston Poulet and the London Symphony Orchestra: Crowell-
Collier Record Guild (LP) G-148; MGM (LP) E-3073;
Odeon (LP) ODX-137

Manuel Rosenthal and the Orchestre du Théâtre National de
l'Opera de Paris: Adès (CD) ADE-202502; Westminster
(LP) XWN-18798

Franz Schultz and the Berliner Rundfunk Sinfonie-Orchester:
Regent (LP) MG-5023

George Sebastian and the Music Treasures Philharmonic
Symphony: Music Treasures of the World (LP) MT-502

George Sebastian and the Orchestre des Concerts Colonne:
Urania (LP) URLP-7085

Vicente Spiteri and the Orquesta Sinfónica de Madrid: Philips
(LP) RPF-761/2,3,4

Eduardo Toldrá and the Orchestre des Concerts Lamoureux:
Epic (LP) 3068; Philips (LP) A-00403-L, N-00699

Yan Pascal Tortelier and the Philharmonia Orchestra: Chandos
(CD) CHAN-8904, (CS) ABTD-1513

Jörg Peter Weigle and the Dresden Philharmonic Orchestra:
Berlin Classics (CD) 9142

207. *Iberia*, orchestrated by Carlos Surinach (complements Arbós).

Jean Morel and the Orchestre du Conservatoire de Paris: RCA
Victor (LP) LM-6094, LSC-6094

208. *Iberia*, orchestrations by Enrique Fernández Arbós and Carlos
Surinach (complete).

Eugene Ormandy and the Philadelphia Orchestra: Columbia (LP)
M2L-237 (ML-5017/18)

209. *Iberia*, "Evocación."

Enrique Fernández Arbós and the Orquesta Sinfónica de Madrid (E. F. Arbós): Columbia (78) 264515, 67708-D, 9605, AG-8009

Pedro de Freitas-Branco and the Orchestre Lamoureux (E. F. Arbós): Gramophone/His Master's Voice (78) DB-11216

Rafael Frühbeck de Burgos and the Orchestre de la Société des Concerts du Conservatoire de Paris: EMI (LP) 1-J-053-00.624

Harry Horlick and the Decca Concert Orchestra (E. F. Arbós): Decca (LP) DL-5070, (78) 18088 in DM-A-150

Juan Lamote de Grignon and the Banda Municipal de Barcelona: Gramophone/His Master's Voice (78) AB-281

George Sebastian and the Orchestre des Concerts Colonne (E. F. Arbós): Urania (LP) URLP-7130

210. *Iberia*, "El puerto."

Enrique Fernández Arbós and the Orquesta Sinfónica de Madrid (E. F. Arbós): Columbia (78) 52068X, 67708-D, 9603, AG-8042

Pedro de Freitas-Branco and the Orchestre Lamoureux (E. F. Arbós): Gramophone/His Master's Voice (78) DB-11216

Enrique Jordá and the Orchestre du Conservatoire de Paris (E. F. Arbós): Decca (LP) LW-5055, LXT-2521; London (LP) LD-9042

George Sebastian and the Orchestre des Concerts Colonne (E. F. Arbós): American Recording Society (LP) MP-124; Nixa (LP) ULP-9085; Urania (LP) URLP-7130

211. *Iberia*, "Fête-Dieu à Séville" ["El Corpus en Sevilla"].

Enrique Fernández Arbós and the Orquesta Sinfónica de Madrid (E. F. Arbós): Columbia (78) 264514, 67709-D, 9604, AG-8041

Matthias Bamert and the BBC Philharmonic: Chandos (CD) CHAN-9349

Antal Doráti and the Minneapolis Symphony Orchestra (E. F. Arbós): Mercury (CD) 434-388, (LP) SR-90361

Frederick Fennell and the Dallas Wind Symphony Orchestra (L. Cailliet): Reference (CD) RR-52CD, RR-S3CD

Pedro de Freitas-Branco and the Orchestre Lamoureux (E. F. Arbós): Gramophone/His Master's Voice (78) DB-11219

Rafael Frühbeck de Burgos and the Orchestre de la Société des Concerts du Conservatoire de Paris: EMI (LP) 1-J-053-00.624

Morton Gould and the London Symphony Orchestra (E. F. Arbós): Chalfont (LP) SDG-302

André Kostelanetz and His Orchestra: Columbia (LP) CL-943

Erich Kunzel and the Cincinnati Pops Orchestra (L. Stokowski): Telarc (CD) CD-80129, CD-80338

Juan Lamote de Grignon and the Banda Municipal de Barcelona: Gramophone/His Master's Voice (78) AB-282

Roy Newsome and the Sun Life Stanshawe Band (arr. for brass band by R. Newsome): Chandos (LP) BBR-1005

Fritz Reiner and the Chicago Symphony Orchestra (E. F. Arbós): Chesky (LP) RC–9; RCA (CD) 09026-62586-2, BVCC-1035, RCD-15404, (CS) 09026-62586-4, AGK-11332, (LP) AGL-11332, LM-2230, LSC-2230

William Revelli and the University of Michigan Symphony Band (L. Cailliet): Golden Crest (LP) CRS-4202

Artur Rodzinski and the Royal Philharmonic Orchestra (E. F. Arbós): Capitol (LP) SG-7176; EMI (CD) 7243-5-68742-0, CDZB-68742; Seraphim (LP) S-60021

George Sebastian and the Orchestre des Concerts Colonne (E. F. Arbós): Nixa (LP) ULP-9085; Urania (LP) URLP-7130

Leopold Stokowski and the National Philharmonic Orchestra (L. Stokowski): Columbia (CS) MT-34543, (LP) M-34543

Leopold Stokowski and the Philadelphia Orchestra (L. Stokowski): Biddulph (CD) 047; Gramophone/His Master's Voice (78) AB-675, D-1888; Pearl (CD) GEMM-9276; RCA (78) 7158

Unknown orchestra: RCA (LP) LE-6003

212. *Iberia,* "Rondeña."

Carlos Surinach and L'Orchestre Radio-Symphonique de Paris (C. Surinach): Montilla (CD) MNT-3018, (LP) FM-162

213. *Iberia*, "Almería."

Carlos Surinach and the Orchestre Radio-Symphonique de Paris:
Montilla (LP) FM-141; Musidisc (LP) 30-RC-776/7

214. *Iberia*, "Triana."

Enrique Fernández Arbós and the Orquesta Sinfónica de Madrid
(E. F. Arbós): Columbia (78) 264513, 67710-D, 9603, AG-
8039
Arthur Fiedler and the Boston Promenade Orchestra (E. F.
Arbós): La Voz de su Amo (LP) 7ERL-1053; RCA Victor
(78) 12-0920; Victor (45) 49-0437
José María Franco and the Orquesta Sinfónica Española (Pilar
López, footwork): Capitol (LP) P-18020; La Voz de su Amo
(LP) LDLP-1011, (45) 7EPL-13028
Pedro de Freitas-Branco and the Orchestre Lamoureux (E. F.
Arbós): Gramophone/His Master's Voice (78) DB-11217
Rafael Frühbeck de Burgos and the Orchestre de la Société des
Concerts du Conservatoire de Paris: EMI (LP) 1-J-053-
00.624
Eugene Goosens and the New Light Symphony (E. F. Arbós):
Gramophone/His Master's Voice (78) C-1554
Morton Gould and the London Symphony Orchestra (E. F.
Arbós): Chalfont (LP) SDG-302
Enrique Jordá and the Orchestre du Conservatoire de Paris (E. F.
Arbós): Decca (LP) LW-5055, LXT-2521; London (LP)
LD-9042
Juan Lamote de Grignon and the Banda Municipal de Barcelona:
Gramophone/His Master's Voice (78) AB-281
Fritz Reiner and the Chicago Symphony Orchestra (E. F. Arbós):
Chesky (LP) RC–9; RCA (CD) 09026-62586-2, BVCC-
1035, RCD-15404, (CS) 09026-62586-4, AGK-11332, (LP)
AGL-11332, LSC-2230
Artur Rodzinski and the Royal Philharmonic Orchestra: EMI
(CD) 7243-5-68742-0, CDZB-68742
George Sebastian and the Orchestre des Concerts Colonne (E. F.
Arbós): American Recording Society (LP) MP-124; Nixa
(LP) ULP-9085; Urania (LP) URLP-7130

Felix Slatkin and the Hollywood Bowl Orchestra (E. F. Arbós):
Capitol (LP) P-8357, SP-8679

215. *Iberia,* "El Albaicín."

Enrique Fernández Arbós and the Orquesta Sinfónica de Madrid
(E. F. Arbós): Columbia (78) AG-8001
F. Delta and the Orquesta Sinfónica Española (with footwork by
Pilar López, Paco de Ronda, and Antonio Montoya): Capitol
(LP) 18003; La Voz de su Amo (LP) LCLP-102, (45) 7EPL-
13041
Pedro de Freitas-Branco and the Orchestre Lamoureux (E. F.
Arbós): Gramophone/His Master's Voice (78) DB-11217/8
George Sebastian and the Orchestre des Concerts Colonne (E. F.
Arbós): American Recording Society (LP) MP-124; Nixa
(LP) ULP-9085; Urania (LP) URLP-7130

216. *Iberia,* "El polo."

Carlos Surinach and the Orchestre Radio-Symphonique de Paris
(C. Surinach): Montilla (LP) FM-142; Musidisc (LP) 30-
RC-776/7

217. *Iberia,* "Lavapies."

Carlos Surinach and L'Orchestre Radio-Symphonique de Paris
(C. Surinach): Montilla (CD) MNT-3018, (LP) FM-162

218. *Iberia,* "Málaga."

Carlos Surinach and the Orchestre Radio-Symphonique de Paris:
Montilla (LP) FM-141; Musidisc (LP) 30-RC-776/7; Zacosa
(LP) GML-2006

219. *Iberia,* "Jerez."

Carlos Surinach and L'Orchestre Radio-Symphonique de Paris
(C. Surinach): Montilla (CD) MNT-3018, (LP) FM-162

220. *Iberia,* "Eritaña."

José María Franco and the Orquesta Sinfónica Española (Pilar López, footwork): Capitol (LP) P-18020; La Voz de su Amo (LP) LDLP-1011, (45) 7EPL-13029

Carlos Surinach and the Orchestre Radio-Symphonique de Paris: Montilla (LP) FM-141; Musidisc (LP) 30-RC-776/7

221. *Navarra*, orchestrated by Enrique Fernández Arbós.

Ernest Ansermet and the Orchestre de la Suisse Romande: Ace of Diamonds (LP) SDD-180; Decca (LP) 6594116.9, SDD-180; London (CD) 433905-2-LM2, (LP) CM-9263, CS-6194, STS-15374

Enrique Fernández Arbós and the Orquesta Sinfónica de Madrid: Columbia (78) 264501, 52052X, 67821-D, AG-8040, D-12540; InSyc (CS) 4141

Ataúlfo Argenta and the Orquesta Nacional de España: Alhambra (LP) MCC-30042; Columbia (LP) SCLL-14027; Everest (LP) 3325; London (LP) LL-1585; Zacosa (LP) GML-2004; Zafiro (LP) ZTV-37

Enrique Bátiz and the London Symphony Orchestra: Angel (LP) S-37878; EMI (CD) CDC-7-49405-2; EMI/Angel (CS) 4XS-37878; IMG/Pickwick (CD) IMGCD-1607

Enrique Bátiz and the Orquesta Sinfónica del Estado de México: ASV (CD) DCA-888

Coppola and the Orchestre de la Société des Concerts du Conservatoire de Paris (shortened version): Gramophone/His Master's Voice (78) DB-4815

Pedro de Freitas-Branco and the Orchestre Lamoureux: Gramophone/His Master's Voice (78) DB-11218

Fritz Reiner and the Chicago Symphony Orchestra: Chesky (LP) RC–9; RCA (CD) 09026-62586-2, BVCC-1035, RCD-15404, (CS) 09026-62586-4, AGK-11332, (LP) AGL-11332, LSC-2230

Artur Rodzinski and the Royal Philharmonic Orchestra: Capitol (LP) SG-7176; EMI (CD) 7243-5-68742-0, CDZB-68742; Seraphim (LP) S-60021

Carlos Surinach and the Orchestre Radio-Symphonique de Paris: Musidisc (LP) 30-RC-776/7; Zacosa (LP) GML-2006

Organ

222. *España: Six Feuilles d'album* [*España: Seis hojas de album*], "Tango."

   Kees Van Houten: Emergo (CD) 3996

223. *España: Six Feuilles d'album* [*España: Seis hojas de album*], "Malagueña."

   Kees Van Houten: Emergo (CD) 3996

Piano Quintet

224. *España: Six Feuilles d'album* [*España: Seis hojas de album*], "Tango."

   I Salonisti: EMI/Deutsche Harmonia Mundi (CD) CDC-7-47536-2
   Viveza: Skylark (CD) 9001-CD

Saxophone(s)

225. *Suite española No. 1,* "Sevilla (Sevillanas)."

   G. Chauvet, F. L'Homme, M. Mule, P. Romby: Clarinet Classics (CD) CC-0013
   Chicago Saxophone Quartet (M. Mule): Centaur (CD) CRC-2086
   Quatuor "Adolphe Sax" de Paris: Philips (LP) N-00616-R
   Quatuor de la Garde Republicaine de Paris: Columbia (78) DF-1461

226. *Suite española No. 1,* "Asturias (Leyenda)."

   Steve Douglas (with an instrumental ensemble): Mercury (LP) SR-61217

227. *Rêves* [*Sueños*], "Berceuse."

   Chicago Saxophone Quartet (M. Mule): Brewster Records (CS) BRS-184, (LP) BRS-184

New York Saxophone Quartet: Stash (CD) ST-CD-15, (LP) ST-220
Roth Saxophone Quartet (M. Mule): Pan Extra (CD) 510-529

228. *Rêves* [*Sueños*], "Chant d'amour."

Chicago Saxophone Quartet (M. Mule): Brewster Records (CS) BRS-184, (LP) BRS-184
New York Saxophone Quartet: New York Saxophone Quartet (LP) 022880; Stash (CD) ST-CD-15, (LP) ST-210
Paul Brodie Saxophone Quartet: Golden Crest (LP) CRSQ-4154
Quatuor "Adolphe Sax" de Paris: Philips (LP) N-00616-R
Roth Saxophone Quartet (M. Mule): Pan Extra (CD) 510-529

229. *Album of Miniatures* [*Les Saisons*] (three selections).

Northern Saxophone Quartet (M. Mule): Foxglove (LP) FOX-013

230. *Album of Miniatures* [*Les Saisons*], "L'Éte."

Chicago Saxophone Quartet (M. Mule): Brewster Records (CS) BRS-184, (LP) BRS-184

231. *Album of Miniatures* [*Les Saisons*], "L'Hiver."

Roth Saxophone Quartet (M. Mule): Pan Extra (CD) 510-529

Saxophone and Piano

232. *España: Six Feuilles d'album* [*España: Seis hojas de album*], "Tango."

Paul Brodie and Myriam Shechter: Golden Crest (LP) RE-7103; Musica Viva (CD) MVCD-1005 (LP) MVC-1005

String Bass and Guitar

233. *Mallorca.*

Frano Kakarigi and Hiroto Yamaya: S-Tone (CD) AH-0004-2231

String Bass and Piano

234. *España: Six Feuilles d'album* [*España: Seis hojas de album*], "Malagueña."

Jorma Katrama and Margit Rahkonen: Finlandia (CD) 4509-95605-2; Fuga (LP) 3025

Trombone and Piano

235. *España: Six Feuilles d'album* [*España: Seis hojas de album*], "Malagueña."

Kyryl Ribarski and Milica Sperovic-Ribarski: Discover (CD) DICD-920188

Viola and Piano

236. *Recuerdos de viaje*, "Puerta de tierra (Bolero)."

Ellen Rose and Katherine Collier: Centaur (CD) CRC-2315

Violin and Accordion

237. *España: Six Feuilles d'album* [*España: Seis hojas de album*], "Tango."

Violacord: Aurophon (LP) AU-11-187

Violin and Guitar

238. *España: Six Feuilles d'album* [*España: Seis hojas de album*], "Tango."

Jaap Van Zweden and Robby Favery: Attacca (LP) Babel-8424-9

239. *Chants d'Espagne* [*Cantos de España*], "Córdoba."

Alma Duo (Phyllis Kamrin and Michael Goldberg): Kameleon (CD) KA-9001

Violin and Orchestra

240. *Suite española No. 1* "Granada (Serenata)"

Josef Suk and the Prague Chamber Ensemble: Lotos (CD) LT-0023

Violin and Piano

241. *Suite española No. 1*, "Sevilla (Sevillanas)."

Jascha Heifetz and Arpad Sandor: EMI (CD) ZDHB-64929; Gramophone/His Master's Voice (78) DB-2220; Pearl (CD) GEMM-CD-9023; RCA (CD) 61733
Leonid Kogan and Andrei Mitnik or Arnold Kaplan (J. Heifetz): Westminster (LP) number not available on WorldCat
Itzhak Perlman and Samuel Sanders: EMI/Angel (CD) CDC-49604, (CS) 4DS-49604

242. *Suite española No. 1*, "Cádiz (Canción)."

Lees Kooper and Mary Louise Boehm: Dot (CS) DLP-3040

243. *Suite española No. 1*, "Aragón (Fantasía)."

Samuel Dushkin and Max Pirani: Gramophone/His Master's Voice (78) E-523

244. *Recuerdos de viaje*, "Rumores de la caleta (Malagueña)."

Giucci and Miguel Raucheisen: Telefunken (78) A-2109
Ida Haendel and Josef Hassid (F. Kreisler): Pearl (CD) GEMM-CD-9939
Ida Haendel and Adela Kotowska: Columbia (78) RG-120039; Decca (78) K-1073; Odeon (78) 263772
Fritz Kreisler and Carl Lamson: Gramophone/His Master's Voice (78) DA-1354; Pearl (CD) GEMM-9324; RCA (78) 1244
Dmitry Sitkovetsky and Pavel Gililov (F. Kreisler): Virgin (CD) VC7-90842-2, (CS) VC7-90842-4
Jacques Thibaud and Tasso Janapolou: Gramophone/His Master's Voice (78) DB-2011

245. *España: Six Feuilles d'album [España: Seis hojas de album]*, "Tango."

Khalida Akhtyamova and Leonid Blok: Melodiya (LP) C10-
15537, ROCT-5289-88
Alfredo Campoli and Norihiko Wada: Decca (LP) LW-5180,
(78) T-2512; London (LP) STS-15239
Miguel Candela (pianist unknown): Columbia (78) LF-32
Peter Csaba and Zoltan Kocsis (F. Kreisler): Hungaroton (LP)
SLPX-12437
Yelly d'Aranyi (pianist unknown): Columbia (78) 2144-C
Samuel Dushkin and Max Pirani: Gramophone/His Master's
Voice (78) E-523
Mischa Elman and Joseph Bonime (M. Elman): Biddulph (CD)
LAB-037
Devy Erlih and F. Bureau: Ducretet (LP) DTL-93106
Simone Filon: Polydor (78) PD-524288
J. Fournier and A. Collard: Vega (LP) C-30-A-38
Zino Francescatti and Arthur Balsam: Columbia (LP) ML-4310;
Philips (LP) N-02101-L, S-06602
Ida Haendel and Noel Newton-Wood (F. Kreisler): Pearl (CD)
GEMM-CD-9939
Kornelija Kaliauskaite and Halina Znaidzilauskaite (S.
Duskinas): Melodiya (LP) S10-22741-000
Kimon Daeshik Kang and Margit Rahkonen (F. Kreisler):
Nimbus (CD) NI-5358
Ani Kavafian and Charles Wadsworth (F. Kreisler): Musical
Heritage Society (LP) MHS-3760
David Kim and Gail Niwa (F. Kreisler): SKC (CD) SKCD-C-
0382
Fritz Kreisler and Carl Lamson (F. Kreisler): Gramophone/His
Master's Voice (78) DA-1009, DA-1354; Pearl (CD)
GEMM-CD-9324; RCA (78) 1339
Georg Kulenkampff and Franz Rupp: Discopaedia (LP) MB-
1015; Telefunken (78) A-2551
T. Magyatr and W. Hielkema: Philips (LP) S-06049-R
Shlomo Mintz and Clifford Benson (F. Kreisler): Deutsche
Grammophon (CS) 3301-305, (LP) 2531-305
Roland Muller and Philippe Reymond: Sonpact (CD) SPT-95016
Itzhak Perlman and Samuel Sanders (F. Kreisler): Angel (CS)
4XS-37171, (LP) S-37171

Manuel Quiroga and Mme. Quiroga (F. Kreisler): Pathé (78) X-9938; Symposium (CD) SYM-1131
Benno Rabinof and Sylvia Rabinof (F. Kreisler): Decca (LP) DL-710-101
Dmitry Sitkovetsky and Bruno Canino (F. Kreisler): Orfeo (CD) C-048-831-A, (LP) S-048831
Henryk Szeryng and Tasso Janapolou: Odeon (LP) ODX-129
Mela Tenenbaum and Anton Neli: Ess.a.y (CD) CD-1042
Jacques Thibaud and Tasso Janapolou: Appian Publications and Recordings (CD) APR-7028; Gramophone/His Master's Voice (78) DA-1339; Music Memoria (CD) MMA-30321; Pearl (CD) GEMM-CD-BVA-1
Heinz Trutzschler and Lillian Rogers Gilbreath: World Wide Records (LP) W.W.-1045-B
Ingolf Turban and Jean-Jacques Dünki: Claves (CD) CD-508917
Pinchas Zukerman and Marc Neikrug: Philips (CD) 416158-2, (CS) 416158-4, (LP) 416158-1
Pinchas Zukerman and Lawrence Smith: Columbia (LP) M-31378

246. *España: Six Feuilles d'album* [*España: Seis hojas de album*], "Malagueña."

Augustín León Ara and Felix Lavilla (F. Kreisler): Zacosa (LP) GML-2033
Peter Csaba and Zoltan Kocsis (F. Kreisler): Hungaroton (LP) SLPX-12437
Ida Haendel and Noel Newton-Wood: Pearl (CD) GEMM-9939
Fritz Kreisler and Carl Lamson (F. Kreisler): Discopaedia (LP) MB-1012; Pearl (CD) GEMM-CD-9324
Itzhak Perlman and Samuel Sanders (F. Kreisler): EMI (CD) CDM-7-63533-2, EG-63533, (CS) EG-63533
Michel Schwalbe and Horst Kurzbach: Hör zu (LP) SHZE-320
Dmitry Sitkovetsky and Pavel Gililov (F. Kreisler): Virgin (CD) VC7-90842-2, (CS) VC7-90842-4
Jacques Thibaud and Tasso Janapolou: Appian Publications and Recordings (CD) APR-7028; Music Memoria (CD) MMA-30321
Unknown performer: His Master's Voice (LP) 1C-037-46-176

247. *Rêves* [*Sueños*], "Chant d'amour."

Salvatore Accardo and Bruno Canino: EMI/His Master's Voice
(LP) EL-27-0186-1, (CS) E-27-0186-4
David Oistrakh and V. Topilin or Vladimir Yampolsky (entitled
"Love Song"): Colosseum (LP) 105, CRLP-249, CRLP-
10050; Melodiya (CD) 40710, (LP) 33D-028807/8; Monitor
(CD) MCD-72003, (LP) MC-2003

248. *Iberia*, "Evocación."

Lees Kooper and Mary Louise Boehm: Dot (CS) DLP-3040

249. *Iberia*, "El puerto."

Leonid Kogan and Andrei Mitnik or Arnold Kaplan (J. Heifetz):
Westminster (LP) no number available on WorldCat

250. *Iberia*, "Triana."

Lees Kooper and Mary Louise Boehm: Dot (CS) DLP-3040

Voice and Piano or Orchestra

251. *Suite española No. 1* "Granada (Serenata)," arranged by Cuenca.

J. Blanch (pianist unknown): Columbia (78) 4713
Conchita Supervía (pianist unknown): Lebendige Vergangenheit
(LP) LV-150; Odeon (78) 121146; Pathé (78) R-20130;
Pearl (CD) GEMM-9975
Conchita Velázquez (pianist unknown): Regal (78) PKX-3015

252. *Suite española No. 1* "Cádiz (Canción)," arranged by Cuenca.

Conchita Velázquez (pianist unknown): Regal (78) PKX-3015

253. *Douze Pièces caractéristiques pour piano* [*Doce piezas
características*], "Torre Bermeja (Serenata)."

Consuelo Rubio and the Orquesta Teatro de la Zarzuela de
Madrid (F. Moreno Torroba): Decca (LP) 9817; Deutsche
Grammophon (LP) LPEM-19082

254. *España: Six Feuilles d'album* [*España: Seis hojas de album*], "Tango."

Beniamino Gigli (pianist unknown) (entitled "Quisiera olvidar tus ojos" ["I would like to forget your eyes"]): Gramophone/His Master's Voice (78) DA-1295; RCA (78) 1646; Romophone (CD) GBK-82005
Ninon and Vallin (in French, arr. by Dark and Thuillier): Odeon (78) 281037; Parlophone (78) RO-20326
John Raitt with the Osser Orchestra: Capitol (LP) T-714

Woodwind Ensemble

255. *Suite española No. 1*, "Sevilla (Sevillanas)."

Double Reed Ensemble of Iowa: Contemporary Record Society (CD) 9460

256. *Suite española No. 1*, "Cádiz (Canción)."

Double Reed Ensemble of Iowa: Contemporary Record Society (CD) 9460

Miscellaneous

Unspecified Selections (unlisted on WorldCat or MUZE)

257. Ernesto Bitetti (guitar): Musical Heritage Society (CS) MHC-5621

258. Ernesto Bitetti (guitar), Alicia de Larrocha (piano), and Enrique Jordá conducting the Orquesta de Conciertos de Madrid: Hispavox (LP) S-66.317 (3)

259. Frank Corrales (guitar): Iago (CD) IAG-205

260. Alicia de Larrocha (piano): Erato (LP) STU-70562

261. Susanne Mebes (guitar): Saturn (LP) YA-8203

262. Carlo Vidusso (piano): Fonit Cetra (LP) LAR-24

Unspecified Instrumentation and Performers (unlisted on WorldCat or MUZE)

263. *Suite española No. 1*, "Granada (Serenata)."

EMI (CD) CMS-7-64467-2

264. *Suite española No. 1*, "Sevilla (Sevillanas)."

Time-Life Records (LP) SLT-161

265. *Suite española No. 1*, "Asturias (Leyenda)."

Audivis Valois (CD) V-4780
CBS (LP) MK-42404
Time-Life Records (LP) SLT-161

266. *España: Six Feuilles d'album* [*España: Seis hojas de album*], "Tango."

Allegretto (CD) ACD-8723
Audio Education (78) AS-30
Madacy (CD) HCD-2-3408

267. *Iberia* ("Evocación," "El puerto," "Rondeña," "El Albaicín").

EMI (CD) CMS-7-64467-2

268. *Iberia*, "Evocación."

EMI/Angel (CD) CDM-65620

269. *Iberia*, "El puerto."

Audivis Valois (CD) V-4780

Unspecified Selections, Instrumentation, and Performers (unlisted on WorldCat or MUZE)

270. "Deux pièces."

Ensembles at the University of New Mexico: Century (LP) V-14237

271. "Dos piezas españolas" (from the *Suite española No. 1*?)

Hispavox (LP) HH-10-209

272. "Five Pieces for Guitar."

Various guitarists: London (CD) 433935-2

Chronology of Albéniz's Life

1860.   Albéniz born on May 29 in the town of Camprodon, near the French border in Catalonia. His father, Ángel, is Basque; his mother, Dolors, is Catalan.

1863.   The Albéniz family moves to Barcelona in December.

1864-7.   Albéniz studies piano with his sister Clementina and with Narciso Olivares, a local teacher. Gives his first public performance, at the Teatre Romea. Sister Enriqueta dies of typhoid in late 1867.

1868.   Family relocates to Madrid around the time of the revolution, in the fall. Albéniz begins study at the Real Conservatorio.

1869.   Publication of Albéniz's first composition, the *Marcha militar* for piano solo, which is dedicated to the Vizconde del Bruch (the twelve-year-old son of General Prim) and presented to him in person.

1872-5.   Albéniz's studies at the conservatory are desultory as he travels throughout Spain giving concerts. The young prodigy creates a sensation wherever he goes. Concertizing comes to a halt after his sister Blanca commits suicide on October 16, 1874. Touring resumes in 1875 and culminates in successful appearances in Puerto Rico and Cuba in the summer and fall of 1875, where he accompanies his father after the latter's appointment as Inspector General in the revenue department in Havana.

1876.   Begins studies in May at the Hochschule für Musik in Leipzig, but leaves after less than two months. Upon gaining financial support from King Alfonso XII in Madrid, commences studies at the Conservatoire Royal in Brussels.

1879.   Completes his studies at the Conservatoire and ties with Arthur de Greef for first prize, "with distinction," in the piano class of Louis Brassin.

1880.   After a triumphal return to Spain, travels to Budapest, ostensibly to study with Liszt. But Liszt is not in Budapest at this time, and Albéniz returns to Spain and then Cuba to give more concerts.

1882.   Successful premieres of his zarzuelas *Cuanto más viejo* (in Bilbao) and *Catalanes de gracia* (in Madrid). Concertizes throughout Spain.

1883.   Moves to Barcelona from Madrid. Studies composition with Felip Pedrell and marries Rosina Jordana Lagarriga, one of his students and the daughter of a wealthy businessman in Barcelona.

1884.   Birth of his first child, Blanca, in Barcelona.

1885.   Birth of his second child, Alfonso, during the summer in Tiana outside Barcelona. Moves with his growing family to Madrid, where he enjoys great celebrity as a performer and composer.

1886.   Triumphant concert at the Salón Romero in January and the appearance of the first biography of Albéniz, by the journalist Guerra y Alarcón. Death of his daughter Blanca in April. Gives numerous concerts throughout Spain.

1887-9.   Continued residence in Madrid and increasing output of works, published by houses in Madrid and Barcelona. Series of twenty recitals at the Universal Exposition in Barcelona in the summer and fall of 1888. Birth of his daughter Enriqueta in 1889. Well-received performance at the Salle Erard in Paris in 1889 attracts many of that city's finest musicians. Begins touring in England that same year.

1890.   Moves to London. Birth of his daughter Laura. Enters into a contractual agreement with the businessman Henry Lowenfeld, who becomes his manager. Numerous concerts in London are lauded by the critics, who appreciate his technical mastery, "velvety touch," and sensitive interpretations.

1892.   Composes the Act II finale "Oh Horror, Horror" for the operetta *Incognita*. Composes his own operetta, *The Magic Opal*. Concerts in Berlin mark the apex of his concert career and the turning point after which he will devote himself mostly to serious composition.

1893.   Premiere of *The Magic Opal* at the Lyric Theatre in January. Run ends soon thereafter, in late February. Though the critics praised the work, it did not draw large enough audiences. Touring company is formed to take it throughout Britain, and it is a success on the road. Revised and renamed *The Magic Ring*, it opens at the Prince of Wales's Theatre in April, but again it fails to achieve popularity. Writes several numbers for and conducts a production of Millöcker's *Poor Jonathan* at the Prince of Wales's Theatre. The independently wealthy poet Francis Money-Coutts enters into the contract between Albéniz and Lowenfeld (who drops out of it the following year). Albéniz agrees to set Money-Coutts's librettos to music in exchange for a generous income. Albéniz then leaves London for Spain to give concerts.

1894.   After giving several concerts in Barcelona, settles permanently in Paris in mid-year. Completes work on the zarzuela *San Antonio de la Florida*, which premieres to negative notices in Madrid in October. The Madrid premiere of a Spanish version of *The Magic Opal* (*La sortija*) is a fiasco and closes after three nights in November. Begins work on the opera *Henry Clifford*.

1895.   Premiere of *Henry Clifford* in May at the Liceu in Barcelona, to mixed reviews. Begins work on the opera *Pepita Jiménez*. November production of *San Antonio de la Florida* in Barcelona unsuccessful.

1896.   Premiere of *Pepita Jiménez* in January at the Liceu. The most successful of all his operas, it nonetheless finds no permanent place on the stage in Spain.

1897.   Production of *Pepita Jiménez* in Prague at the Neues Deutsches Theater in June. Meets with mixed reaction in the press and does not remain in the repertoire of that theater. Composes "La vega." Begins work on *Merlin*.

1898.   Onset of Bright's disease and gradual decline in health. Premiere of the Prelude to Act I of *Merlin* in Barcelona, conducted by Vincent d'Indy.

1899.   Premiere of "La vega" at the Société Nationale de Musique in January. Premiere of *Catalonia* at the Société Nationale de Musique in May. Commences reorchestration of *Pepita Jiménez*.

1901.   Catalan Lyric Theatre project in Barcelona collapses when Enric Morera withdraws from the contract with Enric Granados and Albéniz.

1902.   Finishes *Merlin* and reorchestration of *Pepita Jiménez*. Leaves Barcelona for Madrid but fails to gain a production of either opera in Madrid. Returns to Paris.

1904.   Publication in Leipzig of the new version of *Pepita Jiménez*.

1905.   Production of *Pepita Jiménez* (new version) and *San Antonio de la Florida* (*L'Hermitage fleuri*) at the Monnaie in Brussels. Greatest stage triumph of his career. Begins work on *Iberia*.

1906-09. Publication of *Merlin* in 1906. Despite increasing illness, completes work on *Iberia*, whose four books are premiered by Blanche Selva in France. Several numbers premiered in Spain by Joaquim Malats. Leaves *Navarra* and *Azulejos* incomplete upon his death from kidney failure on May 18, 1909, in Cambo-les-Bains, in the French Pyrenees.

Index 1: Proper Names
(Authors and Subjects in Chapters One and Two)

(Principal bibliographic entries of authors and editors appear in boldface type)

Index 2: Works

(All Chapters)

(Individual movements are indexed only when and where they appear outside the Catalogue of Works)

Index 3: Performers

(Individuals and Groups in Chapter Four)

WALTER AARON CLARK is Associate Professor of Musicology at the University of Kansas. He received his doctorate at the University of California, Los Angeles, and specializes in the music of Spain and Latin America from 1800 to the present. In addition to writing articles, reviews, and entries in reference works, he is the author of *Isaac Albéniz: Portrait of a Romantic* (Oxford: Clarendon Press, 1998) and the chapter on music in *Latin America: A Panorama* (New York: Peter Lang Publishing, 1998).

Composer Resource Manuals
Guy A. Marco, *General Editor*